D0596449

A
FAMILIAR
EXPOSITION OF THE CONSTITUTION
OF THE
UNITED STATES

A
Regnery Gateway
Bicentennial Edition

950 North Shore Drive,
Lake Bluff, Illinois 60044.

Regnery Books is a Division of Regnery Gateway, Inc.
All inquiries concerning this book should be directed to Regnery Books,
950 North Shore Drive, Lake Bluff, IL 60044.

Library of Congress Cataloging-in-Publication Data

Story, Joseph, 1779-1845.
  A familiar exposition of the Constitution of the United States.

  Reprint. Originally published: New York: Harper, 1859.
  Includes index.
  1. United States—Constitutional law. I. title
KF4550.S77 1986   34.73'023   86-17907
ISBN 0-89526-796-9   347.30223

TO

THE PEOPLE

OF THE

COMMONWEALTH OF MASSACHUSETTS,

THIS WORK,

DESIGNED TO AID

THE CAUSE OF EDUCATION,

AND

TO PROMOTE AND ENCOURAGE THE STUDY

OF THE

CONSTITUTION OF THE UNITED STATES,

BY HER INGENUOUS YOUTH,

IS RESPECTFULLY DEDICATED,

BY ONE

WHO GRATEFULLY ACKNOWLEDGES, THAT HER
TERRITORY IS

THE LAND OF HIS BIRTH,

AND THE

HOME OF HIS CHOICE,

THE AUTHOR,

Cambridge, January 1840.

CONTENTS.

	Page
FOREWORD (by Edwin Meese III),	9
PREFACE,	15
INTRODUCTION,	17

CHAPTER I.
History of the Colonies, ... 27

CHAPTER II.
Colonial Governments, ... 33

CHAPTER III.
Origin of the Revolution, ... 39

CHAPTER IV.
Revolutionary Government, ... 43

CHAPTER V.
History of the Confederation, ... 47

CHAPTER VI.
Origin of the Constitution, ... 53

CHAPTER VII.
Exposition of the Constitution.—The Preamble, ... 57

CHAPTER VIII.
Distribution of Powers.—The Legislative Department, ...67

CHAPTER IX.
The House of Representatives, ...73

CHAPTER X.
The Senate, ...87

CHAPTER XI.
Impeachments, ...101

CHAPTER XII.
Elections, and Meetings of Congress, ...115

CHAPTER XIII.
Powers and Privileges of both Houses, ...117

CHAPTER XIV.
Mode of Passing Laws, ...125

CHAPTER XV.
Powers of Congress.—Taxation, ...131

CHAPTER XVI.
Power to borrow Money and regulate Commerce, ...139

CHAPTER XVII.
Naturalization, Bankruptcy, and Coinage of Money, ...147

CHAPTER XVIII.
Post Office and Post Roads.—Patents for Inventions, ...151

CHAPTER XIX.
Punishment of Piracies and Felonies.
—Declaration of War, ...155

CHAPTER XX.
Power as to Army and Navy, ...159

CHAPTER XXI.
Power over Militia, ...163

CONTENTS

CHAPTER XXII.
Seat of Government, and other Ceded Places, ...167

CHAPTER XXIII.
General Power to make Necessary and Proper Laws, ...171

CHAPTER XXIV.
Punishment of Treason.—State Records, ...175

CHAPTER XXV.
Admission of New States.—Government of Territories, ...179

CHAPTER XXVI.
Prohibitions on the United States, .185

CHAPTER XXVII.
Prohibitions on the States, ...189

CHAPTER XXVIII.
The Executive Department, ...203

CHAPTER XXIX.
Powers and Duties of the President, ...215

CHAPTER XXX.
The Judicial Department, ...225

CHAPTER XXXI.
Powers and Jurisdiction of the Judiciary, ...233

CHAPTER XXXII.
Trial by Jury, and its Incidents.—Definition of treason, ...277

CHAPTER XXXIII.
Privileges of Citizens.—Fugitive Criminals and Slaves, ...291

CHAPTER XXXIV.
Guaranty of Republican Government—Mode of making
Amendments, ...295

CHAPTER XXXV.
Public Debt.—Supremacy of the Constitution and Laws, ...301

CHAPTER XXXVI.
Oath of Office.—Religious Test.—Ratification of the
Constitution, ...305

CHAPTER XXXVII.
Amendments to the Constitution, .309

CHAPTER XXXVIII.
Conciuding Remarks, ...323

APPENDIX.
Declaration of Rights of the Continental Congress, 1774, . . .327
Declaration of Independence, ...331
Articles of Confederation, ...335
Constitution of the United States, .344
Washington's Farewell Address, ...361
Definitive Treaty of Peace between the United States
of America and his Britannic Majesty, ...378
An Ordinance for the Government of the Territory
of the United States, Northwest of the River Ohio, ...383
Glossary, ...393

FOREWORD.

In 1836, after having served nearly twenty-five years on the Supreme Court of the United States, Justice Joseph Story remarked:

> If I do not live otherwise to posterity, I shall at all events live in my children in the law. While that endures I am content to be known through my pupils.

Despite his incomparable achievements as a jurist, an advocate, and a politician, Story plainly believed that his most enduring legacy would come from his work as a legal educator. It is a privilege for me to be associated with the continued advancement of this legacy through the republication of this treatise on our Constitution, a study Story specifically designed for lay readers and as a text for the high school students of his day.

Although this work will undoubtedly command respect from every generation that values our constitutional democracy, this republication is particularly timely for two reasons. First, we are preparing to celebrate the Bicentennial of our basic charter, described by William Gladstone in 1878 as "the most wonderful work ever struck off at a given time by the brain and purpose of man." It is entirely fitting that Justice Story should play a significant role in educating us as to its

9

meaning and its genius. He was a remarkably prolific writer, producing scholarly commentaries not only on the Constitution but on eight other areas of the law (agency, bailments, bills of exchange, conflict of laws, equity jurisprudence, equity pleadings, partnerships, and promissory notes), as well as countless other essays, articles, and reviews. Not content with edifying only those within his own profession, Story prepared this *Familiar Exposition of the Constitution* in 1840 by revising a lengthier treatise he had written for constitutional scholars. That lengthier treatise, *Commentaries on the Constitution of the United States* (1833), remains today as one of the most thorough expositions ever on the substance of our constitutional law. Few things would have pleased him more than to have the abridged treatise widely circulated to enhance our knowledge and appreciation of the Constitution on its 200th anniversary.

Second, a republication of this volume is especially appropriate now as we inaugurate a newly constituted Supreme Court under the leadership of Chief Justice William H. Rehnquist. On the first Monday of October 1986, the Supreme Court officially began the first term of what future historians will call the Rehnquist Court. We stand at the threshold of a promising era, one that I hope will see a return to the rigorous approach to constitutional interpretation espoused by Story in this book, as well as in his lengthier *Commentaries*. As Story makes plain, the Constitution is our fundamental law, and federal judges are obliged to apply its provisions in accordance with the plain meaning of their terms as understood by the society that ratified them. His eloquent statement of this theory deserves to be quoted at length:

> We shall treat [our Constitution], not as a mere compact, or league, or confederacy, existing at the mere will of any one or more of the States, during their good pleasure; but, (as it purports on its face to be,) as a Constitution of Government, framed and adopted by the people of the United States, and obligatory upon all the States, until it is altered, amended, or abolished by the people, in the manner pointed

out in the instrument itself. It is to be interpreted, as all other solemn instruments are, by endeavoring to ascertain the true sense and meaning of all the terms; and we are neither to narrow them, nor to enlarge them, by straining them from their just and natural import, for the purpose of adding to, or diminishing its powers, or bending them to any favorite theory or dogma of party. It is the language of the people, to be judged of according to common sense, and not by mere theoretical reasoning. It is not an instrument for the mere private interpretation of any particular men. The people have established it and spoken their will; and their will, thus promulgated, is to be obeyed as the supreme law.

Why should we continue to adhere to the Constitution as our fundamental law? Justice Story provides the answer on the title page of these commentaries by quoting from George Washington's *Farewell Address*. The Constitution, and the government it establishes, Washington stated, "has a just claim to [our] confidence and respect" because it is

the offspring of our own choice, uninfluenced and unawed, adopted upon full investigation and mature deliberation, completely free in its principles, in the distribution of its powers uniting security with energy, and containing, within itself, a provision for its own amendment***.

In other words, the Constitution is fundamental law because it is *our* law, law established by "we the people," law that permits social progress while preventing political tyranny, and law that we can adjust through amendment under the Fifth Article as time and experience demand.

Unfortunately, several modern jurists and scholars have rejected Justice Story's vision of the Constitution, and would probably find the very notion of a "commentary" on the meaning of the Constitution somewhat archaic, perhaps even quaint. They view constitutional provisions not as having a fixed meaning that can be identified and applied, but as nothing more than vague generalities and empty vessels that can be made to carry the political values of the judges who interpret them. They probably do not see the value in an interpretive guide to a text that they believe has so little content.

Justice Story knew better. He recognized that departure from the text of the Constitution as originally understood would permit unelected and unaccountable, life-tenured federal judges to impose their personal values on the rest of us, and would ultimately result in judicial tyranny. Because the Constitution expresses the will of the people, only fidelity to its original meaning ensures that our country will remain self-governing. If a judge departs from the original meaning—if he acts solely on his personal notion of the public good or wise policy—he usurps powers not given to him by the people through their Constitution. He is no longer interpreting the Constitution, but amending it in a way contrary to the amendment process set forth in the document itself.

Story realized that, if the Constitution is to remain our basic law, all citizens (not just the lawyers) must understand its provisions and protect against its infringement by those who would disregard it. Accordingly, he produced this treatise, dedicated to the people of his home state of Massachusetts, with the hope of inspiring "a more warm and devoted attachment to the National Union, and a more deep and firm love of the National Constitution." The essential role of an educated citizenry in ensuring fidelity to our Constitution is emphasized in his concluding remarks, where he warns that our constitutional democracy might "perish in an hour, by the folly, or corruption, or negligence of its only keepers, THE PEOPLE."

Perhaps no one was better suited to the task of producing an enduring commentary on our Constitution than Justice Story. Born in 1779, three years after the birth of our republic, his life was imbued with the ideals of the American Revolution. His father participated in the Boston Tea Party, and fought at Concord, Lexington, and Bunker Hill. As one of eighteen children, Story's boyhood must have been filled with inspiring conversation and speculation as to the fate of our new country. His intellectual prowess manifested itself at an early age. Largely through self-study, he secured early enrollment at Harvard, graduating second in his class when he was just eighteen years old.

In 1810, Story was thrust into national prominence when he vindicated the claims of certain Massachusetts land investors before the Supreme Court in the landmark case of *Fletcher v. Peck*. The famous "Yazoo" lands at issue in that case had been sold by the Georgia legislature, and then subsequently purchased by Story's clients. When the original grant was challenged as having been procured through bribery, the Georgia legislature attempted to nullify it. But Story convinced the Supreme Court that his clients' property rights were protected against state infringement by the Contract Clause of the Constitution. His role in *Fletcher* might well have contributed to his understanding that economic liberty and individual liberty are inextricably linked, a belief to which he adhered throughout his life.

The following year, Story became the youngest person ever to serve on our nation's highest court when, at the age of 32, he was confirmed as an Associate Justice. While on the Court, he encountered perhaps the most important influence on his constitutional jurisprudence, the phenomenal mind of Chief Justice John Marshall. The two quickly forged an abiding friendship, and more often than not they stood united on the great constitutional issues of their day. It is to Marshall that Story's unabridged work on the Constitution is dedicated, and it was Marshall—together with *The Federalist*—that Story described as the "two great sources" for his constitutional commentaries.

Justice Story's fidelity to the text of the Constitution is perhaps best revealed by examining his greatest judicial pronouncement, his opinion in *Martin v. Hunter's Lessee* (1816). In that case, the Court upheld the legitimacy of Supreme Court review of state court decisions that interpret federal law. Story began his opinion by insisting that the Constitution, "like every other grant [of power], is to have a reasonable construction, according to the import of its terms." Adhering strictly to the text, his interpretation was not cramped. "The words," he wrote, "are to be taken in their natural and obvious sense, and not in a sense unreasonably restricted or enlarged." He recognized that "[t]he constitution unavoidably deals in general language" and that "where a power is expressly given in general terms, it is not to be restrained to particular cases, unless that construction grow out of the context expressly, or by necessary implication." In *Hunter's Lessee*, Story sought to ensure that the Constitution would be viewed as the supreme national law of the people, and he established the Supreme Court as the final arbiter of federal law over and above state tribunals. But he demanded that federal judges *interpret* the law as established by the people through their representatives, not *make* new law by enforcing their own views as to how the country should be governed.

Much more could be said regarding Story's extraordinary legal career, but the reader's time would be better spent studying his writings and the Constitution itself. Story's lengthier *Commentaries on the Constitution* ran to five editions and was translated into French, Spanish, and German. Through this republication of the abridged version for the general public, Story will continue to "inspire the rising generation with a more ardent love of their country, an unquenchable thirst for liberty, and a profound reverence for the Constitution and the Union," as he so fervently desired. We can hope that it will also lead to a return to the jurisprudence that Story knew is essential to our constitutional democracy. As we continue Justice Story's legacy as legal educator and constitutional scholar, let us keep in mind the admonition that concludes these commentaries:

> Republics are created by the virtue, public spirit, and intelligence of the citizens. They fall, when the wise are banished from the public councils, because they dare to be honest, and the profligate are rewarded, because they flatter the people, in order to betray them.

Edwin Meese III

14

PREFACE.

THE present Work is designed, not only for private reading, but as a text book for the highest classes in our Common Schools and Academies. It is also adapted to the use of those, who are more advanced, and have left school, after having passed through the common branches of education. It may also be studied with advantage by those, who have arrived at maturer years, but whose pursuits have not allowed them leisure to acquire a thorough knowledge of the Republican Constitution of Government, under which they live. Some of the subjects, which are here treated of, may seem remote from those topics, which ordinarily engage the attention of our youth, and some of them may seem to be of such an abstract political nature, that the full value of them can scarcely be felt, except by persons, who have had some experience of the duties and difficulties of social life. But, I think, that it will be found, upon closer examination, that an objection of this sort can properly apply to very few passages in the Work; and that even those, which fall within the scope of the objection, will furnish sources of reflection, and means of knowledge, which will essentially aid the student in his future progress, and place him, as it were, upon the vantage ground, to master the leading principles of politics, and public policy. The Work has been framed upon the basis of my larger Commentaries on the Constitution, which are already before the Public. And one of the advantages, which it possesses, is, that the reader will find every one of the topics here discussed, examined almost in the same order, far more completely in those Commentaries, if his curiosity or his leisure shall prompt him to more thorough researches. I have endeavored, as far as practicable, to make the remarks intelligible to every class of readers, by embodying them in plain and unambitious language, so as to give the Work a just claim to the title of being "A Familiar Exposition of the Constitution of the United States." If it shall tend to awaken in the bosoms of American Youth, a more warm and devoted attachment to the National Union, and a more deep and firm love of the National Constitution, it will afford me very sincere gratification, and be an ample compensation for the time, which has necessarily been withdrawn from my other pressing avocations, in order to prepare it.

An Appendix has been added, containing some important public Documents, which may serve to confirm or illustrate the Text.

With these few suggestions, I submit the Work to the indulgent consideration of the Public, adopting the expressive motto of the poet,—

> "Content, if here th' unlearned their wants may view,
> The learned reflect on what before they knew."

JOSEPH STORY.

Cambridge, January 1, 1840.

INTRODUCTION.

Judged by the variety of his contributions to American law and the quality of his work, Joseph Story stands out in the annals of history as the foremost jurist America has produced. During his long tenure on the Supreme Court (1811–1845), he wrote some of the most important opinions of the period, including a number of notable dissents. His opinion in *Martin v. Hunter's Lessee* (1816), for example, has been described by one Supreme Court historian as "the keystone of the whole arch of Federal judicial power." Story also delivered hundreds of significant opinions from the First Circuit Court (of Appeals); for in those days members of the Supreme Court not only sat in Washington but also "rode circuit" and participated in the proceedings of lower Federal courts.

A prolific writer, Story edited and published four books of law before his appointment to the Supreme Court. While performing his judicial responsibilities, he produced nine major treatises within the space of twelve years—*Bailments* (1832), *Commentaries on the Constitution* (3 Vols., 1833), *Conflict of Laws* (1834), *Equity Jurisprudence* (2 Vols., 1836), *Equity Pleadings* (1838), *Agency* (1839), *Partnership* (1841), *Bills of Exchange* (1843), and *Promissory Notes* (1845). These commentaries, each a pioneering endeavor, went through many editions. Judge Story was also the author of valuable notes on prize, admiralty, maritime, and patent law contained in appendices to Supreme Court reports, and a frequent contributor to the *North American Review*, in which he published legal essays.

Story's *Miscellaneous Writings,* first published in 1835, shows the full panoply of his wide-ranging interests and contains a rich selection of his public addresses, articles, and book reviews on art, science, literature, education, government, and the law. Not the least of his scholarly achievements were the essays he prepared for Francis Lieber's *Encyclopedia Americana* (1836), those on *Natural Law* and *Law, Legislation and Codes* being especially noteworthy. Truly the father of American law, Story wove a whole *corpus juris* into the American legal system. Indeed, his judicial opinions and writings laid the foundation for admiralty law, equity jurisprudence, and commercial law in the United States.

Though a member of the judiciary, Story also worked diligently to clarify and improve Federal laws. He drafted legislation to extend the jurisdiction of the circuit courts and revise the bankruptcy laws. In collaboration with Daniel Webster, he worked successfully behind the scenes to reform the criminal code of the United States in 1825. In 1827, he prepared and superintended the publication of the three volume edition of the *Laws of the United States*. He was also a delegate, it should be noted, to the Massachusetts Constitutional Convention of 1820.

In addition to these labors, Judge Story also served as Dane Professor of Law at Harvard University from 1829 until the time of his death. He was proudest of his title "Professor," and he placed it on the title pages of all his books. Only at the insistence of his publisher, we are told, did he finally consent to add, "Justice of the Supreme Court of the United States." Story may justly be regarded as the real founder of the Harvard Law School; for his appointment marked an important turning point in the history of an institution that was faltering until

Story took command. As a result of his leadership, enrollment increased, the quality of instruction improved, and the school's reputation for excellence grew rapidly.

Joseph Story, it may thus be seen, was a remarkable individual—a jurist, author, and teacher, a renaissance man of many talents and indefatigable industry. But it was in writing and discoursing on the Constitution—his greatest love—that Story achieved his greatest and most enduring fame. His *Commentaries on the Constitution,* regularly republished well into the twentieth century, is appropriately listed by the Library of Congress as "a legal classic of continuing importance and reputation." Story's *Commentaries* began to appear as authority in arguments of counsel and in opinions from the bench within a year of its publication. By 1860, he was cited in four opinions of the Supreme Court, twice in concurring opinions, and eight times in dissents. In all, Story was cited by the bench and bar during this period in 42 separate cases—on issues covering almost the entire range of constitutional law.

Reliance upon Judge Story's authoritative exposition of the Constitution has continued down to the present. His explanation of the original meaning and purpose of the Establishment Clause of the First Amendment is central to the current debate within the Federal judiciary over the constitutionality of school prayer, and his "rules of interpretation" are quoted with approbation and increasing frequency by the critics of judicial activism—a rather ironic development when we recall that Judge Story's *Commentaries* endorsed the principles of John Marshall and broad construction and were roundly condemned by Calhoun and the strict constructionists throughout the nineteenth century. This turn of events is hardly surprising, however, given the fact that the Supreme Court long ago not only abandoned strict construction but also moved well beyond the limits of broad construction that John Marshall and Joseph Story crafted during our formative era. In these respects, little of the Story or the Calhoun legacies survives in today's "living Constitution."

We are now in a fever pitch of constitution-making and

wholesale revision of our basic law, the symptoms of which first appeared some fifty years ago and have gone untreated, in any meaningful and effective manner, until recently. But today, the political agenda has changed, the proponents of original intent and limited constitutional government have seized the initiative, and there is now public debate throughout the land on the proper role of the judiciary in our political system. The American people—and this includes members of the bench and bar—seem almost caught up in a spontaneous effort to re-educate themselves about their Constitution. Indeed, scarcely a day goes by that these issues are not discussed by the media.

While much of this intellectual ferment may be attributed to the politics of judicial selection, it is clear enough that the root causes go deeper. For the first time in this century we are witnessing a sudden effusion of scholarship that is both critical of the modern Court and intent on preserving the original design of the Constitution. In sharp contrast to the constitutional revolution of the New Deal era, which produced only scattered dissent, the changes wrought by the Warren-Burger Courts have elicited an outpouring of protest, and there is now an increasingly informed and informative body of opinion calling for a return to basic principles. Issues considered nondebatable just a decade ago, such as the applicability of the Bill of Rights to the States, have become a common topic of constitutional discussion.

There is no indication, however, that this renewed interest in preserving the integrity of the Constitution has filtered down to secondary education or stimulated a reconsideration of teaching materials that are used for the instruction of the young. A recent study published by the Center for Judicial Studies, entitled *Democracy at Risk: The Rising Tide of Political Illiteracy and Ignorance of the Constitution,* shows that there has been a marked decline of constitutional understanding among high school students. According to surveys conducted in 1976 by the National Assessment of Educational Progress, for example, every indicator points to a retrogression of knowledge about the Constitution and its basic principles

among seventeen-year-olds since 1969: only seventy-four percent could identify Congress as part of the legislative branch,
and twelve percent did not even recognize the Senate as part
of the Congress; about half thought the President could appoint members of Congress, and less than half knew that the
Senate confirms presidential appointments; only sixty-two
percent understood that the Supreme Court has the power to
declare acts of Congress unconstitutional; and only seven percent knew that a simple majority of the Justices is sufficient for
the Supreme Court to overturn a Federal statute. The situation
is no more encouraging among the adult population. A review
of the data led the author of a 1981 study jointly published by
the American Historical Association and American Political
Science Association to the morbid conclusion that "most people know very little about the Constitution [and] very little
about anything other than the most basic tenets of our constitutional system."

A number of developments explain the cause of the problem, including the decline of reading comprehension, poor
teacher training and the drift away from a structured core cur-
riculum, but certainly a key factor is the inferior quality of
many high school civics textbooks currently in use. As Michael
Novak, Jeane Kirkpatrick, and Anne Crutcher noted in a
thoughtful study published in 1978 by the Ethics and Public
Policy Center, "liberal bias" permeates much of the literature.
Various studies produced by the American Historical Association and American Political Science Association also complain
about the quality of today's civics textbooks, superficiality being the principal criticism.

This timely republication of Judge Story's *Familiar Exposition of the Constitution* offers an alternative to the present
crop of civics textbooks, and if adopted in the schools would
contribute mightily to the educational effort to improve public
understanding of our constitutional system. It is an abridgement of his *Commentaries on the Constitution* and is based in
large measure on the essays in *The Federalist*. Although it is
not the first civics textbook printed in the United States, it is

surely one of the best. Originally published in 1840, the book went through a number of editions. It has been estimated that as many as seventy "civil government" textbooks were published in the United States before 1890, Story's *Familiar Exposition* serving as the standard for others that followed.

Early attempts to teach American youth about the Constitution were only mildly successful. The American Philosophical Society sponsored an essay contest in 1797 on the question of what system of education the new republic should encourage, and the two prize winners—Samuel Harrison Smith and Samuel Knox—both emphasized the need for constitutional study. But only a handful of textbooks were written in the years that followed. They were less than satisfactory, and there was no solid effort to establish the study of civil government in the early republic.

Judge Story addressed the problem in a lecture on "The Science of Government As a Branch of Popular Education," which he delivered in 1834 before the American Institute of Instruction. That same year, he expanded the lecture and published it as his *Constitutional Classbook*. Though superseded six years later by his *Familiar Exposition,* this first effort to spark an interest in constitutional studies is noteworthy because it reveals Story's general plan and rationale for the study of civil government—and, we may further note, the two books establish Joseph Story as a leader of educational reform in early nineteenth century America.

He believed that an understanding of the Constitution must begin with an inquiry into the origin, purpose, and function of the basic principles of the document, a task, he urged, that "may be brought within the comprehension of the most common minds." The text of the Constitution is sufficiently brief and intelligible that any youth "of ordinary capacity may be made fully to understand it between his fourteenth and sixteenth year, if he has an instructor of reasonable ability and qualifications."

A striking contrast to today's civics books, Judge Story's *Familiar Exposition* seeks to explain why the Founding Fathers structured the Constitution the way they did, and why they deliberately designed "the most complicated frame of republican government...ever offered to the world." It is, then, a true primer, designed to familiarize the student with the rationale of the system and to encourage loyalty and support for its basic principles and values. Unlike today's prolix textbooks on American government, the focus is on the original text of the Constitution itself. The bulk of the book is devoted to an explanation of the Framers' intent, not to discussions about transitory political issues, interest group politics, and the latest decisions of the Supreme Court. It is thus a manageable book about fundamental principles that the student knows he can handle in a school term, not a massive encyclopedia of current events topics. No less significant, Story's *Familiar Exposition* is eloquently written and a pleasure to read; and it is orderly and logical because Story follows the order of the Constitution itself—article by article. Even the general reader and the accomplished scholar will find Story's elucidations to be insightful and instructive.

Although Story is unashamedly patriotic and does not hesitate to defend as well as explain the political values that are embodied in the Constitution, his treatment of the controversial constitutional issues of his day is appropriately brief and remarkably free of partisanship. Witness, for example, his closing remarks in the section where he illuminates the original meaning and purpose of the "elastic" or Necessary and Proper Clause:

> There are many cases...in which Congress have acted upon implied powers, some of which have given rise to much political discussion, and controversy; but it is not within the design of this work to examine those cases, or to express any opinion respecting them. It is proper, however, that the reader should be apprized, that among them, are the questions respecting the power of Congress to establish a national bank; to make national roads, canals, and other internal national improvements; to purchase

cessions of foreign territory, (such, for example, as Louisiana and Florida) to lay embargoes, without any fixed limitation of the time of their duration; and to prohibit intercourse or commerce with a foreign nation for an unlimited period.

The Supreme Court, of course, had already addressed some of these questions; but a complete and accurate understanding of the Constitution, as Story realized, must *begin* with an examination of the Constitution itself and the original sources that produced and shaped it, not with the opinions of judges, legislators, executives, and other authorities far removed from the creation. That, perhaps, is the primary lesson of this book, a lesson that has often been forgotten or ignored today, but one that can be relearned in these pages from America's greatest jurist.

James McClellan
President
Center for Judicial Studies
    & The Joseph Story Society
Washington, D.C.

A

FAMILIAR

EXPOSITION OF THE CONSTITUTION

OF THE

UNITED STATES:

CONTAINING

A BRIEF COMMENTARY

ON EVERY CLAUSE, EXPLAINING THE TRUE NATURE, REASONS, AND
OBJECTS THEREOF; DESIGNED FOR THE USE OF SCHOOL LIBRARIES
AND GENERAL READERS.

WITH

AN APPENDIX,

CONTAINING IMPORTANT PUBLIC DOCUMENTS, ILLUSTRATIVE OF
THE CONSTITUTION.

BY JOSEPH STORY, LL.D.

DANE PROFESSOR OF LAW IN HARVARD UNIVERSITY

"The Government, the offspring of our own choice, uninfluenced and unawed,
adopted upon full investigation and mature deliberation, completely free in its principles, in the distribution of its powers uniting security with energy, and containing,
within itself, a provision for its own amendment, has a just claim to your confidence
and respect."—*President Washington's Farewell Address to the People of the United
States.*

NEW YORK:

HARPER & BROTHERS, PUBLISHERS,

329 & 331 PEARL STREET,

FRANKLIN SQUARE.

1859.

A

FAMILIAR EXPOSITION

OF THE

CONSTITUTION OF THE UNITED STATES.

CHAPTER I.

History of the Colonies.

§1. BEFORE entering upon the more immediate object of this work, which is, to present to the general reader a familiar exposition of the nature and objects of the different provisions of the Constitution of the United States, it seems proper to take a brief review of the origin and settlement of the various States, originally composing the Union, and their political relations to each other at the time of its adoption. This will naturally conduct us back to the American Revolution, and to the formation of the Confederation of the States, consequent thereon. But if we stop here, we shall still be surrounded by difficulties, unless we understand the political organization of the various colonies during their common dependence upon the sovereignty of Great Britain, and we are in some degree made acquainted with the domestic institutions, policy, and legislation, which impressed upon each of them some peculiar habits, interests, opinions, attachments, and even prejudices, which may still be traced in the actual jurisprudence of each State, and are openly or silently referred to in some of the provisions of the Constitution of Government, by which they are now united. This review will, however, contain but a rapid glance at these various important topics, and the reader must be left to satisfy his further inquiries by the study of the works of a more large and comprehensive character.

§2. The thirteen American Colonies which, on the fourth day of July, 1776, declared themselves free and independent States were New Hampshire, Massachusetts, Rhode Island, Connecticut, New York, New Jersey, Pennsylvania, Delaware, Maryland, Virginia, North Carolina, South Carolina, and Georgia. All these colonies were originally settled by British subjects, under the express or implied authority of the government of Great Britain, except New York, which was originally settled by emigrants from Holland, and Delaware, which, although at one time an appendage to the Government of New York, was at first principally inhabited by the Dutch and Swedes. The British government, however, claimed the territory of all these colonies by the right of original discovery, and at all times resisted the claim of the Dutch to make any settlement in America. The Colony of New York became, at an early period, subject to British authority by conquest from the Dutch. Delaware was soon separated from New York, and was afterwards connected with, and a dependency upon, the proprietary government of Pennsylvania. The other States, now belonging to the Union, had no existence at the time of the Declaration of Independence; but have been established within the territory, which was ceded to the United States by the Treaty of Peace with Great Britain in 1783, or within the territory, which has been since acquired by the United States, by purchase from other nations.

§3. At the time of the discovery of America, towards the close of the fifteenth century, (1492,) the various Indian tribes, which then inhabited it, maintained a claim to the exclusive possession and occupancy of the territory within their respective limits, as sovereign proprietors of the soil. They acknowledged no obedience, nor allegiance, nor subordination to any foreign nation whatsoever; and, as far as they have possessed the means, they have ever since constantly asserted this full right of dominion, and have yielded it up only, when it has been purchased from them by treaty, or obtained by force of arms and consent. In short, like all the civilized nations of the earth, the Indian tribes deemed themselves rightfully possessed, as sovereigns, of all the territories, within which they were accustomed to hunt, or to exercise other acts of ownership, upon the common principle, that the exclusive use gave them an exclusive right to the soil, whether it was cultivated or not.

§4. It is difficult to perceive, why their title was not, in this respect, as well founded as the title of any other nation, to the soil within its own boundaries. How, then, it may be asked, did the European nations acquire the general title, which they have always asserted to the whole soil of America, even to that in the occupancy of the Indian tribes? The only answer, which can be given, is, their own assertion, that they acquired a general title thereto in virtue of their being the first discoverers thereof, or, in other words, that their title was founded upon the right of discovery. They established the doctrine (whether satisfactorily or not is quite a different question) that discovery is sufficient foundation for the right to territory. As between themselves, with a view to prevent contests, where the same land had been visited by the subject of different European nations, each of which might claim it as its own, there was no inconvenience in allowing the first discoverer to have the priority of right, where the territory was at the time desert and uninhabited. But as to nations, which had not acceded to the doctrine, and especially as to countries in the possession of native inhabitants and tribes at the time of the discovery, it seems difficult to perceive, what ground of right any discovery could confer. It would seem strange to us, if, in the present times, the natives of the South Sea Islands, or of Cochin China, should, by making a voyage to, and a discovery of, the United States, on that account set up a right to the soil within the boundaries.

§5. The truth is, that the European nations paid not the slightest regard to the rights of the native tribes. They treated them as mere barbarians and heathens, whom, if they were not at liberty to extirpate, they were entitled to deem mere temporary occupants of the soil. They might convert them to Christianity; and, if they refused conversion, they might drive them from the soil, as unworthy to inhabit it. They affected to be governed by the desire to promote the cause of Christianity, and were aided in this ostensible object by the whole influence of the Papal power. But their real object was, to extend their own power, and increase their own wealth, by acquiring the treasures, as well as the territory, of the New World. Avarice and ambition were at the bottom of all their original enterprises.

§6. The right of discovery, thus asserted, has become the settled foundation, on which the European nations rest their title to territory in America; and it is a right, which, under our governments, must now be deemed incontestable, however doubtful in its origin, or unsatisfactory in its principles. The Indians, indeed, have not been treated as mere intruders, but as entitled to a qualified right of property in the territory. They have been deemed to be the lawful occupants of the soil, and entitled to a temporary possession thereof, subject to the superior sovereignty of the particular European nation, which actually held the title of discovery. They have not, indeed, been permitted to alienate their possessory right to the soil, except to the nation, to whom they were thus bound by a qualified dependence. But in other respects, they have been left to the free exercise of internal sovereignty, in regard to the members of their own tribe, and in regard to their intercourse with other tribes; and their title to the soil, by way of occupancy, has been generally respected, until it has been extinguished by purchase, or by conquest, under the authority of the nation, upon which they were dependent. A large portion of the territory in the United States, to which the Indian title is now extinguished, has been acquired by purchase; and a still larger portion by the irresistible power of arms, over a brave, hardy, but declining race, whose destiny seems to be, to perish as fast as the white man advances upon their footsteps.

§7. Having thus traced out the origin of the title to the soil of America, asserted by the European nations, we may now enter upon a brief statement of the times and manner, in which the different settlements were made, in the different colonies, which originally composed the Union, at the time of the Declaration of Independence. The first permanent settlement made in America, under the auspices of England, was under a charter granted by King James I., in 1606. By this charter, he granted all the lands lying on the seacoast between the thirty-fourth and the forty-fifth degrees of north latitude, and the islands adjacent, within one hundred miles, which were not then belonging to, or possessed by, any Christian prince or people. The first associates were divided into two companies; one, the First, or Southern Colony, to which was granted all the lands between the thirty-fourth and the forty-first degrees of north latitude; and the other, the Second, or Northern Colony, to which was granted all the lands between the thirty-eight and forth-fifth degrees of north latitude, but not within one hundred miles of the prior Colony. Each Colony was declared to have the exclusive propriety or title in all the territory within fifty miles from the seat of its first plantation. The name of Virginia was in general confined exclusively to the Southern Colony; and the name of the Plymouth Company (from the place of residence of the original grantees in England) was assumed by the Northern Colony. From the former, the States south of the Potomac may be said to have had their origin; and from the latter, the States of New England.

§8. Some of the provisions of this charter deserve a particular consideration, from the light, which they throw upon the civil and political condition of the persons, who should become inhabitants of the Colonies. The two companies were authorized to engage, as colonists, any of the subjects of England, who should be disposed to emigrate. All persons, being English subjects, and inhabitants in the Colonies, and their children born therein, were declared to have and possess all liberties, franchises, and immunities of subjects within any dominions of the Crown of England, to all intents and purposes, as if they were born and abiding within the realm or other dominions of that Crown. The original grantees, or patentees, were to hold the lands and other territorial rights in the Colonies, of the King, his heirs and successors, in the same manner as the manner of East Greenwich, in the county of Kent, and not, in capite, (as it was technically called,) that is to say, by a free and certain tenure, as contradistinguished from a military and a servile tenure,—a privilege of inestimable value, as those, who are acquainted with the history of the feudal tenures, well know.* The patentees were also authorized to grant the same lands to the inhabitants of the Colonies in such form and manner, and for such estates, as the Council of the Colony should direct. These provisions were, in substance, incorporated into all the charters subsequently granted by the Crown to the different Colonies, and constituted also the basis, upon which all the subsequent settlements were made.

§9. The Colony of Virginia was the earliest in its origin, being settled in 1606. The Colony of Plymouth (which afterwards was united with Massachusetts in 1692) was settled in 1620; the Colony of Massachusetts in 1628; the Colony of New Hampshire in 1629; the Colony of Maryland in 1632; the Colony of Connecticut in 1635; the Colony of Rhode Island in 1636; the Colony of New York in 1662; the Colonies of North and South Carolina in 1663; the Colony of Georgia in 1732. In using these dates, we refer not to any sparse and disconnected settlements in these Colonies, (which had been made at prior periods,) but to the permanent settlements made under distinct and organized governments.

---

*On this subject, the reader can consult the history of the ancient and modern English tenures in Blackstone's Commentaries, vol. ii chs. 5 and 6, p. 59 to p. 103.

CHAPTER II.

Colonial Governments.

§10. LET us next proceed to the consideration of the political Institutions and forms of Government, which were established in these different Colonies, and existed here at the commencement of the Revolution. The governments originally formed in these different Colonies may be divided into three sorts, viz., Provincial, Proprietary, and Charter, Governments. First, Provincial Governments. These establishments existed under the direct and immediate authority of the King of England, without any fixed constitution of government; the organization being dependent upon the respective commissions issued from time to time by the Crown to the royal governors, and upon the instructions, which usually accompanied those commissions. The Provincial Governments were, therefore, wholly under the control of the King, and subject to his pleasure. The form of government, however, in the Provinces, was at all times practically the same, the commissions being issued in the same form. The commissions appointed a Governor, who was the King's representative, or a deputy; and a Council, who, besides being a part of the Legislature, were to assist the Governor in the discharge of his official duties; and both the Governor and the Council held their offices during the pleasure of the Crown. The commissions also contained authority to the Governor to convene a general assembly of the representatives of the freeholders and planters in the Province; and under this authority, Provincial Assemblies, composed of the Governor, the Council, and the Representatives, were, from time to time, constituted and held. The Representatives composed the lower house, as a distinct branch; the Council composed the upper house; and the Governor had a negative upon all their proceedings, and the power to prorogue and dissolve them. The Legislature, thus constituted, had power to make all local laws and ordinances not repugnant to the laws of England, but, as near as might conveniently be, agreeable thereto, subject to the ratification or disapproval of the Crown. The Governor appointed the judges and magistrates, and other officers of the Province, and possessed other general executive powers. Under this form of government, New Hampshire, New York, Virginia, North Carolina, South Carolina, and Georgia, were governed, as provinces, at the commencement of the American Revolution; and some of them had been so governed from an early period of their settlement.

§ 11. Secondly, Proprietary Governments. These were grants by letters patent (or open, written grants under the great seal of the kingdom) from the Crown to one or more persons as Proprietary or Proprietaries, conveying to them not only the rights of the soil, but also the general powers of government within the territory so granted, in the nature of feudatory principalities, or dependent royalties. So that they possessed within their own domains nearly the same authority, which the Crown possessed in the Provincial Governments, subject, however, to the control of the Crown, as the paramount sovereign, to whom they owed allegiance. In the Proprietary Governments, the Governor was appointed by the Proprietary or Proprietaries; the Legislature was organized and convened according to his or their will; and the appointment of officers, and other executive functions and prerogatives, were exercised by him or them, either personally, or by the Governors for the time being. Of these Proprietary governments, three only existed at the time of the American Revolution, *viz.*, Maryland, held by Lord Baltimore, as Proprietary, and Pennsylvania and Delaware, held by William Penn, as Proprietary.

§12. Thirdly, Charter Governments. These were great political corporations, created by letters patent, or grants of the Crown, which conferred on the grantees and their associates not only the soil within their territorial limits, but also all the high powers of legislation and government. The charters contained, in fact, a fundamental constitution for the Colony, distributed the powers of government into three great departments, legislative, executive, and judicial; provided for the mode, in which these powers should be vested and exercised; and securing to the inhabitants certain political privileges and rights. The appointment and authority of the Governor, the formation and structure of the Legislature, and the establishment of courts of justice, were specially provided for; and generally the powers appropriate to each were defined. The only Charter Governments existing at the time of the American Revolution, were Massachusetts, Rhode Island, and Connecticut.

§13. The Charter Governments differed from the Provincial, principally in this, that they were not immediately under the authority of the Crown, nor bound by any of its acts, which were inconsistent with their charters; whereas the Provincial Governments were entirely subjected to the authority of the Crown. They differed from the Proprietary Governments in this, that the latter were under the control and authority of the Proprietaries, as substitutes of the Crown, in all matters, not secured from such control and authority by the original grants; whereas, in the Charter Governments, the powers were parcelled out among the various departments of government, and permanent boundaries were assigned by the charter to each.

§14. Notwithstanding these differences in their original and actual political organization, the Colonies, at the time of the American Revolution, in most respects, enjoyed the same general rights and privileges. In all of them, there existed a Governor, a Council, and a Representative Assembly, composed of delegates chosen by the people, by whom the legislative and executive functions were exercised according to the particular organization of the Colony. In all of them, the legislative power extended to all local subjects, and was subject only to this restriction, that the laws should not be repugnant to, but, as far as conveniently might be, agreeable to, the law and customs of England. In all of them, express provision was made, that all subjects, and their children, inhabiting in the Colonies, should be deemed natural-born subjects, and should enjoy all the privileges and immunities thereof. In all of them, the common law of England, as far as it was applicable to their situation, was made the basis of their jurisprudence; and that law was asserted at all times by them to be their birthright and inheritance.

§15. It may be asked, how the common law of England came to be the fundamental law of all the Colonies. It may be answered in a few words, that, in all the Proprietary and Charter Governments, there was an express restriction, that no laws should be made repugnant to those of England, but, as near as they might conveniently be, should be consonant and conformable thereto, and, either expressly or by necessary implication, it was provided, that the law of England, so far as it was applicable to the rest of the Colonies, should be in force there. In the Provincial Governments the same provisions were incorporated into all the royal commissions. It may be added, that the common law of England was emphatically the law of a free nation, and secured the public and private rights and liberties of the subjects against the tyranny and oppression of the Crown. Many of these rights and liberties were proclaimed in Magna Charta, (as it is called,) that instrument containing a declaration of rights by the peers and commons of England, wrung from King John, and his son, Henry III, by the pressure of stern necessity. But Magna Charta would itself have been but a dead letter, if it had not been sustained by the powerful influences of the common law, and the right of trial by jury. Accordingly, our ancestors at all times strenuously maintained, that the common law was their birthright, and (as we shall presently see) in the first revolutionary Continental Congress, in 1774, unanimously resolved, that the respective Colonies are entitled to the common law, and more especially to the great and inestimable privilege of being tried by their peers of the vicinage according to the course of that law.

§16. Independently, however, of the special recognitions of the Crown, there is a great conservative principle in the common law of England, which would have insured to our ancestors the right to partake of its protection, its remedial justice, and its extensive blessings. It is a well-settled doctrine of that law, that, if an uninhabited country is discovered and planted by British subjects, the laws of England, so far as they are applicable, are there held immediately in force; for, in all such cases, the subjects, wherever they go, carry those laws with them. This doctrine has been adopted, to save the subjects, in such desert places, from being left in a state of utter insecurity, from the want of all laws to govern them, and from being thus reduced to a mere state of nature. On the contrary, where new countries are obtained by cession or conquest, a different rule exists. The Crown has the sole and exclusive right to abrogate the existing laws, and to prescribe, what new laws shall prevail there; although, until the pleasure of the Crown is made known, the former laws are deemed to remain in force. Attempts were made to hold the American Colonies to be in this latter predicament, that is, to be territories ceded by or conquered from the Indians. But the pretension was always indignantly repelled; and it was insisted, that the sole claim of England thereto being founded on the mere title of discovery, the colonists brought thither all the laws of the parent country, which were applicable to their situation.

§17. We may thus see, in a clear light, the manner, in which the common law was first introduced into the Colonies, and also be better enabled to understand the true nature and reason of the exceptions to it, which are to be found in the laws and usages of the different Colonies. The general basis was the same in all the Colonies. But the entire system was not introduced into any one Colony, but only such portions of it, as were adapted to its own wants, and were applicable to its own situation. Hence the common law can hardly be affirmed to have been exactly, in all respects, the same in all the Colonies. Each Colony selected for itself, and judged for itself, what was most consonant to its institutions, and best adapted to its civil and political arrangements; and, while the main principles were everywhere the same, there were endless minute usages and local peculiarities, in which they differed from each other.

§18. Thus limited and defined by the colonists themselves, in its actual application, the common law became the guardian of their civil and political rights; it protected their infant liberties; it watched over their maturer growth; it expanded with their wants; it nourished in them that spirit of independence, which checked the first approaches of arbitrary power; it enabled them to triumph in the midst of dangers and difficulties; and by the good providence of God, we, their descendants, are now enjoying, under its bold and manly principles, the blessings of a free and enlightened administration of public justice.

§19. Having made these preliminary observations, we may now advance to the consideration of the political state of the Colonies at the time of the Revolution and trace its origin and causes. The natural inquiries here are: What, at this period, were their admitted rights and prerogatives? What were their civil and political relations with the parent country? To what extent were they dependent upon the parent country? What were the limits of the sovereignty, which either Parliament, or the King, might rightfully exercise over them? These are questions of deep importance; but they are more easily put, than answered. A full explanation of them is incompatible with the narrow limits prescribed to the present work; but a brief summary of some of the leading views may not be without use.

CHAPTER III.

Origin of the Revolution.

§20. THE Colonies, at the time of the Revolution, considered themselves, not as parcel of the realm of Great Britain, but as dependencies of the British Crown, and owing allegiance thereto, the King being their supreme and sovereign lord. In virtue of this supremacy, the King exercised the right of hearing appeals from the decisions of the courts of the last resort in the Colonies; of deciding controversies between the Colonies as to their respective jurisdictions and boundaries; and of requiring each Colony to conform to the fundamental laws and constitution of its own establishment, and to yield due obedience in all matters belonging to the paramount sovereignty of the Crown.

§21. Although the Colonies had a common origin and common right, and owed a common allegiance, and the inhabitants of all of them were British subjects, they had no direct political connection with each other. Each colony was independent of the others; and there was no confederacy or alliance between them. The legislature of one could not make laws for another, nor confer privileges to be enjoyed in another. They were also excluded from all political connection with foreign nations; and they followed the fate and fortunes of the parent country in peace and in war. Still the colonists were not wholly alien to each other. On the contrary, they were fellow subjects, and, for many purposes, one people. Every colonist had a right to inhabit, if he pleased, in any other Colony; to trade therewith; and to inherit and hold lands there.

§22. The nature and extent of their dependency upon the parent country is not so easily stated; or, rather, it was left in more uncertainty; the claims on either side not being always well defined, nor clearly acquiesced in. The Colonies claimed exclusive authority to legislate on all subjects of local and internal interest and policy. But they did not deny the right of Parliament to regulate their foreign commerce, and their other external concerns, or to legislate upon the common interests of the whole empire. On the other hand, the Crown claimed a right to exercise many of its prerogatives in the Colonies; and the British Parliament, although it practically interfered little with their internal affairs, yet theoretically maintained the right to legislate over them in all cases whatsoever.

§23. As soon as any systematic effort was made by the British Parliament practically to exert over the Colonies the power of internal legislation and taxation, as was attempted by the Stamp Act, in 1765, it was boldly resisted; and it brought on the memorable controversy, which terminated in their Independence, first asserted by them in 1776, and finally admitted by Great Britain by the Treaty of 1783. At an early period of that controversy, the first Continental Congress, in 1774, drew up and unanimously adopted a declaration of the rights of the Colonies, the substance of which is as follows: (1.) That they are entitled to life, liberty, and property; and they have never ceded to any sovereign power, whatever, a right to dispose of either without their consent. (2.) That our ancestors, who first settled the Colonies, were, at the time of their emigration from the mother country, entitled to all the rights, liberties, and immunities of free and natural-born subjects within the realm of England. (3.) That by such emigration they by no means forfeited, surrendered, or lost any of those rights; but that they were, and their descendants now are, entitled to the exercise and enjoyment of all such of them, as their local and other circumstances enable them to exercise and enjoy. (4.) That the foundation of English liberty is a right in the people to participate in their legislative councils; and as the English colonists are not represented, and, from their local and other circumstances, cannot properly be represented, in the British Parliament, they are entitled to a free and exclusive power of legislation in their several provincial assemblies, where their right of representation can alone be preserved, in all cases of taxation and internal polity, subject only to the negative of their sovereign, in such manner as has been heretofore used and accustomed. But from the necessity of the case, and a regard to the mutual interests of both countries, they cheerfully consent to the operation of such acts of the British Parliament, as are *bonâ fide* restrained to the regulation of their external commerce, for the purpose of securing the commercial advantages of the whole empire to the mother country, and the commercial benefits of its respective members, excluding every action of taxation, internal or external, for raising a revenue on the subjects in America without their consent. (5.) That the respective Colonies are entitled to the common law of England, and more especially, the great and inestimable privilege of being tried by their peers of the vicinage, according to the course of that law, (meaning the trial by jury). (6.) That the Colonies are entitled to the benefit of such of the English statutes, as existed at the time of their colonization, and which they have, by experience, respectively found applicable to their several local and other circumstances. (7.) That they are likewise entitled to all the immunities and privileges granted and confirmed to them by royal charters, or secured to them by their several codes of provincial law. (8.) That they have a right peaceably to assemble, consider of their grievances, and petition the King; and that all prosecutions, prohibitory proclamations, and commitments for the same, are illegal. (9.) That the keeping of a standing army in these Colonies in times of peace, without the consent of the legislature of that Colony, in which such army is kept, is against law. (10.) That it is indispensably necessary to good government, and rendered essential by the English constitution, that the constituent branches of the legislature be independent of each other; that, therefore, the exercise of legislative power in several Colonies by a Council appointed during pleasure by the Crown, is unconstitutional, dangerous, and destructive to the freedom of American legislation.

§24. Such is, in substance, the Bill of Rights claimed in behalf of all the Colonies by the Continental Congress, the violation of which, constituted the main grounds, upon which the American Revolution was founded; and the grievances, under which the Colonies labored, being persisted in by the British government, a resort to arms became unavoidable. The result of the contest is well known and has been already stated; and it belongs to the department of history, and not of constitutional law, to enumerate the interesting events of that period.

CHAPTER IV.

Revolutionary Government.

§25. BUT it may be asked, and it properly belongs to this work to declare: What was the political organization, under which the Revolution was carried on and accomplished? The Colonies being, as we have seen, separate and independent of each other in their original establishment, and down to the eve of the Revolution, it became indispensable, in order to make their resistance to the British claims either formidable or successful, that there should be harmony and unity of operations under some common head. Massachusetts, in 1774, recommended the assembling of a Continental Congress at Philadelphia, to be composed of delegates chosen in all the Colonies, for the purpose of deliberating on the common good, and to provide a suitable scheme of future operations. Delegates were accordingly chosen in the various Colonies, some by the legislative body, some by the popular representative branch thereof, and some by conventions of the people, according to the several means and local circumstances of each Colony. This first great Continental Congress assembled on the 4th of September, 1774, chose their own officers, and adopted certain fundamental rules to regulate their proceedings. The most important rule then adopted was, that each Colony should have one vote only in Congress, whatever might be the number of its delegates; and this became the established course throughout the whole Revolution. They adopted such other measures, as the exigency of the occasion seemed to require; and proposed another Congress, to be assembled for the like purpose, in May, 1775, which was accordingly held. The delegates of this last Congress were chosen in the same manner as the preceding; but principally by conventions of the people in the several Colonies. It was the same Congress, which, after voting other great measures, all leading to open war, finally, in 1776, made the Declaration of Independence, which was unanimously adopted by the American people. Under the recommendations of the same Congress, suitable arrangements were made to organize the State governments, so as to supply the deficiencies in the former establishments; and henceforth the delegates to the Continental Congress from time to time assembled, were appointed by the State legislatures.

§26. The Continental Congress, thus organized by a voluntary association of the States, and continued by the successive appointments of the State legislatures, constituted, in fact, the National Government, and conducted the national affairs until near the close of the Revolution, when, as we shall presently see, the Articles of Confederation were adopted by all the States. Their powers were nowhere defined or limited. They assumed, among others, the power to declare war and make peace, to raise armies and equip navies, to form treaties and alliances with foreign nations, to contract public debts, and to do all other sovereign acts essential to the safety of the United Colonies. Whatever powers they assumed were deemed legitimate. These powers originated from necessity and were only limited by events; or, in other words, they were revolutionary powers. In the exercise of these powers, they were supported by the people, and the exercise of them could not, therefore, be justly questioned by any inferior authority. In an exact sense, then, the powers of the Continental Congress might be said to be coextensive with the exigencies and necessities of the public affairs; and the people, by their approbation and acquiescence, justified all their acts, having the most entire reliance upon their patriotism, their integrity, and their political wisdom.

§27. But it was obvious to reflecting minds, upon the slightest consideration, that the union thus formed, was but of a temporary nature, dependent upon the consent of all the Colonies, now become States, and capable of being dissolved, at any time, by the secession of any one of them. It grew out of the exigencies and dangers of the times; and, extending only to the maintenance of the public liberties and independence of all the States during the contest with Great Britain, it would normally terminate with the return of peace, and the accomplishment of the ends of the revolutionary contest. As little could it escape observation, how great would be the dangers of the separation of the confederated States into independent communities, acknowledging no common head, and acting upon no common system. Rivalries, jealousies, real or imaginary wrongs, diversities of local interests and institutions, would soon sever the ties of a common attachment, which bound them together, and bring on a state of hostile operations, dangerous to their peace, and subversive of their permanent interests.

CHAPTER V.

History of the Confederation.

§28. ONE of the first objects, therefore, beyond that of the immediate public safety, which engaged the attention of the Continental Congress, was to provide the means of a permanent union of all the Colonies under a General Government. The deliberations on this subject were coeval with the Declaration of Independence, and, after various debates and discussions, at different sessions, the Continental Congress finally agreed, in November, 1777, upon a frame of government, contained in certain Articles of Confederation, which were immediately sent to all the States for their approval and adoption. Various delays and objections, however, on the part of some of the States, took place; and as the government was not to go into effect, until the consent of all the States should be obtained, the Confederation was not finally adopted until March, 1781, when Maryland (the last State) acceded to it. The principal objections taken to the Confederation were to the mode prescribed by it for apportioning taxes among the States, and raising the quota or proportions of the public forces; to the power given to keep up a standing army in time of peace; and, above all, to the omission of the reservation of all the public lands, owned by the Crown, within the boundaries of the

United States, to the National Government, for national purposes. This latter subject was one of a perpetually recurring and increasing irritation; and the Confederation would never have been acceded to, if Virginia and New York had not at last consented to make liberal cessions of the territory within their respective boundaries for national purposes.

§29. The Articles of Confederation had scarcely been adopted, before the defects of the plan, as a frame of national government, began to manifest themselves. The instrument, indeed, was framed under circumstances very little favorable to a just survey of the subject in all its proper bearings. The States, while colonies, had been under the controlling authority of a foreign sovereignty, whose restrictive legislation had been severely felt, and whose prerogatives, real or assumed, had been a source of incessant jealousy and alarm. Of course, they had nourished a spirit of resistance to all external authority, and having had no experience of the inconveniences of the want of some general government to superintend their common affairs and interests, they reluctantly yielded anything, and deemed the least practicable delegation of power quite sufficient for national purposes. Notwithstanding the Confederation purported on its face to contain articles of perpetual union, it was easy to see, that its principal powers respected the operations of war, and were dormant in times of peace; and that even these were shadowy and unsubstantial, since they were stripped of all coercive authority. It was remarked, by an eminent statesman, that by this political compact the Continental Congress has exclusive power for the following purposes, without being able to execute one of them:—It may make and conclude treaties; but can only recommend the observance of them. It may appoint ambassadors; but it cannot defray even the expense of their tables. It may borrow money in its own name, or the faith of the Union; but it cannot pay a dollar. It may coin money; but it cannot import an ounce of bullion. It may make war, and determine what number of troops are necessary; but it cannot raise a single soldier. In short, it may declare everything, but it can do nothing. And, strong as this description may seem, it was literally true; for Congress had little more than the power of recommending its measures to the good will of the States.

§30. The leading defects of the Confederation were the following: In the first place, there was an utter want of all coercive authority in the Continental Congress, to carry into effect any of its constitutional measures. It could not legislate directly upon persons; and, therefore, its measures were to be carried into effect by the States; and of course, whether they were executed or not, depended upon the sole pleasure of the legislatures of the latter. And, in point of fact, many of the measures of the Continental Congress were silently disregarded; many were slowly and reluctantly obeyed; and some of them were openly and boldly refused to be executed.

§31. In the next place, there was no power in the Continental Congress to punish individuals for any breaches of its enactments. Its laws, if laws they might be called, were without any penal sanction; the Continental Congress could not impose a fine, or imprisonment, or any other punishment, upon refractory officers, or even suspend them from office. Under such circumstances, it might naturally be supposed, that men followed their own interests, rather than their duties. They obeyed, when it was convenient, and cared little for persuasions, and less for conscientious obligations. The wonder is, not that such a scheme of government should fail; but, that it should have been capable even of a momentary existence.

§32. In the next place, the Continental Congress had no power to lay taxes, or to collect revenue, for the public service. All that it could do was, to ascertain the sums necessary to be raised for the public service, and to apportion its quota or proportion upon each State. The power to lay and collect the taxes was expressly and exclusively reserved to the States. The consequence was, that great delays took place in collecting the taxes; and the evils from this source were of incalculable extent, even during the Revolutionary War. The Continental Congress was often wholly without funds to meet the exigencies of the public service; and if it had not been for its good fortune, in obtaining money by some loans in foreign countries, it is far from being certain, that this dilatory scheme of taxation would not have been fatal to the cause of the Revolution. After the peace of 1783, the States relapsed into utter indifference on this subject. The requisitions of the Continental Congress for funds, even for the purpose of enabling it to pay the interest of the public debt, were openly disregarded; and, notwithstanding the most affecting appeals, made from time to time by the Congress, to the patriotism, the sense of duty, and the justice of the States, the latter refused to raise the necessary supplies. The consequence was, that the national treasury was empty; the credit of the Confederacy was sunk to a low ebb; the public burdens were increasing; and the public faith was prostrated and openly violated.

§33. In the next place, the Continental Congress had no power to regulate commerce, either with foreign nations, or among the several States composing the Union. Commerce, both foreign and domestic, was left exclusively to the management of each particular State, according to its view of its own interests, or its local prejudices. The consequence was, that the most opposite regulations existed in the different States; and, in many cases, and especially between neighboring States, there was a perpetual course of retaliatory legislation, from their jealousies and rivalries in commerce, in agriculture, or in manufactures. Foreign nations did not fail to avail themselves of all the advantages accruing to themselves from this suicidal policy, tending to the common ruin. And as the evils grew more pressing, the resentments of the States against each other, and the consciousness, that their local interests were placed in opposition to each other, were daily increasing the mass of disaffection, until it became obvious, that the dangers of immediate warfare between some of the States were imminent; and thus, the peace and safety of the Union were made dependent upon measures of the States, over which the General Government had not the slightest control.

§34. But the evil did not rest here. Our foreign commerce was not only crippled, but almost destroyed, by this want of uniform laws to regulate it. Foreign nations imposed upon our navigation and trade just such restrictions, as they deemed best to their own interest and policy. All of them had a common interest to stint our trade, and enlarge their own; and all of them were well satisfied, that they might, in the distracted state of our legislation, pass whatever acts they pleased on this subject, with impunity. They did not fail to avail themselves, to the utmost, of their advantages. They pursued a system of the most rigorous exclusion of our shipping from all the benefits of their own commerce; and endeavored to secure, with a bold and unhesitating confidence, a monopoly of ours. The effects of this system of operations, combined with our political weakness, were soon visible. Our navigation was ruined; our mechanics were in a state of inextricable poverty; our agriculture was withered; and the little money still found in the country was gradually finding its way abroad, to supply our immediate wants. In the rear of all this, there was a heavy public debt, which there was no means to pay; and a state of alarming embarrassment, in that most difficult and delicate of all relations, the relation of private debtors and creditors, threatened daily an overthrow even of the ordinary administration of justice. Severe, as were the calamities of the war, the pressure of them was far less mischievous, than this slow but progressive destruction of all our resources, all our industry, and all our credit.

§35. There were many other defects in the Confederation, of a subordinate character and importance. But these were sufficient to establish its utter unfitness, as a frame of government, for a free, enterprising, and industrious people. Great, however, and manifold as the evils were, and, indeed, so glaring and so universal it was yet extremely difficult to induce the States to concur in adopting any adequate remedies to redress them. For several years, efforts were made by some of our wisest and best patriots to procure an enlargement of the powers of the Continental Congress; but, from the predominance of State jealousies, and the supposed incompatibility of State interests with each other, they all failed. At length, however, it became apparent, that the Confederation, being left without resources and without powers, must soon expire of its own debility. It had not only lost all vigor, but it had ceased even to be respected. It had approached the last stages of its decline; and the only question, which remained, was, whether it should be left to a silent dissolution, or an attempt should be made to form a more efficient government, before the great interests of the Union were buried beneath its ruins.

CHAPTER VI.

Origin of the Constitution.

§36. In 1785, commissioners were appointed by the legislatures of Maryland and Virginia, to form a compact, relative to the navigation of the rivers Potomac and Roanoke, and the Chesapeake Bay. The commissioners met, accordingly, at Alexandria, in Virginia; but, feeling the want of adequate powers, they recommended proceedings of a more enlarged nature. The legislature of Virginia accordingly, in January, 1786, proposed a convention of commissioners from all the States, for the purpose of taking into consideration the state of trade, and the propriety of a uniform system of commercial relations, for their permanent harmony and common interest. Pursuant to this proposal, commissioners were appointed by five States, who met at Annapolis, in September, 1786. They framed a Report, to be laid before the Continental Congress, advising the latter to call a General Convention, of commissioners from all the States, to meet in Philadelphia, in May, 1787, for a more effectual revision of the Articles of Confederation.

§37. Congress adopted the recommendation of the Report, and in February, 1787, passed a resolution for assembling a Convention accordingly. All the States, except Rhode Island, appointed delegates; and they met at Philadelphia. After very protracted deliberations, and great diversities of opinion, they finally, on the 17th of September, 1787, framed the present Constitution of the United States, and recommended it to be laid by the Congress before the several States, to be by them considered and ratified, in conventions of the representatives of the people, to be called for that purpose. The Continental Congress accordingly took measures for this purpose. Conventions were accordingly called in all the States, except Rhode Island, and, after many warm discussions, the Constitution was ratified by all of them, except North Carolina and Rhode Island.

§38. The assent of nine States only being required to put the Constitution into operation, measures were taken for this purpose, by Congress, in September, 1788, as soon as the requisite ratifications were ascertained. Electors of President and Vice President were chosen, who subsequently assembled and gave their votes; and the necessary elections of Senators and Representatives being made, the first Congress under the Constitution assembled at New York, (the then seat of government,) on Wednesday, the 4th day of March, 1789, for commencing proceedings under the Constitution. A quorum, however, of both Houses, for the transaction of business generally, did not assemble until the 6th of April following, when, the votes of the Electors being counted, it was found, that George Washington was unanimously elected President, and John Adams was elected Vice President. On the 30th of April, President Washington was sworn into office; and the government immediately went into full operation. North Carolina afterwards, in a new convention, held in November, 1789, adopted the Constitution; and Rhode Island, also, by a convention, held in May, 1790. So that all the thirteen States, by the authority of the people thereof, finally became parties under the new government.

§39. Thus was achieved another, and still more glorious, triumph, in the case of liberty, even than that, by which we were separated from the parent country. It was not achieved, however, without great difficulties and sacrifices of opinion. It required all the wisdom, the patriotism, and the genius of our best statesmen, to overcome the objections, which, from various causes, were arrayed against it. The history of those times is full of melancholy instruction, at once to admonish us of the dangers, through which we have passed, and of the necessity of incessant vigilance, to guard and preserve, what has been thus hardly earned. The Constitution was adopted unanimously in New Jersey, Delaware, and Georgia. It was supported by large majorities in Connecticut, Pennsylvania, Maryland, and South Carolina. In the remaining States, it was carried by small majorities; and especially, in Massachusetts, New York, and Virginia, by little more than a mere preponderating vote. What a humiliating lesson is this, after all our sufferings and sacrifices, and after our long and sad experience of the evils of disunited councils, and of the pernicious influence of State jealousies, and local interests! It teaches us, how slowly even adversity brings the mind to a due sense of what political wisdom requires. It teaches us, how liberty itself may be lost, when men are found ready to hazard its permanent blessings, rather than submit to the wholesome restraints, which its permanent security demands.

§40. To those great men, who thus framed the Constitution, and secured the adoption of it, we owe a debt of gratitude, which can scarcely be repaid. It was not then, as it is now, looked upon, from the blessings, which, under the guidance of Divine Providence, it has bestowed, with general favor and affection. On the contrary, many of those pure and disinterested patriots, who stood forth, the firm advocates of its principles, did so at the expense of their existing popularity. They felt, that they had a higher duty to perform, than to flatter the prejudices of the people, or to subserve selfish, or sectional, or local interests. Many of them went to their graves, without the soothing consolation, that their services and their sacrifices were duly appreciated. They scorned every attempt to rise to power and influence by the common arts of demagogues; and they were content to trust their characters, and their conduct, to the deliberate judgement of posterity.

§41. If, upon a close survey of their labors, as developed in the actual structure of the Constitution, we shall have reason to admire their wisdom and forecast, to observe their profound love of liberty, and to trace their deep sense of the value of political responsibility, and their anxiety, above all things, to give perpetuity, as well as energy, to the republican institutions of their country; then, indeed, will our gratitude kindle into a holier reverence, and their memories will be cherished among those of the noblest benefactors of mankind.

CHAPTER VII.

Exposition of the Constitution.—The Preamble.

§42. HAVING given this general sketch of the origin of the Colonies, of the rise and fall of the Confederation, and of the formation and adoption of the Constitution of the United States, we are now prepared to enter upon an examination of the actual structure and organization of that Constitution, and the powers belonging to it. We shall treat it, not as a mere compact, or league, or confederacy, existing at the mere will of any one or more of the States, during their good pleasure; but, (as it purports on its face to be,) as a Constitution of Government, framed and adopted by the people of the United States, and obligatory upon all the States, until it is altered, amended, or abolished by the people, in the manner pointed out in the instrument itself. It is to be interpreted, as all other solemn instruments are, by endeavoring to ascertain the true sense and meaning of all the terms; and we are neither to narrow them, nor to enlarge them, by straining them from their just and natural import, for the purpose of adding to, or diminishing its powers, or bending them to any favorite theory or dogma of party. It is the language of the people, to be judged of according to common sense, and not by mere theoretical reasoning. It is not an instrument for the mere private interpretation of any particular men. The people have established it and spoken their will; and their will, thus promulgated, is to be obeyed as the supreme law. Every department of the Government must, of course, in the first instance, in the exercise of its own powers and duties, necessarily construe the instrument. But, if the case admits of judicial cognizance, every citizen has a right to contest the validity of that construction before the proper judicial tribunal; and to bring it to the test of the Constitution. And, if the case is not capable of judicial redress, still the people may, through the acknowledged means of new elections, or proposed amendments, check any usurpation of authority, whether wanton, or unintentional, and thus relieve themselves from any grievances of a political nature.

§43. For a right understanding of the Constitution of the United States, it will be found most convenient to examine the provisions, generally, in the order, in which they are stated in the instrument itself; and thus, the different parts may be made mutually to illustrate each other. This order will, accordingly, be adopted in the ensuing commentaries.

§44. We shall begin then, with the Preamble, which is in the following words:—

"WE, the people of the United States, in order to form a more perfect union, establish justice, insure domestic tranquility, provide for the common defence, promote the general welfare, and secure the blessings of liberty to ourselves and our posterity, do ordain and establish this Constitution for the United States of America."

§45. This Preamble is very important, not only as explanatory of the motives and objects of framing the Constitution; but, as affording the best key to the true interpretation thereof. For it may well be presumed, that the language used will be in conformity to the motives, which govern the parties, and the objects to be attained by the Instrument. Every provision in the instrument may therefore fairly be presumed to have reference to one or more of these objects. And consequently, if any provision is susceptible of two interpretations, that ought to be adopted, and adhered to, which best harmonizes with the avowed intentions and objects of the authors, as gathered from their declarations in the instrument itself.

§46. The first object is, "to form a more perfect union." From what has been already stated, respecting the defects of the Confederation, it is obvious, that a further continuance of the Union was impracticable, unless a new government was formed, possessing more powers and more energy. That the Union of the States is in the highest degree desirable, nay, that it is almost indispensable to the political existence of the States, is a proposition, which admits of the most complete moral demonstration, so far as human experience and general reasoning can establish it. If the States were wholly separated from each other, the very inequality of their population, territory, resources, and means of protecting their local interests, would soon subject them to injurious rivalries, jealousies, and retaliatory measures. The weak would be wholly unable to contend successfully against the strong, and would be compelled to submit to the terms, which the policy of their more powerful neighbors should impose upon them. What could Rhode Island, or New Jersey, or Delaware, accomplish against the will, or the resentments, of the formidable States, which surround them? But, in a more general view, the remark of the Abbe Mably may be appealed to, as containing the result of all human experience. "Neighboring states (says he) are naturally enemies of each other, unless their common weakness forces them to league in a confederative republic, and their Constitution prevents the differences, that neighborhood occasions, extinguishing that secret jealousy, which disposes all states to aggrandize themselves, at the expense of their neighbors."

§47. On the other hand, if the States should separate into distinct confederacies, there could scarcely be less than three, and most probably, there would be four; an Eastern, a Middle, a Southern, and a Western Confederacy. The lines of division would be traced out by geographical boundaries between the slave-holding and the non-slave-holding States, a division, in itself, fraught with constant causes of irritation and alarm. There would also be marked distinctions between the commercial, the manufacturing, and the agricultural States, which would perpetually give rise to real or supposed grievances and inequalities. But the most important consideration is, that, in order to maintain such confederacies, it would be necessary to clothe the government of each of them with summary and extensive powers, almost incompatible with liberty, and to keep up large and expensive establishments, as well for defence as for offence, in order to guard against the sudden inroads, or deliberate aggressions of their neighbors and rivals. The evils of faction, the tendencies to corrupt influence, the pressure of taxation, the necessary delegation of arbitrary powers, and the fluctuations of legislation, would thus be immeasurably increased. Foreign nations, too, would not fail to avail themselves, in pursuit of their own interests, of every opportunity to foster our intestine divisions, since they might thus more easily command our trade, or monopolize our products, or crush our manufactures, or keep us in a state of dependence upon their good will for our security.

§48. The Union of the States, "the more perfect union" of them, under a National Government, is, then, and forever must be, invaluable to the whole country, in respect to foreign and domestic concerns. It will diminish the causes of war, that scourge of the human race; it will enable the National Government to protect and secure the rights of the whole people; it will diminish public expenditures; it will insure respect abroad, and confidence at home; and it will unite in one common bond the interests of agriculture, of commerce, and of manufactures.

§49. The next object is, "to establish justice." This, indeed, is the first object of all good and rational forms of government. Without justice being fully, freely, and impartially administered, neither our persons, nor our rights, nor our property, can be protected. Call the form of government whatever you may, if justice cannot be equally obtained by all the citizens, high and low, rich and poor, it is a mere despotism. Of what use is it to have wise laws to protect our rights or property, if there are no adequate means of enforcing them? Of what use are constitutional provisions or prohibitions, if they may be violated with impunity? If there are no tribunals of justice established to administer the laws with firmness and independence, and placed above the reach of the influence of rulers, or the denunciations of mobs, what security can any citizen have for his personal safety or for his public or private rights? It may, therefore, be laid down as a fundamental maxim of all governments, that justice ought to be administered freely and fully between private persons; and it is rarely departed from, even in the most absolute despotisms, unless under circumstances of extraordinary policy or excitement. Doubtless, the attainment of justice is the foundation, on which all our State governments rest; and, therefore, the inquiry may naturally present itself, in what respects the formation of a National Government would better tend to establish justice.

§50. The answer may be given in a few words. In the administration of justice, citizens of the particular State are not alone interested. Foreign nations, and their subjects, as well as citizens of other States, may be deeply interested. They may have rights to be protected; wrongs to be redressed; contracts to be enforced; and equities to be acknowledged. It may be presumed, that the States will provide adequate means to redress the grievances, and secure the rights of their own citizens. But, it is far from being certain, that they will at all times, or even ordinarily, take the like measures to redress the grievances, and secure the rights of foreigners, and citizens of other States. On the contrary, one of the rarest occurrences in human legislation is, to find foreigners, and citizens of other States, put upon a footing of equality with the citizens of the legislating State. The natural tendency of every government is, to favor its own citizens; and unjust preferences, not only in the administration, but in the very structure of the laws, have often arisen, and may reasonably be presumed hereafter to arise. It could not be expected, that all the American States, left at full liberty, would legislate upon the subject of rights and remedies, preferences and contracts, exactly in the same manner. And every diversity would soon bring on some retaliatory legislation elsewhere. Popular prejudices and passions, real or supposed injuries, or inequalities, the common attachment to persons, whom we know, as well as to domestic pursuits and interests, and the common indifference to strangers and remote objects, are often found to interfere with a liberal policy in legislation. Now, precisely, what this reasoning would lead us to presume as probable, actually occurred, not only while we were colonies of Great Britain, but also under the Confederation. The legislation of several of the States gave a most unjust preference to the debts of their own citizens in cases of insolvency, over those due to the citizens of other States and to foreigners.

§51. But there were other evils of a much greater magnitude, which required a National Government, clothed with powers adequate to the more effectual establishment of justice. There were territorial disputes between the States, as to their respective boundaries and jurisdiction, constantly exciting mutual irritations, and introducing border warfare. Laws were perpetually made in the States, interfering with the sacred rights of private contracts, suspending the remedies in regard to them, or discharging them by a payment or tender in worthless paper money, or in some depreciated or valueless property. The debts due to foreigners were, notoriously, refused payment; and many obstructions were put in the way of the recovery of them. The public debt was left wholly unprovided for; and a disregard of the public faith had become so common a reproach among us, that it almost ceased to attract observation. Indeed, in some of the States, the operation of private and public distresses was felt so severely, that the administration, even of domestic justice, was constantly interfered with; the necessity of suspending it was boldly vindicated; and in some cases, even a resort to arms was encouraged to prevent it. Nothing but a National Government, capable, from its powers and resources, of overawing the spirit of rebellion, and of aiding in the establishment of a sound currency, just laws, and solid public credit, could remedy the existing evils.

§52. The next object is, "to insure domestic tranquility." From what has been already stated, it is apparent, how essential an efficient National Government is, to the security of the States against foreign influence, domestic dissensions, commercial rivalries, legislative retaliations, territorial disputes, and the perpetual irritations of a border warfare, for privileges, or exemptions, or smuggling. In addition to these considerations, it is well known, that factions are far more violent in small than in large communities; and that they are even more dangerous and enfeebling; because success and defeat more rapidly succeed each other in the changes of their local affairs, and foreign influences can be more easily brought into play to corrupt and divide them. A National Government naturally tends to disarm the violence of domestic factions in small states, by its superior influence. It diminishes the exciting causes, and it leaves fewer chances of success to their operations.

§53. The next object is, "to provide for the common defence." One of the surest means of preserving peace is always to be prepared for war. One of the safest reliances against foreign aggression is the possession of numbers and resources, capable of repelling any attack. A nation of narrow territory, and small population, and moderate resources, can never be formidable; and must content itself with being feeble and unenviable in its condition. On the contrary, a nation or a confederacy, which possesses large territory, abundant resources, and a dense population, can always command respect, and is almost incapable, if true to itself, of being conquered. In proportion to the size and population of a nation, its general resources will be; and the same expenditures, which may be easily borne by a numerous and industrious people, would soon exhaust the means of a scanty population. What, for instance, would be more burdensome to a State like New Jersey, than the necessity of keeping up a large body of troops, to protect itself against the encroachments of the neighboring States of Pennsylvania and New York? The same military force, which would hardly be felt in either of the latter States, would press heavily upon the resources of a small State, as a permanent establishment. The ordinary expenditures, necessary for the protection of the whole Union with its present limits, are probably less than would be required for a single State, surrounded by jealous and hostile neighbors.

§54. But, in regard to foreign powers, the States separately would sink at once into the insignificance of the small European principalities. In the present situation of the world, a few great powers possess the command of commerce, both on land and at sea. No effectual resistance could be offered by any of the States singly, against any monopoly, which the great European Powers might choose to establish, or any pretensions, which they might choose to assert. Each State would be compelled to submit its own commerce to all the burdens and inequalities, which they might impose; or purchase protection, by yielding up its dearest rights, and, perhaps, its own independence. A National Government, containing, as it does, the strength of all the States, affords to all of them a competent protection. Any navy, or army, which could be maintained by a single State, would be scarcely formidable to any second-rate power in Europe; and yet it would be an intolerable public burden upon the resources of that State. A navy, or army, competent for all the purposes of our home defence, and even for the protection of our commerce on the ocean, is within the compass of the actual means of the General Government, without any severe exaction upon its finances.

§55. The next object is, "to promote the general welfare." If it should be asked, why this may not be effectually accomplished by the States, it may be answered; first, that they do not possess the means; and secondly, if they did, they do not possess the powers necessary to carry the appropriate measures into execution. The means of the several States will rarely be found to exceed their actual domestic wants, and appropriations to domestic improvements. Their resources by internal taxation must necessarily be limited; and their revenue from imports would, if there were no national government, be small and fluctuating. Their whole system would be defeated by the jealousy, or competitions, or local interests of their neighbors. The want of uniformity of duties in all the States, as well as the facility of smuggling goods, imported into one State, into the territory of another, would render any efficient collection of duties almost impracticable. This is not a matter of mere theory. It was established by our own history and experience under the Confederation. The duties imposed upon the importation of goods by Massachusetts, were completely evaded or nullified by their free admission into the neighboring State of Rhode Island.

§56. But, if the means were completely within the reach of the several States, the jurisdiction would still be wanting, completely to carry into effect any great or comprehensive plan for the welfare of the whole. The idea of a permanent and zealous cooperation of all the States in any one scheme for the common welfare, is visionary. No scheme could be devised, which would not bear unequally upon some particular sections of the country; and these inequalities could not be, as they now are, meliorated and corrected under the general government, by other correspondent benefits. Each State would necessarily legislate singly; and it is scarcely possible, that various changes of councils should not take place, before any scheme could receive the sanction of all of them. Infinite delays would intervene, and various modifications of measures would be proposed, to suit particular local interests, which would again require reconsideration. After one or two vain attempts to accomplish any great system of improvements, there would be a general abandonment of all efforts to produce a general system for the regulation of our commerce, or agriculture, or manufactures; and each State would be driven to consult its own peculiar convenience and policy only, in despair of any common concert. And even if it were practicable, from any peculiar conjuncture of circumstances, to bring about such a system at one time, it is obvious, that it would be liable to be broken up, without a moment's warning, at the mere caprice, or pleasure, or change of policy, of a single State.

§57. The concluding object, stated in the Preamble, is, "to secure the blessings of liberty to us, and our posterity." And surely nothing of mere earthly concern is more worthy of the profound reflection of wise and good men, than to erect structures of government, which shall permanently sustain the interests of civil, political, and religious liberty, on solid foundations. The great problem in human governments has hitherto been, how to combine durability with moderation in powers, energy with equality of rights, responsibility with a sense of independence, steadiness in councils with popular elections, and a lofty spirit of patriotism with the love of personal aggrandizement; in short, how to combine the greatest happiness of the whole with the least practicable restraints, so as to insure permanence in the public institutions, intelligent legislation, and incorruptible private virtue. The Constitution of the United States aims at the attainment of these ends, by the arrangements and distributions of its powers; by the introduction of checks and balances in all its departments; by making the existence of the State governments an essential part of its own organization; by leaving with the States the ordinary powers of domestic legislation; and, at the same time, by drawing to itself those powers only, which are strictly national, or concern the general welfare. Its duties and its powers thus naturally combine to make it the common guardian and friend of all the States; and in return, the States, while they may exercise a salutary vigilance for their own self-protection, are persuasively taught, that the blessings of liberty, secured by the national government, are far more certain, more various, and more extensive, than they would be under their own distinct and independent sovereignties.

§58. Let us now enter upon a more close survey of the structure and powers of the national Constitution, that we may see, whether it is as wisely framed as its founders believed; so as to justify our confidence in its durability, and in its adaptation to our wants, and the great objects proposed in the Preamble. If it be so wisely framed, then, indeed, it will be entitled to our most profound reverence; and we shall accustom ourselves to repel with indignation every attempt to weaken its powers, or obstruct its operations, or diminish its influence, as involving our own degradation, and, ultimately, the ruin of the States themselves.

CHAPTER VIII.

Distribution of Powers.—The Legislative Department.

§59. IN surveying the general structure of the Constitution of the United States, we are naturally led to an examination of the fundamental principles, on which it is organized, for the purpose of carrying into effect the objects disclosed in the Preamble. Every government must include within its scope, at least if it is to possess suitable stability and energy, the exercise of the three great powers, upon which all governments are supposed to rest, *viz.*, the executive, the legislative, and the judicial powers. The manner and extent, in which these powers are to be exercised, and the functionaries, in whom they are to be vested, constitute the great distinctions, which are known in the forms of government. In absolute governments, the whole executive, legislative, and judicial powers are, at least in their final result, exclusively confided to a single individual; and such a form of government is denominated a Despotism, as the whole sovereignty of the State is vested in him. If the same powers are exclusively confided to a few persons, constituting a permanent sovereign council, the government may be appropriately denominated an absolute or despotic Aristocracy. If they are exercised by the people at large in their original sovereign assemblies, the government is a pure and absolute Democracy. But it is more common to find these powers divided, and separately exercised by independent functionaries, the executive power by one department, the legislative by another, and the judicial by a third; and in these cases the government is properly deemed a mixed one; a mixed monarchy, if the executive power is hereditary in a single person; a mixed aristocracy, if it is hereditary in several chieftains or families; and a mixed democracy or republic, if it is delegated by election, and is not hereditary. In mixed monarchies and aristocracies, some of the functionaries of the legislative and judicial powers are, or at least may be, hereditary. But in a representative republic, all power emanates from the people, and is exercised by their choice, and never extends beyond the lives of the individuals, to whom it is intrusted. It may be intrusted for any shorter period; and then it returns to them again, to be again delegated by a new choice.

§60. The first thing, that strikes us, upon the slightest survey of the national Constitution, is, that its structure contains a fundamental separation of the three great departments of government, the legislative, the executive, and the judicial. The existence of all these departments has always been found indispensable to due energy and stability in a government. Their separation has always been found equally indispensable, for the preservation of public liberty and private rights. Whenever they are all vested in one person or body of men, the government is in fact a despotism, by whatever name it may be called, whether a monarchy, or an aristocracy, or a democracy. When, therefore, the Convention, which framed the Constitution, determined on a more efficient system than the Confederation, the first resolution adopted by them was, that "a national government ought to be established, consisting of a supreme legislative, judiciary, and executive."

§61. In the establishment of free governments, the division of the three great powers of government, the executive, the legislative, and the judicial, among different functionaries, has been a favorite policy with patriots and statesmen. It has by many been deemed a maxim of vital importance, that these powers should forever be kept separate and distinct. And, accordingly, we find it laid down, with emphatic care, in the Bill of Rights of several of the State Constitutions.

§62. The general reasoning, by which the maxim is supported, independently of the just weight of the authority in its support, seems entirely satisfactory. What is of far more value than any mere reasoning, experience has demonstrated it to be founded in a just view of the nature of government, and of the safety and liberty of the people. It is no small commendation of the Constitution of the United States, that, instead of adopting a new theory, it has placed this practical truth, at the basis of its organization. It has placed the legislative, executive, and judicial powers in different hands. It has, as we shall presently see, made the term of office and the organization of each department different. For objects of permanent and paramount importance, it has given to the judicial department a tenure of office during good behavior; while it has limited each of the others to a term of years.

§63. But when we speak of a separation of the three great departments of government, and maintain, that that separation is indispensable to public liberty, we are to understand this maxim in a limited sense. It is not meant to affirm, that they must be kept wholly and entirely separate and distinct, and have no common link of connection or dependence, the one upon the other, in the slightest degree. The true meaning is, that the whole power of one of these departments should not be exercised by the same hands, which possess the whole power of either of the other departments; and that such exercise of the whole by the same hands would subvert the principles of a free constitution.

§64. How far the Constitution of the United States, in the actual separation of these departments, and the occasional mixtures of some of the powers of each, has accomplished the great objects of the maxim, which we have been considering, will appear more fully, when a survey is taken of the particular powers confided to each department. But the true and only test must, after all, be experience, which corrects at once the errors of theory, and fortifies and illustrates the eternal judgements of Nature.

§65. The first section, of the first article, begins with the structure of the Legislature. It is in these words:—

"All legislative powers, herein granted, shall be vested in a Congress of the United States; which shall consist of a Senate and House of Representatives." Under the Confederation, the whole legislative power of the Union was confided to a single branch; and, limited as that power was, this concentration of it, in a single body, was deemed a prominent defect. The Constitution, on the other hand, adopts, as a fundamental rule, the exercise of the legislative power by two distinct and independent branches. The advantages of this division are, in the first place, that it interposes a great check upon undue, hasty, and oppressive legislation. In the next place, it interposes a barrier against the strong propensity of all public bodies to accumulate all power, patronage, and influence in their own hands. In the next place, it operates, indirectly, to retard, if not wholly to prevent, the success of the efforts of a few popular leaders, by their combinations and intrigues in a single body, to carry their own personal, private, or party objects into effect, unconnected with the public good. In the next place, it secures a deliberate review of the same measures, by independent minds, in different branches of government, engaged in the same habits of legislation, but organized upon a different system of elections. And, in the last place, it affords great securities to public liberty, by requiring the cooperation of different bodies, which can scarcely ever, if properly organized, embrace the same sectional or local interests, or influences, in exactly the same proportion, as a single body. The value of such a separate organization will, of course, be greatly enhanced, the more the elements, of which each body is composed, differ from each other, in the mode of choice, in the qualifications, and in the duration of office of the members, provided due intelligence and virtue are secured in each body. All these considerations had great weight in the Convention, which framed the Constitution of the United States. We shall presently see, how far these desirable modifications have been attained in the actual composition of the Senate and House of Representatives.

CHAPTER IX.

The House of Representatives.

§66. THE second section, of the first article, contains the structure and organization of the House of Representatives. The first clause is—"The House of Representatives shall be composed of members chosen every second year by the people of the several States; and the electors in each State shall have the qualifications, requisite for electors of the most numerous branch of the State legislature."

§67. First, the principle of representation. The Representatives are to be chosen by the people. No reasoning was necessary, to satisfy the American people of the advantages of a House of Representatives, which should emanate directly from themselves, which should guard their interests, support their rights, express their opinions, make known their wants, redress their grievances, and introduce a pervading popular influence throughout all the operations of the national government. Their own experience, as colonists, as well as the experience of the parent country, and the general deductions of theory, had settled it, as a fundamental principle of a free government, and especially of a republican government, that no laws ought to be passed without the consent of the people, through representatives, immediately chosen by, and responsible to them.

§68. The *indirect* advantages, from this immediate agency of the people in the choice of their Representatives, are of incalculable benefit, and deserve a brief mention in this place, because they furnish us with matter for most serious reflection, in regard to the actual operations and influences of republican governments. In the first place, the right confers an additional sense of personal dignity and duty upon the mass of the people. It gives a strong direction to the education, studies, and pursuits of the whole community. It enlarges the sphere of action, and contributes, in a high degree, to the formation of the public manners, and national character. It procures to the common people courtesy and sympathy from their superiors, and diffuses a common confidence, as well as a common interest, through all the ranks of society. It awakens a desire to examine, and sift, and debate all public proceedings; and it thus nourishes a lively curiosity to acquire knowledge, and, at the same time, furnishes the means of gratifying it. The proceedings and debates of the legislature; the conduct of public officers, from the highest to the lowest; the character and conduct of the Executive and his ministers; the struggles, intrigues, and conduct of different parties; and the discussion of the great public measures and questions which agitate and divide the community;—are not only freely canvassed, and thus improve and elevate conversation, but they gradually furnish the mind with safe and solid materials for judgement upon all public affairs, and check that inpetuosity and rashness, to which sudden impulses might otherwise lead the people, when they are artfully misguided by selfish demagogues, and plausible schemes of change.

§69. Secondly, the qualifications of electors. These were various in the different States. In some of them, none but freeholders were entitled to vote; in others, only persons, who had been admitted to the privileges of freemen; in others, a qualification of property was required of voters; in others, the payment of taxes; and in others, again, the right of suffrage was almost universal. This consideration had great weight in the Convention; and the extreme difficulty of agreeing upon any uniform rule of voting, which should be acceptable to all the States, induced the Convention, finally, after much discussion to adopt the existing rule in the choice of Representatives in the popular branch of the State legislatures. Thus, the peculiar wishes of each State, in the formation of its own popular branch, were consulted; and some not unimportant diversities were introduced into the actual composition of the national House of Representatives. All the members would represent the people, but not exactly under influences precisely of the same character.

§70. Thirdly, the term of service of the Representatives. It is two years. This period, with reference to the nature of the duties to be performed by the members, to the knowledge and experience essential to a right performance of them, and to the periods, for which the members of the State legislatures are chosen, seems as short as an enlightened regard to the public good could require. A very short term of service would bring together a great many new members, with little or no experience in the national business; the very frequency of the elections would render the office of less importance to able men; and some of the duties to be performed would require more time, and more mature inquiries, than could be gathered, in the brief space of a single session, from the distant parts of so extensive a territory. What might be well begun by one set of men, could scarcely be carried on, in the same spirit, by another. So that there would be great danger of new and immature plans succeeding each other, without any well-established system of operations.

§71. But the very nature and objects of the national government require far more experience and knowledge, than what may be thought requisite in the members of a State legislature. For the latter, a knowledge of local interests and opinions may ordinarily suffice. But it is far different with a member of Congress. He is to legislate for the interest and welfare, not of one State only, but of all the States. It is not enough, that he comes to the task with an upright intention and sound judgement; but he must have a competent degree of knowledge of all the subjects, on which he is called to legislate; and he must have skill, as to the best mode of applying it. The latter can scarcely be acquired, but by long experience and training in the national councils. The period of service ought, therefore, to bear some proportion to the variety of knowledge and practical skill, which the duties of the station demand.

§72. The most superficial glance at the relative duties of a member of a State legislature and of those of a member of Congress, will put this matter in a striking light. In a single State, the habits, manners, institutions, and laws, are uniform, and all the citizens are more or less conversant with them. The relative bearings of the various pursuits and occupations of the people are well understood, or easily ascertained. The general affairs of the State lie in a comparatively narrow compass, and are daily discussed and examined by those, who have an immediate interest in them, and, by frequent communication with each other, can interchange opinions. It is very different with the general government. There, every measure is to be discussed with reference to the rights, interests, and pursuits of all the States. When the Constitution was adopted, there were thirteen, and there are now twenty-six States, having different laws, institutions, employments, products, and climates, and many artificial, as well as natural differences in the structure of society, growing out of these circumstances. Some of them are almost wholly agricultural; some commercial; some manufacturing; some have a mixture of all; and in no two of them are there precisely the same relative adjustments of all these interests. No legislation for the Union can be safe or wise, which is not founded upon an accurate knowledge of these diversities, and their practical influence upon public measures. What may be beneficial and politic, with reference to the interests of a single State, may be subversive of those of other States. A regulation of commerce, wise and just for the commercial States, may strike at the foundation of the prosperity of the agricultural or manufacturing States. And, on the other hand, a measure beneficial to agriculture or manufactures, may disturb, and even overwhelm the shipping interest. Large and enlightened views, comprehensive information, and a just attention to the local peculiarities, and products, and employments of different States, are absolutely indispensable qualifications for members of Congress. Yet it is obvious, that if very short periods of service are to be allowed to members of Congress, the continual fluctuations in the public councils, and the perpetual changes of members, will be very unfavorable to the acquirement of the proper knowledge, and the due application of it for the public welfare. One set of men will just have mastered the necessary information, when they will be succeeded by a second set, who are to go over the same grounds, and then are to be succeeded by a third. So that inexperience, instead of practical wisdom, hasty legislation, instead of sober deliberation, and imperfect projects, instead of well-constructed systems, would characterize the national government.

§73. Fourthly, the qualifications of Representatives. The Constitution declares—"No person shall be a Representative, who shall not have attained to the age of twenty-five years; and been seven years a citizen of the United States; and who shall not, when elected, be an inhabitant of that State, in which he shall be chosen." These qualifications are few and simple. They respect only age, citizenship, and inhabitancy.

§74. First, in regard to age. That some qualification, as to age, is desirable, cannot well be doubted, if knowledge, or experience, or wisdom, is of any value in the administration of public affairs. And if any qualification is required, what can be more suitable than twenty-five years of age? The character and principles of young men can scarcely be understood at the moment of their majority. They are then new to the rights even of self-government; warm in their passions; ardent in their expectations; and too eager in their favorite pursuits, to learn the lessons of caution, which riper years inculcate. Four years of probation, is but a very short space, in which to try their virtues, to develop their talents, to enlarge their intellectual resources, and to give them a practical knowledge of the true principles of legislation. Indeed, it may be safely said, that a much longer period will scarcely suffice to furnish them with that thorough insight into the business of human life, which is indispensable to a safe and enlightened exercise of public duties.

§75. Secondly, in regard to citizenship. No person will deny the propriety of excluding aliens from any share in the administration of the affairs of the national government. No persons, but citizens, can be presumed to feel that deep sense of the value of our domestic institutions, and that permanent attachment to the soil and interests of our country, which are the true sources of a healthy patriotism. The only practical question would seem to be, whether foreigners, even after they were naturalized, should be permitted to hold office. Most nations studiously exclude them, from policy, or from jealousy. But the peculiar circumstances of our country were supposed to call for a less rigorous course; and the period of seven years was selected as one, which would enable naturalized citizens to acquire a reasonable familiarity with the principles of our institutions and with the interests of the people; and which, at the same time, would justify the latter in reposing confidence in their talents, virtues, and patriotism.

§76. Thirdly, in regard to inhabitancy. The Representative is required to be an inhabitant of the State, at the time when he is chosen. The object of this clause, doubtless, is to secure, on the part of the Representative, a familiar knowledge of the interests of the people whom he represents, a just responsibility to them, and a personal share in all the local results of the measures, which he shall support. It is observable, that inhabitancy is required in the State only, and not in any particular election district; so that the Constitution leaves a wide field of choice open to the electors. And if we consider, how various the interests, pursuits, employments, products, and local circumstances of the different States are, we can scarcely be surprised, that there should be a marked anxiety to secure a just representation of all of them in the national councils.

§77. Subject to these reasonable qualifications, the House of Representatives is open to persons of merit of every description, whether native or adopted citizens, whether young or old, whether rich or poor, without any discrimination of rank, or business, or profession, or religious opinion.

§78. The next clause of the Constitution respects the apportionment of Representatives among the States. It declares,— "Representatives, and direct taxes, shall be apportioned among the several States, which may be included within this Union, according to their respective numbers, which shall be determined by adding to the whole number of free persons, including those bound to service for a term of years, and excluding Indians not taxed, three fifths of all other persons. The actual enumeration shall be made within three years after the first meeting of the Congress of the United States, and within every subsequent term of ten years, in such manner, as they shall by law direct. The number of Representatives shall not exceed one for every thirty thousand; but each State shall have at least one Representative. And until such enumeration shall be made, the State of New Hampshire shall be entitled to choose three; Massachusetts, eight; Rhode Island and Providence Plantations, one; Connecticut, five; New York, six; New Jersey, four; Pennsylvania, eight; Delaware, one; Maryland, six; Virginia, ten; North Carolina, five; South Carolina, five; and Georgia, three."

§79. Under the Confederation, each State was entitled to one vote only, but might send as many delegates to Congress, as it should choose, not less than two, nor more than seven; and of course, the concurrence of a majority of its delegates was necessary to every vote of each State. In the House of Representatives, each member is entitled to one vote, and therefore the apportionment of Representatives became, among the States, a subject of deep interest, and of no inconsiderable diversity of opinion in the Convention. The small States insisted upon an equality of representation in the House of Representatives, as well as in the Senate, which was strenuously resisted by the large States. The slave-holding States insisted on a representation strictly according to the number of inhabitants, whether they were slaves or free persons, within the State. The non-slave-holding States contended for a representation according to the number of free persons only. The controversy was full of excitement, and was maintained with so much obstinacy, on each side, that the Convention was more than once on the eve of a dissolution. At length, the present system was adopted, by way of compromise. It was seen to be unequal in its operation, but was a necessary sacrifice to that spirit of conciliation, on which the Union was founded. The exception of Indians was of no permanent importance; and the persons bound to service for a term of years were too few to produce any sensible effect in the enumeration. The real difficulty was, as to slaves, who were included under the mild appellation of "all other persons." Three fifths of the slaves are added to the number of free persons, as the basis of the apportionment.

§80. In order to reconcile the non-slave-holding States to this arrangement, it was agreed, that *direct* taxes (the nature of which we shall hereafter consider) should be apportioned in the same manner as Representatives. This provision is more specious than solid; for, in reality, it exempts the remaining two fifths of the slaves from direct taxation. But, in the practical operations of the government, a far more striking inequality has been developed. The principle of representation is uniform and constant; whereas, the imposition of direct taxes is occasional and rare; and, in fact, three direct taxes only have been laid, at distant periods from each other, since the adoption of the Constitution. The slave-holding States have, at the present time, in Congress, twenty-five Representatives more than they would have upon the basis of an enumeration of free persons only. The apportionment, however, viewed as a matter of compromise, is entitled to great praise, for its moderation, its aim at practical utility, and its tendency to satisfy the people of every State in the Union, that the Constitution ought to be dear to all, by the privileges, which it confers, as well as by the blessings, which it secures. It has sometimes been complained of as a grievance, founded in a gross inequality and an unjustifiable surrender of important rights. But whatever force there may be in the suggestion, abstractly considered, it should never be forgotten that it was a necessary price paid for the Union; and if it had been refused, the Constitution never would have been recommended for the adoption of the people, even by the Convention, which framed it.

§81. In order to carry into effect this principle of apportionment, it was indispensable, that some provision should be made for ascertaining, at stated times, the population of each State. Unless this should be done, it is obvious, that, as the growth of the different States would be in very unequal proportions, the representation would soon be marked by a corresponding inequality. To illustrate this, we need only to look at Delaware, which now sends only one Representative, as it did in the first Congress, and to New York, which then sent six, and now sends forty Representatives. Similar, though not as great, diversities exist in the comparative representation of several other States. Some have remained nearly stationary, and others have had a very rapid increase of population. The Constitution has, therefore, wisely provided, that there shall be a new enumeration of the inhabitants of all the States, every ten years, which is commonly called the decennial census.

§82. There is one question of great practical importance, as to the apportionment of Representatives, which has constantly been found to involve much embarrassment and difficulty; and that is, how and in what manner the apportionment is to be made. The language of the Constitution is that "Representatives and direct taxes shall be apportioned among the several States, &c., according to their respective numbers;" and at the first view it would not seem to involve the slightest difficulty. A moment's reflection will dissipate the illusion, and teach us, that there is a difficulty intrinsic in the very nature of the subject. In regard to direct taxes, the natural course would be to assume a particular sum to be raised, as three millions of dollars; and to apportion it among the States according to their relative numbers. But even here, there will always be a very small fractional amount incapable of exact distribution, since the numbers in each State will never exactly coincide with any common divisor, or give an exact aliquot part for each State without any remainder. But, as the amount may be carried through a long series of descending money fractions, it may be ultimately reduced to the smallest fraction of any existing, or even imaginary coin.

§83. But the difficulty is far otherwise in regard to Representatives. Here, there can be no subdivision of the unit; each State must be entitled to an entire Representative, and a fraction of a Representative is incapable of apportionment. Yet it will be perceived at once, that it is scarcely possible, and certainly is wholly improbable, that the relative numbers in each State should bear such an exact proportion to the aggregate, that there should exist a common divisor for all, which should leave no fraction in any State. Such a case never yet has existed; and in all human probability it never will. Every common divisor, hitherto applied, has left a fraction, greater or smaller, in every State; and what has been, in the past, must continue to be, for the future. Assume the whole population to be three, or six, or nine, or twelve million, or any other number; if you follow the injunctions of the Constitution, and attempt to apportion the Representatives according to the numbers in each State, it will be found to be absolutely impossible. The theory, however true, becomes practically false in its application. Each State may have assigned to it a relative proportion of Representatives, up to a given number, the whole being divisible by some common divisor; but the fraction of population belonging to each beyond that point is left unprovided for. So that the apportionment is, at best, only an approximation to the rule laid down by the Constitution, and not a strict compliance with the rule. The fraction in one State may be ten times as great, as that in another; and so may differ in each State in any assignable mathematical proportion. What then is to be done? Is the Constitution to be wholly disregarded on this point? Or is it to be followed out in its true spirit, though unavoidably differing from the letter, by the nearest approximation to it? If an additional Representative can be assigned to one State beyond its relative proportion to the whole population, it is equally true, that it can be assigned to all, that are in a similar predicament. If a fraction admits of representation in any case, what prohibits the application of the rule to all fractions? The only constitutional limitation seems to be, that no State shall have more than one Representative for every thirty thousand persons. Subject to this, the truest rule seems to be, that the apportionment ought to be the nearest practical approximation to the terms of the Constitution; and the rule ought to be such, that it shall always work the same way in regard to all the States, and be as little open to cavil, or controversy, or abuse, as possible.

§84. But it may be asked, What are the first steps to be taken in order to arrive at a constitutional apportionment? Plainly, by taking the aggregate of population in all the States, (according to the constitutional rule,) and then ascertain the relative proportion of the population of each State to the population of the whole. This is necessarily so in regard to direct taxes; and there is no reason to say, that it can, or ought to be otherwise in regard to Representatives; for that would be to contravene the very injunctions of the Constitution, which require the like rule of apportionment in each case. In the one, the apportionment may be run down below unity; in the other, it cannot. But this does not change the nature of the rule, but only the extent of its application.

§85. It is difficult to make this subject clear to the common understanding, without introducing some tabular statements, which the nature of this work seems absolutely to prohibit. But it may be stated, as an historical fact, that in every apportionment hitherto made of Representatives, whatever has been the number of inhabitants assumed as the ratio to govern the number of Representatives, whether thirty thousand or any higher number, there has always been a fraction in each State less than that number, and of course an unrepresented fraction. In some of the States, the fraction has been very small; in others, very large; and in others, intermediate numbers constantly varying from each other. So that, in fact, there never has been any representation of each State, apportioned in exact proportion to its numbers, as the Constitution requires. The rule adopted has been, to assume a particular number of inhabitants as the ratio to give a single Representative, and to give to each State as many Representatives, as its population contained of that ratio or particular number; and to disregard all fractions below that.

§86. There remained two important points to be settled in regard to representation. First, that each State should have at least one Representative; for otherwise, it might be excluded from any share of the legislative power in one branch; and secondly, that there should be some limitation of the number of Representatives; for otherwise, Congress might increase the House to an unreasonable size. If Congress were left free to apportion the Representatives according to any basis of numbers they might select, half the States in the Union might be deprived of Representatives, if the whole number of their inhabitants fell below that basis. On the other hand, if the number selected for the basis were small, the House might become too unwieldly for business. There is, therefore, great wisdom in restricting the representation, so that there shall not be more than one Representative for every thirty thousand inhabitants in a State; and on the other hand, by a positive provision, securing to each State a constitutional representative in the House, by at least one Representative, however small its own population may be. It is curious to remark, that it was originally thought a great objection to the Constitution, that the restriction of Representatives, to one for every thirty thousand, would give too small a House to be a safe depository of power; and that, now the fear is, that a restriction to double that number will hardly, in the future, restrain the size of the House within sufficiently moderate limits, for the purposes of an efficient and enlightened legislation. So much has the growth of the country, under the auspices of the national Constitution, outstripped the most sanguine expectations of its friends.

§87. The next clause is: "When vacancies happen in the representation of any State, the executive authority thereof shall issue writs of election to fill such vacancies." It is obvious, that such a power ought to reside in some public functionary. The only question is, in whom it can, with most safety and convenience, be lodged. If vested in the general government, or in any department of it, it was thought, that there might not be as strong motives for an immediate exercise of the power, or as thorough a knowledge of local circumstances, to guide the exercise of it wisely, as if vested in the State government. It is, therefore, left to the latter, and to that branch of it, the State Executive, which is best fitted to exercise it with promptitude and discretion. And thus, one source of State jealousy is effectually dried up.

§88. The next clause is: "The House of Representatives shall choose their Speaker, and other officers; and shall have the sole power of impeachment." Each of these privileges is of great practical importance. In Great Britain, the Speaker is elected by the House of Commons; but he must be approved by the King; and a similar power of approval belonged to some of the Governors in the Colonies, before the Revolution. An independent and unlimited choice by the House of Representatives of all their officers is every way desirable. It secures, on the part of their officers, a more efficient responsibility, and gives to the House a more complete authority over them. It avoids all the dangers and inconveniences, which may arise from differences of opinion between the House and the Executive, in periods of high party excitement. It relieves the Executive from all the embarrassments of opposing the popular will, and the House from all the irritations of not consulting the wishes of the Cabinet.

§89. Next, the Power of Impeachment. "The House of Representatives shall have the sole power of impeachment;" that is, the right to present a written accusation against persons in high offices and trusts, for the purpose of bringing them to trial and punishment for gross misconduct. The power, and the mode of proceeding, are borrowed from the practice of England. In that Kingdom, the House of Commons (which answers to our House of Representatives) has the right to present articles of impeachment against any person, for the gross misdemeanor, before the House of Lords, which is the court of the highest criminal jurisdiction in the realm. The articles of impeachment, are a sort of indictment; and the House, in presenting them, acts as a grand jury, and also as a public prosecutor. The great object of this power is, to bring persons to justice, who are so elevated in rank or influence, that there is danger, that they might escape punishment before the ordinary tribunals; and the exercise of power is usually confined to political or official offences. These prosecutions are, therefore, conducted by the Representatives of the nation, in their public capacity, in the face of the nation, and upon a responsibility, which is felt and reverenced by the whole community. We shall have occasion, hereafter, to consider the subject of impeachment more at large, in another place; and this may suffice here, as an explanation of the nature and objects of the power. No one can well doubt, that, if the power is to be exercised at all, by any popular body, it is most appropriately confided to the representatives of the people.

CHAPTER X.

The Senate.

§90. WE come next to the organization and powers of the Senate, which are provided for in the third section of the first article of the Constitution.

§91. We have already had occasion to refer, in a brief manner, to the general reasoning, by which the division of the legislative power between two distinct branches has been justified in the actual organization of free governments. And here seems the proper place to enter somewhat more at large, into the reasonings, by which the establishment of the Senate of the United States was supported as an independent branch of the national government. In order to justify the existence of a Senate with coordinate powers, it was said, first, that it was a misfortune incident to republican governments, though in a less degree than to other governments, that those, who administer it, may forget their obligations to their constituents, and prove unfaithful to their important trust. In this point of view, a Senate, as a second branch of the legislative assembly, distinct from, and dividing the power with a first, must be in all cases a salutary check on the government. It doubles the security to the people by requiring the concurrence of two distinct bodies, in schemes of usurpation or perfidy; whereas the ambition or corruption of one would otherwise be sufficient. This precaution, it was added, was founded on such clear principles, as so well understood in the United States, that it was superfluous to enlarge on it. As the improbability of sinister combinations would be in proportion to the dissimilarity in the genius of the two bodies, it must be politic to distinguish them from each other by every circumstance, which would consist with a due harmony in all proper measures, and with the genuine principles of republican government.

§92. Secondly. The necessity of a Senate was not less indicated by the propensity of all single and numerous assemblies to yield to the impulse of sudden and violent passions, and to be seduced by factious leaders into intemperate and pernicious resolutions. Examples of this sort might be cited without number, and from proceedings in the United States, as well as from the history of other nations. A body, which is to correct this infirmity, ought to be free from it, and consequently ought to be less numerous, and to possess a due degree of firmness, and a proper tenure of office.

§93. Thirdly. Another defect, to be supplied by a Senate, lay in the want of a due acquaintance with the objects and principles of legislation. A good government implies two things; first, fidelity to the objects of the government; secondly, a knowledge of the means, by which those objects can be best attained. It was suggested, that in the American governments too little attention had been paid to the last; and that the establishment of a Senate, upon a proper basis, would greatly increase the chances of fidelity, and of wise and safe legislation. What (it was asked) are all the repealing, explaining, and amending laws, which fill and disgrace our voluminous codes, but so many monuments of deficient wisdom; so many impeachments exhibited by each succeeding, against each preceding, session; so many admonitions to the people of the value of those aids, which may be expected from a well-constituted Senate?

§94. Fourthly. Such a body would prevent too great a mutability in the public councils, arising from a rapid succession of new members; for, from a change of men, there must proceed a change of opinions, and from a change of opinions, a change of measures. Such instability in legislation has a tendency to diminish respect and confidence abroad, as well as safety and prosperity at home. It has a tendency to damp the ardor of industry and enterprise; to diminish the security of property; and to impair the reverence and attachment, which are indispensable to the permanence of every political institution.

§95. Fifthly. Another ground, illustrating the utility of a Senate, was suggested to be the keeping alive of a due sense of national character. In respect to foreign nations, this was of vital importance; for in our intercourse with them, if a scrupulous and uniform adherence to just principles was not observed, it must subject us to many embarrassments and collisions. It is difficult to impress upon a single body, which is numerous and changeable, a deep sense of the value of national character. A small portion of the praise, or blame, of any particular measure, can fall to the lot of any particular person; and the period of office is so short, that little responsibility is felt, and little pride is indulged, as to the course of the government.

§96. Sixthly. It was urged, that, paradoxical as it might seem, the want, in some important cases, of a due responsibility in the government arises from that very frequency of elections, which, in other cases, produces such responsibility. In order to be reasonable, responsibility must be limited to objects within the power of the responsible party; and in order to be effectual, it must relate to operations of that power, of which a ready and proper judgement can be formed by the constituents. Some measures have singly an immediate and sensible operation; others again depend on a succession of well-connected schemes, and have a gradual, and perhaps unobserved operation. If, therefore, there be but one Assembly, chosen for a short period, it will be difficult to keep up the train of proper measures, or to preserve the proper connection between the past and the future. And the more numerous the body, and the more changeable its component parts, the more difficult it will be to preserve the personal responsibility, as well as the uniform action, of the successive members, to the great objects of the public welfare.

§97. Lastly. A Senate, duly constituted, would not only operate as a salutary check upon the Representatives, but occasionally upon the people themselves, against their own temporary delusions and errors. The cool, deliberate sense of the community ought, in all governments, and actually will, in all free governments, ultimately prevail over the views of their rulers. But there are particular moments in public affairs, when the people, stimulated by some irregular passion, or some illicit advantage, or misled by the artful misrepresentations of interested men, may call for measures, which they themselves will afterwards be the most ready to lament and condemn. In these critical moments, how salutary will be the interference of a body of respectable citizens, chosen without reference to the exciting cause, to check the misguided career of public opinion, and to suspend the blow, until reason, justice, and truth can regain their authority over the public mind. It was thought to add great weight to all these considerations, that history has informed us of no long-lived republic, which has not a senate. Sparta, Rome, Carthage were, in fact, the only states, to whom that character can be applied.

§98. It will be observed, that some parts of the foregoing reasoning apply to the fundamental importance of an actual division of the legislative power; and other parts to the true principles, upon which that division should be subsequently organized, in order to give full effect to the constitutional check. Some parts go to show the value of a Senate; and others, what should be its structure, in order to insure wisdom, experience, fidelity, and dignity in its members. All of it, however, instructs us, that, in order to give it fair play and influence, as a coordinate branch of government, it ought to be less numerous, more select, and more durable, than the other branch; and be chosen in a manner, which should combine, and represent, different interests, with a varied force. How far these objects are attained by the Constitution, will be better

seen, when the details belonging to each department are successively examined.

§99. The first clause of the third section is—"The Senate of
the United States shall be composed of two Senators from each
State, chosen by the Legislature thereof for six years; and each-
Senator shall have one vote."

§100. First, the nature of the representation and vote in the
Senate. Each State is entitled to two Senators; and each Senator
is entitled to one vote. Of course, there is a perfect equality of
representation and vote of the States in the Senate. In this respect it forms a marked contrast to the House of Representatives. In the latter, the representation is in proportion to the
population of each State, upon a given basis; in the former,
each State, whether it be great or be small, is, in its political capacity, represented upon the footing of equality with every
other, as it would be in a Congress of Ambassadors, or in an Assembly of Peers. The only important difference between the
vote in the Senate, and that in the old Continental Congress under the Confederation, is, that in the latter, the vote was by
States, each having but one vote, whereas, in the Senate, each
Senator has one vote. So that, although the Senators represent
States, they vote as individuals; thus combining the two elements of individual opinion, and of State representation. A majority of the Senators must concur in every vote; but the vote
need not be that of a majority of the States, since the Senators
from the same State, may vote on different sides of the same
question. The Senators from fifteen States may divide in their
votes; and those from eleven, may concur in their votes, and
thus give a decisive majority.

§101. It is obvious, that this arrangement could only arise
from a compromise between the great and the small States,
founded upon a spirit of amity, and mutual deference and con-
cession, which the peculiarity of situation of the United States
rendered indispensable. There was, for a long time, a very ani-
mated struggle in the Convention, between the great and the
small States, on this subject; the latter contending for an equal-

ity of representation in each branch of the Legislature; the former for a representation in each, proportionate to its population and importance. In the discussions, the States were so nearly balanced, that their union in any plan of government, which should provide for a perfect equality, or an inequality, of representation in both Houses, became utterly hopeless. A compromise became indispensable. The small States yielded up an equality of representation in the House of Representatives, and the great States, in like manner, conceded an equality in the Senate. This arrangement, so vital to the peace of the Union, and to the preservation of the separate existence of the States, is, at the same time, full of wisdom, and sound political policy. It introduces, and perpetuates, in the different branches of the Legislature, different elements, which will make the theoretical check, contemplated by the division of the legislative power, more efficient and constant in its operation. The interests, passions, and prejudices of a particular representative district may thus be controlled by the influence of a whole State; the like interests, passions, and prejudices of a State, or of a majority of the States, may thus be controlled by the voice of a majority of the people of the Union.

§102. Secondly, the mode of choosing Senators. They are to be chosen by the Legislature of each State. This mode has a natural tendency to increase the just operation of the check, to which we have already alluded. The people of the States directly choose the Representatives; the Legislature, whose votes are variously compounded, and whose mode of election is different in different States, directly choose the Senators. So that it is impossible, that exactly the same influences, interests, and feelings, should prevail in the same proportions in each branch. Three schemes were presented in the Convention; one was, a choice directly by the people of the States; another was, a choice by the national House of Representatives; and the third was, that which now exists. Upon mature deliberation, the last was thought to possess a decided preference over either of the other two. It was recommended by the double advantage of favoring a select appointment, and of giving to the

State governments such an agency in the formation of the national government, as might secure a due authority to the former, and may well serve as a connecting link between the two systems. Our past experience has fully justified the wisdom of the choice.

§103. The Constitution has not provided for the manner, in which the choice shall be made by the State Legislatures, whether by a joint vote, or by a concurrent vote; the former is, where both branches form one assembly, and give a united vote numerically; the latter is, where each branch gives a separate and independent vote. As each of the State Legislatures now consists of two branches, this is a very important practical question. Generally, but not universally, the choice of Senators is made by a concurrent vote. Another question might be suggested, whether the Executive constitutes a part of the Legislature for such a purpose, in cases where the State constitution gives him a qualified negative upon the laws. But this has been silently and universally settled against the executive participation in the appointment.

§104. Thirdly, the number of Senators. Each State is entitled to two Senators. To insure competent knowledge and ability to discharge all the functions intrusted to the Senate, and, at the same time, to give promptitude and efficiency to their acts, the number should not be unreasonably large or small. The number should be sufficiently large to insure a sufficient variety of talents and experience and practical skill for the just discharge of all the duties of that important branch of the Legislature. A very small body also is more easily overawed and intimidated by external influences, than one of a reasonable size, embracing weight of character, and dignity of talents. Numbers, alone, in many cases, confer power, and encourage firmness. If the number of the Senate were confined to one for each State, there would be danger, that it might be too small for a comprehensive knowledge and diligence in all the business devolved upon the body. And besides; in such a case, the illness, or accidental absence of a Senator might deprive a State of its vote upon an important question, or of its influence in an interesting debate. If, on the other hand, the number were very large, the Senate might become unwieldy, and want despatch, and due responsibility. It could hardly exercise due deliberation in some functions connected with executive duties, which might, at the same time, require prompt action. If any number beyond one be proper, two seems as convenient a number as any, which can be devised. The Senate, upon its present organization, can not probably ever become too large or too small for the fit discharge of all its functions. The benefit is retained, of consultation, and mutual interchange of opinion between the members from the same State; and the number is sufficient to guard against any undue influence over it by the more popular branch of the Legislature.

§105. Fourthly, the term of service of the Senators. It is for six years, although, as we shall presently see, one third of the members is changed every two years. What is the proper duration of the office, is certainly a matter, upon which different minds may arrive at different conclusions. The term should have reference to the nature and extent of the duties to be performed, the experience to be required, the independence to be secured, and the objects to be attained. A very short duration of office, diminishes responsibility, and energy, and public spirit, and firmness of action, by diminishing the motives to great efforts, and also, by diminishing the means of maturing, and carrying into effect, wise measures. The Senate has various highly important functions to perform, besides its legislative duties. It partakes of the executive power of appointment to office, of and the ratification of public treaties. To perform these functions worthily, the members should enjoy public confidence at home and abroad; and they should be beyond the reach of the sudden impulses of domestic factions, as well as of foreign influences. They should not be subject to intimidation by the mere seekers of office; nor should they be deemed by foreign nations, to have no permanent weight in the administration of the government. They should be able, on the one hand, to guard the people against usurpations of authority on the part of the National Government; and on the other hand, to guard the people against the unconstitutional projects of selfish demagogues. They should have the habits of business, and the large experience in the affairs of government, derived from a practical concern in them for a considerable period. They should be chosen for a longer period than the House of Representatives, in order to prevent sudden, and total changes at the same period of all the functionaries of the government, which would necessarily encourage instability in the public councils, and stimulate political agitations and rivalries. In all these respects, the term of office of the Senators seems admirably well adapted to the purposes of an efficient, and yet of a responsible body. It secures the requisite qualifications of skill, experience, information, and independence. It prevents any sudden changes in the public policy. It induces foreign nations to treat the government with more confidence, from the consciousness of the permanence of its councils. It commands a respect at home, which enables it to resist many undue inroads of the popular branch; and, at the same time, its duration is not so long, as to take away a pressing sense of responsibility both to the people, and to the States.

§106. But, in order to quiet the last lingering scruples of jealousy on this head, the next clause of the Constitution provides for a change of one third of the members every two years. It declares—"Immediately after they (the Senators) shall be assembled, in consequence of the first election, they shall be divided, as equally as may be, into three classes. The seats of the Senators of the first class, shall be vacated at the expiration of every second year; of the second calls, at the expiration of every fourth year; and of the third class, at the expiration of every sixth year; so that one third may be chosen every second year." Thus, the whole body is gradually changed in the course of the six years, always retaining a large portion of experience, and yet incapable of combining its members together for any sinister purposes. No person would probably propose a less duration of office for the Senators, than double the period of that of the members of the House. In effect, this provision changes, within the same period, the composition of two thirds of the body.

§107. As vacancies may occur in the Senate during the recess of the State Legislatures, it became indispensable to provide for that exigency, in order to preserve the full right of representation of each State in that body. Accordingly, the same clause declares—"And if any vacancies happen, by resignation, or otherwise, during the recess of the Legislature of any State, the Executive thereof may make temporary appointments, until the next meeting of the Legislature, which shall then fill such vacancies." This mode seems as unexceptionable, as any which would be adopted. It enables the Executive of the State to appoint a temporary Senator, when the State Legislature is not in session. One of three courses, only, seemed open; either to allow the vacancy to remain unfilled, which would deprive the State of its due vote; or to allow the State Legislature prospectively to provide for the vacancy by a contingent appointment, which might be liable to some objections of a different character; or to confide a temporary appointment to the highest State functionary, who might well be presumed to enjoy the public confidence, and be devoted to the public interest, and to have very strong motives to make a judicious appointment.

§ 108. We next come to the qualifications of Senators. "No person shall be a Senator, who shall not have attained the age of thirty years, and been nine years a citizen of the United States, and who shall not, when elected, be an inhabitant of that State, for which he shall be chosen." As the nature of the duties of a Senator require more experience, knowledge, and stability of character, than those of a Representative, the qualification of age is accordingly raised. A person may be a Representative, at twenty-five years; but he cannot be a Senator, until thirty years. Citizenship, also, is required, the propriety of which qualification cannot well be doubted. The term of citizenship of a Representative is seven years; that of a Senator is nine years. The reason, for increasing the term, in the latter case, is, the direct connection of the Senate with foreign nations, in the appointment of ambassadors, and in the formation of treaties. This prolonged term may well be required of a foreigner, not only to give him a more thorough knowledge of the interests of his adopted country; but also to wean him more effectually from those of his native country. The next qualification, is, inhabitancy in the State; and the propriety of this, is almost self-evident, since an inhabitant may not only be presumed to be better acquainted with the local interests, and wants, and pursuits, of the State; but may, also, well be deemed to feel a higher degree of responsibility to the State, than any stranger. He will, also, personally, share more fully in the effects of all measures, touching the sovereignty, rights, and influence, of the State. The only surprise is that provision is not made for his ceasing to represent the State, in the Senate, as soon as he should cease to be an inhabitant of the State.

§109. In concluding this topic, it is proper to remark, that no qualification, whatever, as to property, is required in regard to Senators, any more than in regard to Representatives. Merit and talent have, therefore, the freest access open to them into each branch of the Legislature. Under such circumstances, if the choice of the people is but directed by a suitable sobriety of judgment, the Senate cannot fail of being, distinguished for wisdom, for learning, for exalted patriotism, for incorruptible integrity, and for inflexible independence.

§110. The next clause respects the person who shall preside in the deliberations of the Senate.—"The Vice President of the United States shall be President of the Senate, but shall have no vote, unless they be equally divided. The Senate shall choose their other officers, and also a President pro tempore, in the absence of the Vice President, or when he shall exercise the office of President of the United States."

§111. The propriety of creating the office of Vice President will be reserved for future consideration, when the organization of the executive department shall come under review. The reasons, why he is authorized to preside in the Senate, belong appropriately to this place. The strong motive for this arrangement undoubtedly arose from the desire to moderate State jealousy and to preserve State equality in the Senate. If the presiding officer of the Senate were to be chosen exclusively from its own members, it was supposed, that the State, upon

97

which the choice might fall, might possess either more or less than its due share of influence. If he were not allowed to vote, except upon an equal division of the Senate, then the State would be deprived of his vote; if he were entitled to vote, and also, in such cases, to give a casting vote, then the State would, in effect, possess a double vote. If he could only vote as a member, then, in case of an equality of votes, much inconvenience might arise from the indecision of the Senate. It might give rise to dangerous feuds, or intrigues, and create State, or national agitations. It would be far better, in such an equality of votes, to refer the decision to a common arbiter, like the Vice President, chosen by a vote of the States, and therefore to be deemed the representative of all of them. The permanent appointment of any one of the Senators, as President of the Senate, might give him an undue influence and control over measures during his official term. An appointment for a single session, only, would subject the body to constant agitations, and intrigues, incompatible with its own dignity and convenience, and might introduce irregularities, unfavorable to an impartial course of proceedings, founded upon experience, and an accurate knowledge of the duties of the office. These views appear to have had great weight in the Convention, and have been found entirely satisfactory to the people. The appointment of the Vice President to preside in the Senate has been greatly conducive to the harmony of the States and the dignity of the General Government. As the Senate possesses the power to make rules to regulate its own proceedings, there is little danger that there can ever arise any serious abuse of the presiding power. The danger, if any, is rather the other way, that the presiding power will be silently weakened or openly surrendered, so as to leave to the office little more than the barren honor of the place, without influence, and without action.

§112. The propriety of intrusting the Senate with the choice of its other officers, and also of a President pro tempore in the absence of the Vice President, or when he exercises the office of President, seems never to have been questioned; and indeed is so obvious, that it is wholly unnecessary to vindicate it. Confidence between the Senate and its officers, and the power to make a suitable choice, and to secure a suitable responsibility for the faithful discharge of the duties of office, are so indispensable for the public good, that the provision will command universal assent, as soon as it is mentioned. It has grown into a general practice for the Vice President to vacate the Senatorial chair a short time before the termination of each session, in order to enable the Senate to choose a President pro tempore, who might already be in office, if the Vice President, in the recess, should be called to the chair of State. The practice is funded in wisdom and sound policy, as it immediately provides for an exigency, which may well be expected to occur at any time; and prevents the choice from being influenced by temporary excitements or intrigues, arising from the actual existence of a vacancy. As it is useful in peace to provide for war; so it is likewise useful in times of profound tranquillity to provide for political agitations, which may disturb the public harmony.

CHAPTER XI.

Impeachments.

§ 113. THE next clause respects the judicial power of the Senate to try impeachments. "The Senate shall have the sole power to try all impeachments. When sitting for that purpose, they shall be on oath, or affirmation. When the President of the United States is tried, the Chief Justice shall preside; and no person shall be convicted, without the concurrence of two thirds of the members present." The great objects to be attained in the selection of a tribunal for the trial of impeachments, are impartiality, integrity, intelligence, and independence. If either of these qualities is wanting, the trial is essentially defective. To insure impartiality, the body must be, in some degree, removed from popular power and passions, from the influence of sectional prejudices, and from the still more dangerous influence of party spirit. To secure integrity, there must be a lofty sense of duty, and a deep responsibility to God, as well as to future ages. To secure intelligence, there must be age, experience, and high intellectual powers and attainments. To secure independence, there must be numbers, as well as talents, and a confidence, resulting from permanency of place, dignity of station, and consciousness of patriotism. The Senate, from its very organization, must be presumed to possess all these qualities in a high degree, and, certainly, in a degree not surpassed by any other political body in the country. If it should be asked, why the power to try impeachments might not have been confined to a court of law of the highest grade, it may be answered, that such a tribunal is not, on various accounts, so fit for the purpose. In the first place, the offences to be tried are generally of a political character, such as a court of law is not ordinarily accustomed to examine, and such as its common functions exclude. The Senators, on the contrary, necessarily become familiar with such subjects. In the next place, the strict course of proceedings, in courts of law, is ill adapted to the searching out of political delinquencies. In the next place, such political functions are in no small degree incompatible with the due discharge of other judicial duties. They have a tendency to involve the Judges in party interests and party contests, and thereby to withdraw their minds from those studies and habits, which are most important, in the ordinary administration of justice, to secure independence and impartiality. In the next place, the Judges are themselves appointed by the Executive, and may be called upon to try cases, in which he, or some officer enjoying his confidence, and acting under his orders, is the party impeached. In the last place, a Judge may be the very party impeached; and, under such circumstances, a court of law may be presumed to labor under as strong feelings and sympathies for the accused, as any other body. It could never be desirable to call upon the Supreme Court of the nation to try an impeachment of one of its own members for an official misdemeanor. So that, to say the least, the tribunal selected by the Constitution is as unobjectionable, as any, which could be pointed out.

§114. The mode of trial is also provided for. The Senate, when sitting as a Court of Impeachment, "shall be on oath or affirmation." This is required in all cases of trials in the common courts of law. Jurymen, as well as Judges, are always under oath or affirmation, in the discharge of their respective duties. It is a sanction, appealing to their consciences, and calling upon them to reflect well upon their duties. The provision was deemed the more necessary, because in trials of impeachment in England, the House of Lords (which is the High Court of Impeachment) is not under oath; but each Peer makes a declaration simply upon his honor; although if he were a witness in any common trial, he must give his testimony on oath.

§115. The next provision is: "When the President of the United States is tried, the Chief Justice shall preside." The object of this clause is, to preclude the Vice President, who might be supposed to have a natural desire to succeed to the office of President, from being instrumental, or having any influence, in procuring a conviction of the Chief Magistrate. Under such circumstances, who could be deemed more suitable to preside at the trial, than the highest Judicial magistrate of the nation. His impartiality and independence would be as little liable to suspicion, as those of any other person in the country. The dignity of his station might well be deemed an adequate pledge for his possession of the highest accomplishments; and his various learning and great experience in the law, might well be presumed to enable him to give essential assistance to the Senate, not only in regulating their proceedings in such delicate matters, but also in securing the just rights of the accused, by protecting him against unintentional mistakes and errors of judgement in that body. It is added; "And no person shall be convicted, without the concurrence of two thirds of the members present." The reason for this restriction, doubtless, is, that if a bare majority, only, were sufficient to convict of political offences, there would be danger, in times of high popular commotion, or party spirit, that the influence of the House of Representatives would be found irresistible. In cases of trials by jury, absolute unanimity is required to the conviction of a criminal; in cases of legislation, a majority only is required for a decision; and, here, an intermediate number, between an entire unanimity and a bare majority, is adopted. If anything short of unanimity ought to be allowed, two thirds seems a reasonable limitation.

§116. The next clause respects the judgement to be rendered in cases of impeachment.—"Judgement in cases of impeachment shall not extend further than to removal from office, and disqualification to hold and enjoy any office of honor, trust, or profit, under the United States. But the party convicted shall, nevertheless, be liable and subject to indictment, trial, judgement, and punishment according to law." As the principal object of the power of impeachment is to punish political crimes, the restriction of the punishment to mere removal and disqualification from office, seems appropriate, and sufficient. Probably the abuses, to which an unlimited power of punishment might lead in times of popular excitement, and party strife, introduced this restriction. And the experience of the parent country had demonstrated, that it could be applied against a particular victim with a cruelty and harshness, wholly incompatible with national justice, and public honor. Yet persons, who are guilty of public offences, ought not wholly to escape the proper punishment, affixed by law in other cases. And, therefore, they are made amenable, like their fellow-citizens, to the common course of trial and punishment in the courts of law. This provision was the more necessary, because it might otherwise be contended, that they could not, according to a known maxim of law, be twice tried and punished for the same offence. And here, again, the wisdom of the Constitution, in excluding the courts of law from the trial of impeachments, is shown. For, if the same court should re-try the cause, they would already have decided upon the party's guilt; and, if an inferior court should try it, the influence of the superior court would be apt to have an undue predominance over it.

§ 117. There is wisdom, and sound policy, and intrinsic justice in this separation of the offence, at least, so far as the jurisdiction and trial are concerned, into its proper elements, bringing the political part under the power of the political department of the government, and retaining the civil part for presentment and trial in the ordinary forum. A jury might well be intrusted with the latter; while the former should meet its appropriate trial and punishment before the Senate. If it should be asked, why separate trials should thus be successively had; and why, if a conviction should take place in a court of law, that court might not be intrusted with the power to pronouce a removal from office, and the disqualification to office, as a part of its sentence the answer has been already given in the reasoning against vesting any court of law with merely political functions. In the ordinary course of the administration of criminal justice, no court is authorized to remove or disqualify an offender, as a part of its regular judgement. If it results at all, it results as a consequence, and not as a part of the sentence. But it may be properly urged, that the vesting of such a high and delicate power, to be exercised by a court of law at its discretion, would, in relation to the distinguished functionaries of the government, be peculiarly unfit and inexpedient. What could be more embarrassing, than for a court of law to pronounce for a removal upon the mere ground of political usurpation, or malversation in office, admitting of endless varieties, from the slightest guilt up to the most flagrant corruption? Ought a President to be removed from office at the mere will of a court for political misdemeanors? Is not a political body, like the Senate, from its superior information in regard to executive functions, far better qualified to judge, how far the public weal might be promoted by such a punishment in a given case, than a mere juridical tribunal? Suppose the Senate should still deem the judgement irregular, or unjustifiable, how is the removal to take effect, and how is it to be enforced? A separation of the removing power altogether from the appointing power might create many practical difficulties, which ought not, except upon the most urgent reasons, to be introduced into matters of government. Without attempting to maintain, that the difficulties would be insuperable, it is sufficient to show, that they might be highly inconvenient in practice.

§118. In order to complete our review of the subject of impeachments, it is necessary to cite a clause to be found in a subsequent part of the Constitution (Art. 2, Sect. 4) declaring, who shall be liable to impeachment, and for what offences. "The President, Vice President, and all civil officers of the

United States, shall be removed from office, on impeachment for, and conviction of, treason, bribery, or other high crimes and misdemeanors."

§119. From this clause, it appears, that the power of impeachment does not extend to any, but civil officers of the United States, including the President, and Vice President. In England, it extends to all persons, whether peers or commoners, and whether officers or not. There seems a peculiar propriety, in a republican government, in confining the impeaching power to persons holding office. In such a government, all the citizens are equal, and ought to have the same security of a trial by jury, for all crimes and offences laid to their charge, when not holding any official character. They might, otherwise, be subject to gross political oppressions, and prosecutions, which might ruin their fortunes, or subject them to unjustifiable odium. When a person accepts an office, he may fairly be held to consent to a waiver of this privilege; and there can be no reasonable objection, on his part, to a trial by impeachment, since it can go no further than to a removal from office, and a disqualification of hold office.

§120. Who are "civil officers," within the meaning of this constitutional provision, is an inquiry, which naturally presents itself; and the answer cannot, perhaps, be deemed settled, by any solemn adjudication. The term "civil" has various significations. It is sometimes used, in contradistinction to *barbarous,* or *savage,* to indicate a state of society, reduced to order and regular government. Thus, we speak of civil life, civil society, civil government, and civil liberty; in which cases, it is nearly equivalent, in meaning, to *political.* It is sometimes used in contradistinction to *criminal,* to indicate the private rights and remedies of men, as members of the community, in contrast to those, which are public, and relate to the government. Thus, we speak of civil process and criminal process, civil jurisdiction and criminal jurisdiction. It is sometimes used in contradistinction to *military* or *ecclesiastical,* to *natural* or *foreign.* Thus, we speak of a civil station, as opposed to a military or ecclesiastical station; a civil death, as as opposed to a natural death; a civil war, as opposed to a foreign war. The sense, in which the term is used in the Constitution, seems to be in contradistinction to *military,* to indicate the rights and duties relating to citizens generally, in contradistinction to those of persons engaged in the land or naval service of the government. It is in this sense, that Sir William Blackstone speaks of the laity in England, as divided into three distinct states: the civil, the military, and the maritime; the two latter embracing the land and naval forces of the government. And in the same sense, the expenses of the civil list of officers are spoken of, in contradistinction to those of the army and navy.

§121. All officers of the United States, therefore, who hold their appointments under the National Government, whether their duties are executive or judicial, in the highest or in the lowest departments of the government, with the exception of officers, in the army and navy, are properly civil officers, within the meaning of the Constitution, and liable to impeachment. The reason for excepting military and naval officers is, that they are subject to trial and punishment according to a peculiar military code, the laws, rules, and usages of war. The very nature and efficiency of military duties and discipline require this summary and exclusive jurisdiction; and the promptitude of its operations is not only better suited to the notions of military men; but they deem their honor and their reputation more safe in the hands of their brother officers, than in any merely civil tribunal. Indeed, in military and naval affairs, it is quite clear, that the Senate could scarcely possess competent knowledge or experience to decide upon the acts of military men; so such are these acts to be governed by mere usage and custom, by military discipline, and military discretion, that the Constitution has wisely committed the whole trust to the decision of courts-martial.

§122. It is observable, that the clause makes the President and Vice President expressly liable to impeachment. And the question arose, upon an impeachment, in 1799, whether a Senator is a civil officer of the United States, in the sense of the

Constitution, so as to be liable to an impeachment. It was on that occasion decided, by the Senate, that he is not; and, of course, the same principle would apply to a Representative in Congress. The ground of this decision seems to have been that a Senator does not derive his appointment from or under the National Government, but from the State Legislature; and that the clause contemplated only such civil officers, as derived their appointment from the National Government, and were responsible for their conduct thereto. Motives of public policy would also conduce to the establishment of this same conclusion, since the impeachment of Legislators for their official acts might have a tendency to overawe or intimidate them in the discharge of their public functions. In the whole history and practice of England and America, no example can be found, of any attempt to introduce such a principle; and this very silence is expressive of the state of public opinion as to the danger and policy of conferring such a power.

§123. The offences, to which impeachments extend, are, "treason, bribery, and other high crimes and misdemeanors." No person can reasonably doubt the propriety of the removal, and disqualification from office, of a person, who is guilty of treason, which aims at the overthrow of the government, or of bribery, which corrupts its due administration. And doubtless there are other high crimes and misdemeanors, to which the power of impeachment may properly be applied, since they may be utterly incompatible with the public safety and interests, or may bring the government itself into disgrace and obloquy.

§124. But an important inquiry still remains, as to the nature and definition of these crimes. What is the crime of treason? What is the crime of bribery? What are high crimes and misdemeanors in the sense of the Constitution? For the definition of treason we may resort to the Constitution itself. For the definition of bribery we must resort to the common law, which alone furnishes the proper exposition of the nature and limits of the offence. But neither the Constitution, nor the statutes of the United States, have in any manner defined any other crimes to be high crimes and misdemeanors, and as such, exposing the party to impeachment. How then are we to ascertain, what offences, besides treason and bribery, are within the scope of the impeaching power? If we say, that there are no other offences, which are impeachable offences, until Congress has enacted some law on the subject, then the Constitution, as to all crimes except treason and bribery, has remained a dead letter, up to the present hour. Such a doctrine would be truly alarming and dangerous.

§125. Congress has unhesitatingly adopted the conclusion, that no previous statute is necessary to authorize an impeachment for any official misconduct; and the rules of proceeding, and the rules of evidence, as well as the principles of decision, have been uniformly regulated by the known doctrines of the common law, and parliamentary usage. In the few cases of impeachment, which have hitherto been tried, no one of the charges has rested upon any statutable misdemeanors. It seems, then, to be the settled doctrine of the high court of impeachment, that though the common law cannot be a foundation of a jurisdiction not given by the Constitution, or laws, that jurisdiction, when given, attaches, and is to be exercised, according to the rules of the common law; and that, what are, and what are not, high crimes and misdemeanors, is to be ascertained by a recurrence to that great basis of American jurisprudence. The reasoning, by which the power of the House of Representatives to punish for contempts (which are breaches of privileges, and offences not defined by any positive laws) has been upheld by the Supreme Court, stands upon similar grounds; for if the House had no jurisdiction to punish for contempts, until the acts had been previously defined, and ascertained by positive law, it is clear, that the process of arrest would be illegal.

§126. This subject may be concluded by a summary statement of the mode of proceeding in the institution and trial of impeachments, as it is of rare occurrence, and is not governed by the formalities of the ordinary prosecution in courts at law.

§127. When, then, an officer is known or suspected to be guilty of malversation in office, some member of the House of Representatives usually brings forward a resolution to accuse the party, or for the appointment of a committee, to consider and report upon the charges laid against him. The latter is the ordinary course; and the report of a committee usually contains, if adverse to the party, a statement of the charges, and recommends a resolution, that he be impeached therefor. If the resolution is adopted by the House, a committee is then appointed to impeach the party at the bar of the Senate, and to state, that the articles against him will be exhibited in due time, and made good before the Senate; and to demand, that the Senate take order for the appearance of the party to answer to the impeachment. This being accordingly done, the Senate signifies its willingness to take such order; and articles are then prepared by a committee, under the direction of the House of Representatives, which, when reported to, and approved by the House, are then presented in the like manner to the Senate; and a committee of managers is appointed to conduct the impeachment. As soon as the articles are thus presented, the Senate issues a process, summoning the party to appear, at a given day, before it, to answer the articles. The process is served by the sergeant-at-arms of the Senate, and due return is made thereof under oath.

§128. The articles thus exhibited, need not, and indeed do not, pursue the strict form and accuracy of an indictment. They are sometimes quite general in the form of the allegations; but always contain, or ought to contain, so much certainty, as to enable the party to put himself upon the proper defence, and also, in case of an acquittal, to avail himself of it, as a bar to another impeachment. Additional articles may be exhibited, perhaps, at any stage of the prosecution.

§129. When the return day of the process for appearance has arrived, the Senate resolve themselves into a court of impeachment, and the Senators are at that time, or before, solemnly sworn, or affirmed, to do impartial justice upon the impeachment, according to the Constitution and laws of the United States. The person impeached is then called to appear and answer the articles. If he does not appear in person, or by attorney, his default is recorded, and the Senate may proceed *ex parte* (that is, on the claim of one side) to the trial of the impeachment. If he does appear in person, or by attorney, his appearance is recorded. Counsel for the parties are admitted to appear, and to be heard upon an impeachment.

§130. When the party appears, he is entitled to be furnished with a copy of the articles of impeachment, and time is allowed him to prepare his answer thereto. The answer, like the articles, is exempted from the necessity of observing great strictness of form. The party may plead, that he is not guilty, as to part, and make a further defence, as to the residue; or he may, in a few words, saving all exceptions, deny the whole charge or charges; or he may plead specially, in justification or excuse of the supposed offences, all the circumstances attendant upon the case. And he is also indulged with the liberty of offering argumentative reasons, as well as facts, against the charges, in support, and as part, of his answer, to repel them. It is usual to give a full and particular answer separately to each article of the accusation.

§131. When the answer is prepared and given in, the next regular proceeding is, for the House of Representatives to file a replication to the answer in writing, in substance denying the truth and validity of the defence stated in the answer, and averring the truth and sufficiency of the charges, and the readiness of the House to prove them at such convenient time and place, as shall be appointed for that purpose by the Senate. A time is then assigned for the trial; and the Senate, at that period or before, adjust the preliminaries and other proceedings proper to be had, before and at the trial, by fixed regulations; which are made known to the House of Representatives, and to the party accused. On the day appointed for the trial, the House of Representatives appear at the bar of the Senate, either in a body, or by the managers selected for that purpose, to proceed with the trial. Process to compel the attendance of witnesses is previously issued at the request of either party, by order of the Senate; and at the time and place appointed, they are bound to appear and give testimony. On the day of trial, the parties being ready, the managers to conduct the prosecution open it on behalf of the House of Representatives, one or more of them delivering an explanatory speech, either of the whole charges, or of one or more of them. The proceedings are then conducted substantially, as they are upon common judicial trials, as to the admission or rejection of testimony, the examination and cross-examination of witnesses, the rules of evidence, and the legal doctrines, as to crimes and misdemeanors. When the whole evidence has been gone through, and the parties on each side have been fully heard, the Senate then proceeds to the consideration of the case. If any debates arise, they are conducted in secret; if none arise, or after they are ended, a day is assigned for a final public decision by yeas and nays upon each separate charge in the articles of impeachment. When the court is assembled for this purpose, the question is propounded to each member of the Senate by name, by the President of the Senate, in the following manner, upon each article, the same being first read by the Secretary of the Senate. "Mr. _____ , how say you, is the respondent guilty, or not guilty, of a high crime and misdemeanor, as charges in the _____ article of impeachment?" Whereupon the member rises in his place, and answers guilty, or not guilty, as his opinion is. If upon no one article, two thirds of the Senate decide, that the party is guilty, he is then entitled to an acquittal, and is declared accordingly to be acquitted by the President of the Senate. If he is convicted of all, or any, of the articles, the Senate then proceeds to fix, and declare the proper punishment. The pardoning power of the President does not, as will be presently seen, extend to judgements upon impeachment; and hence when once pronounced, they become absolute and irreversible.

§132. Having, thus gone through the whole subject of impeachments, it only remains to observe, that a close survey of the system, unless we are egregiously deceived, will completely demonstrate the wisdom of the arrangements made in every part of it. The jurisdiction to impeach is placed, where it should be, in the possession and power of the immediate representative of people. The trial is before a body of great dignity, and ability, and independence, possessing the requisite knowledge and firmness to act with vigor, and to decide with impartially upon the charges. The persons subjected to the trial are officers of the national government; and the offences are such, as may affect the rights, duties, and relations of the party accused, to the public in his political or official character, either directly or remotely. The general rules of law and evidence, applicable to common trials, are interposed, to protect the party against the exercise of wanton oppression, and arbitrary power. And the final judgement is confined to a removal from, and disqualification for, office; thus limiting the punishment to such modes of redress, as are peculiarly fit for a political tribunal to administer, and as will secure the public against political injuries. In other respects, the offence is left to be disposed of by the common tribunals of justice, according to the laws of the land, upon an indictment found by a grand jury, and a trial by a jury of peers, before whom the party is to stand for his final deliverance, like his fellow-citizens.

CHAPTER XII.

Elections and Meetings of Congress.

§133. WE next come to the fourth section of the first article, which treats the elections and meetings of Congress. The first clause is,—"The time, places, and manner of holding elections for Senators and Representatives, shall be prescribed in each State, by Legislation thereof. But Congress may, at any time, by law, make or alter such regulations, except as to the places of choosing Senators." There is great propriety in leaving to the State Legislatures the right, in the first instance, of regulating the times and places of choosing the members of Congress, as every State is then enabled to consult its own local convenience in the choice; and it would be difficult to prescribe any uniform time or place of elections, which would, in all possible changes in the situation of the States, be found convenient for all of them. On the other hand, as the ability of the General Government to carry on its own operations depends upon these elections being duly had, it is plain, that it ought not to be left to the State Governments, exclusively, to decide, whether such elections should be had, or not. The maxim of sound political wisdom is, that every Government ought to contain in itself the means of its own preservation. And, therefore, an ulterior and paramount power is reserved to Congress, to make or alter the regulations as to such elections, so as to preserve the efficiency of the General Government. But, inasmuch as the State Legislatures are to elect Senators, the places of their meetings are left to their own discretion, as most fit to be decided by themselves, with reference to their ordinary duties and convenience. But Congress may still prescribe the times, at which such elections shall be made.

§134. The next clause is—"The Congress shall assemble at least once in every year; and such meeting shall be on the first Monday of December, unless they shall, by law, appoint a different day." The importance of this provision can scarcely be overrated by a free people, accustomed to know their rights, and jealous in the maintenance of them. Unless some time were prescribed for the regular meetings of Congress, they would depend upon the good will and pleasure of Congress itself, or of some other department of the government. In times of violent factions, or military usurpations, attempts might be made to postpone such meetings for an unreasonable length of time, in order to prevent the redress of grievances, or secure the violators of the laws from condign punishment. Annual meetings of the legislature have long been deemed, both in England and America, a great security to liberty and justice; and it was true wisdom to establish the duty of such annual meetings, by a political provision in the Constitution, which could not be evaded or disobeyed.

CHAPTER XIII.

Powers and Privileges of both Houses.

§135. THE fifth section of the first article contains an enumeration of the powers, rights, and duties of each branch of the Legislature, in its separate and distinct organic character. The first clause is—"Each House shall be the judge of the elections, returns, and qualifications, of its own members; and a majority of each shall constitute a quorum to do business; but a smaller number may adjourn, from day to day, and may be authorized to compel the attendance of absent members, in such manner, and under such penalties, as each House may provide."

§136. The powers are common to all the legislative bodies of the States; and, indeed, to those of other free governments. They seem indispensable to the due independence and efficiency of the body. The power to judge the elections, returns, and qualifications, of the members of each House, must be lodged somewhere; for otherwise, any intruder, or usurper, might assume to be a member. It can be safely lodged in no other body, but that, in which the party claims a seat; for otherwise, its independence, its purity, and even its existence, might be under the control of a foreign authority. It is equally important, that a proper quorum for the despatch of business should be fixed, otherwise a cunning, or industrious, minority might, by stratagem, usurp the functions of the majority, and pass laws at their pleasure. On the other hand, if a smaller number were not authorized to adjourn from day to day, or to compel the attendance of other members, all legislation might be suspended at the pleasure of the absentees, and the Legislature itself be virtually dissolved.

§137. The next clause is—"Each House may determine the rules of its proceedings, punish its members for disorderly behavior, and, with the concurrence of two thirds, expel a member." These powers, also, are usually granted to legislative bodies. If they did not exist, it would be utterly impracticable to transact the business of the nation at all, or at least, to transact it with decency, deliberation, and order. Without rules, no public body can suitably perform its functions. If rules are made, they are mere nullities, unless the persons on whom they are to operate, can be compelled to obey them. But, if an unlimited power to punish, even to the extent of expulsion, existed, it might, in factious times, be applied by a domineering majority, to get rid of the most intelligent, virtuous, and efficient of their opponents. There is, therefore, a check interposed, which requires a concurrence of two thirds to expel; and this number can hardly be presumed to concur in exercising the power of expulsion, except in cases of flagrant breaches of the rights of the House.

§138. The next clause is—"Each House shall keep a journal of its proceedings, and from time to time publish the same, except such parts as may, in their judgment, require secrecy. And the yeas and nays of the members of either House, on any question, shall, at the desire of one fifth of those present, be entered on the journal." Each of these provisions has the same object, to insure publicity and responsibility in all the proceedings of Congress, so that the public mind may be enlightened, as to the acts of the members. But cases may exist, where secrecy may be indispensable to the complete operation of the intended acts, either at home or abroad. And, on the other hand, an unlimited power to call the yeas and nays on every question, at the mere will of single member, would interrupt and retard, and, in many cases, wholly defeat, the public business. In each case, therefore, a reasonable limitation is interposed.

§139. The next clause is—"Neither House, during the session of Congress, shall, without the consent of the other, adjourn for more than three days, nor to any other place than that in which the two Houses shall be sitting." Here, again, the object of the clause is manifest, to prevent either House from suspending, at its pleasure, the regular course of legislation, and even of carrying the power to the extent of a dissolution of the session. The duration of the sessions of Congress, subject only to the constitutional expiration of the term of office of the members, thus depends upon their own pleasure, with the single exception (as we shall hereafter see) of the case, where the two Houses disagree, in respect to the time of adjournment, when it is given to the President. So that their independence is effectually guarded against any encroachment on the part of the Executive. In England, the King may prorogue or dissolve Parliament at his pleasure; and, before the Revolution, the same power was generally exercised by the Governors in most of the American Colonies.

§140. These are all the powers and privileges expressly enumerated, as belonging to the two Houses. But other incidental powers may well be presumed to exist. Among these, the power to punish contempts, committed against either House by strangers, has been generally admitted, and insisted upon in practice, as indispensable to the freedom, the deliberative functions, and the personal safety of the members.

§141. The sixth section of the first article contains an enumeration of the personal rights, privileges, and disabilities of the members, as contradistinguished from those of the Houses, of which they are members. The first clause is—"The Senators and Representatives shall receive a compensation for their services, to be ascertained by law, and paid out of the Treasury of the United States. They shall, in all cases, except treason, felony, or breach of the peace, be privileged from arrest, during their attendance at the session of the respective Houses, and in going to, and returning from, the same. And for any speech or debate in either House, they shall not be questioned in any other place."

§142. First, compensation. It has been greatly questioned, whether, on the whole, it is best to allow compensation to members of Congress, or not. On the one hand, it has been said, that it tempts unworthy and avaricious men to intrigue for office, and to defeat candidates of higher talents and virtues. On the other hand, it has been said, that unless compensation be allowed, merit of the highest order may be excluded by poverty from the national councils; and in a republican government nothing can be more impolitic than to give to wealth superior encouragement, and facility in obtaining office. The latter reasoning had its due force, and prevailed in the Convention and with the people.

§143. Next, the privilege from arrest. This is given in all cases (except of crimes) in going to, attending upon, and returning from, any session of Congress. It would be a great mistake to consider it, as in reality a personal privilege, for the benefit of the member. It is rather a privilege for the benefit of his constituents, that they may not be deprived of the presence, services, and influence of their own Representative in the national councils. It might otherwise happen, that he might be arrested from mere malice, or from political persecution, or upon some unfounded claim and thus they might be deprived of his aid and talents during the whole session.

§144. Thirdly, the liberty of speech and debate. This, too, is less to be regarded as a personal privilege, than as a public right, to secure independence, firmness, and fearlessness on the part of the members, so that, in discharging their high trusts, they may not be overawed by wealth, or power, or dread of prosecution. The same privilege is enjoyed in the British Parliament, and also in the several State Legislatures of the Union, founded upon the same reasoning.

§145. The next clause regards the disqualifications of members of Congress. "No Senator or Representative shall, during the time for which he is elected, be appointed to any civil office, under the authority of the United States, which shall have been created, or the emoluments whereof shall have been increased during such time. And no person, holding any office under the United States, shall be a member of either House of Congress during his continuance in office." The object of these provisions is sufficiently manifest. It is, to secure the Legislature against undue influence, and indirect corruption, on the part of the Executive. Whether much reliance can be placed upon guards of this disqualifying nature, has been greatly doubted. It is not easy, by any constitutional or legislative enactments, to shut out all, or even many, of the avenues of undue or corrupt influence upon the human mind. The great securities for society—those, on which it must forever rest in a free government—are responsibility to the people through elections, and personal character, and purity of principle. Where these are wanting, there never can be any solid confidence, or any deep sense of duty. Where these exist, they become a sufficient guarantee against all sinister influences, as well as all gross offences. It has been remarked, with equal profoundness and sagacity, that, as there is a degree of depravity in mankind, which requires a certain degree of circumspection and distrust; so there are other qualities in human nature, which justify a certain portion of esteem and confidence. Republican government presupposes the existence of these qualities in a higher form, than any other. It might well be deemed harsh to disqualify an individual from any office, clearly required by the exigencies of the country, simply because he had done his duty. And, on the other hand, the disqualification might operate upon many persons, who might find their way into the national councils, as a strong inducement to postpone the creation of necessary offices, lest they should become victims of their high discharge of duty. The chances of receiving an appointment to a new office are not so many, or so enticing, as to bewilder many minds; and if they are, the aberrations from duty are so easily traced, that they rarely, if ever, escape the public reproaches. And if influence is to be exerted by the

Executive, for improper purposes, it will be quite as easy, and in its operation less seen, and less suspected, to give the stipulated patronage in another form, either of office, or of profitable employment, already existing.

§146. The other part of the clause, which disqualified persons, holding any office under the United States, from being members of either House, during the continuance in office, has been still more universally applauded; and has been vindicated upon the highest grounds of public policy. It is doubtless founded in a deference to State jealousy, and a sincere desire to obviate the fears, real or imaginary, that the General Government would obtain an undue preference over the State Governments. It has also the strong recommendation, that it prevents any undue influence from office, either upon the party himself, or those, with whom he is associated in legislative deliberations. The universal exclusion of all persons holding office, is (it must be admitted) attended with some inconveniences. The Heads of the Departments are, in fact, thus precluded from proposing, or vindicating their own measures in the face of the nation in the course of debate; and are compelled to submit them to other men, who are either imperfectly acquainted with the measures, or are indifferent to their success or failure. Thus, that open and public responsibility for measures, which properly belongs to the Executive in all governments, and especially in a republican government, as its greatest security and strength, is completely done away. The Executive is compelled to resort to secret and unseen influence, to private interviews, and private arrangements, to accomplish his own appropriate purposes; instead of proposing and sustaining his own duties and measures by a bold and manly appeal to the nation in the face of its representatives. One consequence of this state of things, is, that there never can be traced home to the Executive any responsibility for the measures, which are planned, and carried at his suggestion. Patronage may be quite as effective under a different form. It may confer office on a friend, or a relative, or a dependent. The hope of office, in future, may seduce a man from his duty, as much as its present possession. And, after all, the chief guards against venality, in all governments, must be placed in the high virtue, the unspotted honor, and the pure patriotism of public men. On this account, it has been doubted, whether the exclusion of the Heads of Departments from Congress, has not led to the use of indirect and irresponsible influence, on the part of the Executive, over the measures of Congress, far more than could exist, if the Heads of Departments held seats in Congress, and might be there compelled to avow and defend their own opinions. The provision, however, as it stands, has hitherto been found acceptable to the American people, and ought not lightly to be surrendered.

CHAPTER XIV.

Mode of Passing Laws.

§147. THE seventh section of the first article, declares the mode of passing laws. The first clause is—"All bills for raising revenue, shall originate in the House of Representatives; but the Senate may propose or concur with amendments, as in other bills." This clause had its origin in the known rule of the British Parliament, that all money bills shall originate in the House of Commons. And so jealous are the House of Commons of this valuable privilege, that they will not suffer the House of Lords to make the least alteration or amendment to any such bill. The general reason, assigned for this privilege, in that kingdom, is, that all taxes and supplies, raised upon the people, should originate with their immediate representatives. But, in truth, it was intended by the popular branch of the legislature, by this course, to acquire a permanent importance in the government; and to be able to counterpoise the influence of the House of Lords, a body having hereditary rights and dignity. The same reason does not apply, with the same, force to our republican forms of government. But still, as the same power was exercised under some of the State governments, and as the House of Representatives may be deemed peculiarly well fitted to bring, to such subjects, a full knowledge of the local interests, as well as of the wishes and opinions of the people, there is no inconvenience in allowing to the House the exclusive right to originate all such bills in the course of legislation. But, as taxes and revenue laws may bear with great inequality upon some of the States, and, above all, as direct taxes are, and must, according to the Constitution, be apportioned among the States according to the ratio of their population, as already stated, a power to amend such laws is properly reserved to the Senate, where all the States possess an equal voice. The due influence of all the States is thus preserved over a subject of such vital importance; and it might otherwise happen, that, from the overwhelming representation of some of the large States, in the House of Representatives, taxes might be levied, which would bear, with peculiar severity and hardship, upon the agricultural, commercial, or manufacturing, interests of the smaller States; and thus the equilibrium of power, of influence, and of interest, of the several States; in the National councils, might be practically subverted.

§148. The next clause respects the power of the President to approve and negative laws. It is as follows:—"Every bill, which shall have passed the House of Representatives and the Senate, shall, before it becomes a law, be presented to the President of the United States. If he approves, he shall sign it; but if not, he shall return it, with his objections, to that House, in which it shall have originated, who shall enter the objections at large, on their journal, and proceed to reconsider it. If, after such reconsideration, two thirds of that House shall agree to pass the bill, it shall be sent, together with the objections, to the other House, by which it shall, likewise, be reconsidered; and, if approved by two thirds of that House, it shall become a law. But, in all such cases, the votes of both Houses shall be determined by yeas and nays, and the names of the persons voting for and against the bill, shall be entered on the journal of each House respectively. If any bill shall not be returned by the President within ten days (Sundays excepted) after it shall have been presented to him, the same shall be a law, in like manner, as if he had signed it, unless the Congress, by its adjournment, prevent its return, in which case it shall not be a law."

§ 149. The reasons, why the President should possess a qualified negative (for an absolute negative would be highly objectionable) are, if not quite obvious, at least, when fairly expounded, entirely satisfactory. In the first place, there is a natural tendency, in the legislative department, to intrude upon the rights, and to absorb the powers, of the other departments of the government. If the Executive did not possess this qualified negative, he might gradually be stripped of all his authority, and become, what the Governors of some of the States now are, a mere pageant, and a shadow of magistracy.

§ 150. In the next place, the power is important, as an additional security against the enactment of rash, immature, and improper laws. In the third place, the President may fairly be deemed the representative of the whole nation, the choice being produced by a different modification of interests and opinions and votes, from that by which the choice of either branch of the National Legislature is produced, either that representing the People, or that representing the States. His power, therefore, of a qualified negative, being founded upon the supposition, that he truly represents all the interests and opinions of the Union, introduces a useful element, to check any preponderating interest of any section, in a particular measure. It does not, like an absolute negative, suspend legislation, but it merely refers the subject back, for a more deliberate review of the Senate and House. If two thirds of each branch still concur in favor of the measure, it becomes a law. Thus, a thorough revision of the measure is guaranteed; and, at the same time, the deliberate wishes of the States, and of the people, cannot be disobeyed. If two thirds of each branch do not dissent from the President's opinion, the natural inference is, that the measure is not so far beyond all reasonable objections, that it ought ordinarily to prevail. The negative of the President was undoubtedly designed by the Constitution to be applied only on extraordinary occasions and exigencies; and if it were to be applied to the common course of legislation, it might be fraught with great public mischiefs, and weaken, if not overthrow, the just power of legislation by Congress, since it may be presumed, that it can rarely happen, in a country, having such a diversity of interests, and pursuits, and opinions, as ours, that a clear majority of two thirds of each House can be obtained against the known wishes, and natural influence of the Executive department. On the other hand, if Congress should often be driven, by the frequent use of it, to pass laws, in opposition to the President's negative, it would gradually introduce a disregard of his opinions, and a hostile opposition to his authority. Such a state of things would, certainly, in every view, be most inconvenient and undesirable. The evil, however, could scarcely be of a very long continuance; for, if the President should abuse his power, (as certainly he sometimes may,) the people have the proper remedies in their own hands, and can compel him to relinquish office at no distant period.

§151. But the qualified negative is not left wholly without restraint. The President must properly exercise it, within ten days, excluding Sunday; otherwise, the bill becomes a law. And, on the other hand, Congress is deprived of the power of preventing its due exercise by a hasty adjournment within the ten days, so as to leave the President without sufficient time for due deliberation. If a qualified negative is to be allowed at all, it would seem thus to be as much restrained, as the public good can require, or, at least, as much, as its proper exercise can justify.

§152. The remaining clause provides a like regulation in regard to orders, resolutions, and votes, to which the concurrence of both Houses is necessary. It is—"Every order, resolution, or vote, to which the concurrence of the Senate and House of Representatives may be necessary (except on a question of adjournment) shall be presented to the President of the United States; and, before the same shall take effect, shall be approved by him, or, being disapproved by him, shall be repassed by two thirds of the Senate and House of Representatives, according to the rules and limitations prescribed in the case of a bill." If this provision had not been made, Congress, by adopting the form of an order, or resolution, or vote, instead of a bill, might have effectively defeated the President's negative in many important portions of legislation. The reason of the exception as to adjournments, is, that this power is peculiarly fit to be acted upon by Congress, according to its own discretion; and, therefore, it is (as we have seen) by a preceding clause, vested in both Houses, and devolves on the President, only in case of their disagreement.

§153. We have now completed the review of the structure and organization of the legislative department; and, it has been shown, that it is admirably adapted for a wholesome and upright exercise of the powers confided to it. All the checks, which human ingenuity has been able to devise, or at least all, which, with reference to our habits, our institutions, and our diversities of local interests, seem practicable, to give perfect operation to the machinery, to adjust its movements, to prevent its eccentricities, and to balance its forces; all these have been introduced, with singular skill, ingenuity, and wisdom, into the arrangements. Yet, after all, the fabric may fall; for the work of man is perishable. Nay, it must fall, if there be not that vital spirit in the people, which can alone nourish, sustain, and direct, all its movements. If ever the day shall arrive, in which the best talents, and the best virtues shall be driven from office, by intrigue, or corruption, by the denunciations of the press, or by the persecutions of party factions, legislation will cease to be national. It will be wise by accident, and bad by system.

CHAPTER XV.

Powers of Congress.—Taxation.

§154. WE next come to the consideration of the legislative powers conferred on Congress, which are contained in the eighth section of the first article. The first clause is—"The Congress shall have power to lay and collect taxes, duties, imposts, and excises, to pay the debts, and provide for the common defence and general welfare of the United States. But all duties, imposts, and excises shall be uniform throughout the United States." What is the true interpretation of this clause, has been matter of considerable controversy; that is to say, whether the words, "Congress shall have power to lay and collect taxes, duties, imposts, and excises," constitute a distinct clause and confer a substantive independent power; and the words, "to pay the debts, and provide for the common defence and general welfare of the United States," constitute another, distinct clause, and substantive and independent power; or, whether these latter words are a dependent clause, merely qualifying the former clause, and so the whole to be read together, as if the words stood thus—"Congress shall have power to lay and collect taxes, duties, imposts, and excises," *in order* "to pay the public debts, and to provide for the common defence and general welfare;" that is to say, Congress shall have power to lay taxes, &c., for the purpose of paying the public debts, and providing for the common defence and general welfare. If the former be the true interpretation, then it is obvious, that the powers of the National Government, under color of the authority of the clause to provide for the common defence and general welfare, would be practically unlimited. If the latter be the true interpretation, then the words properly amount to a limitation or qualification of the power of taxation; so that no taxes can be laid by Congress, except to pay the debts, and to provide for the common defence and general welfare. The latter seems the more just and solid interpretation of the words, and most comformable to the true spirit and objects of the instrument.

§155. The necessity of the power of taxation, to the vigorous action of the National Government, would seem to be self-evident. The want of it, was one of the principal defects under the Confederation. A National Government, without the power of providing for its own expenditures, charged with public burdens and duties, and yet deprived of adequate means to sustain and perform them, would soon become wholly inert and imbecile. It would be almost as absurd, as to bind a man immovably to the earth, and yet at the same time to require him to walk abroad. If, then, there is to be a real, effective National Government, there must be a power of taxation given to it, adequate to its wants, its objects, and its duties. The only proper remaining inquiry would be, whether the power of taxation should be limited to particular specified objects and sources, or whether the power should be general and unlimited. It is obvious, that if limited to particular objects and sources, those objects and sources might be exhausted, or might become utterly inadequate to the public wants, or might be taxed to an extent, which would be ruinous to particular employments and interests. Thus, for example, if the power were limited to mere taxes on commerce, and the nation should be engaged in war, or should otherwise be involved in heavy expenditures in the course of unfortunate events, the very attempt to defray the national expenditures, and supply the national wants, by taxes on commerce, might amount to an utter annihilation of all its value, and be equivalent to a total prohibition of all foreign trade. The same would be equally true, if the power of taxation were limited exclusively to lands, or to the products of agriculture, or manufactures, or to taxes on particular articles, such as wheat, corn, cotton, flour, rice, or domestic animals. The power of taxation, on the other hand, if general and unrestricted, will leave to Congress a free choice, from time to time, to select such articles for taxation as shall be most productive, and least burdensome, and thus to supply the public wants, without endangering the interests, or depressing the products, of every section of the Country. For these reasons, the power has been given in unlimited terms; and the wisdom of the provision will scarcely now be called in question, by any considerate mind.

§156. The words used, are, "taxes, duties, imposts, and excises." In a general sense, all contributions, imposed by the Government upon individuals *for the service of the State,* are taxes, by whatever name they may be called. In this sense, they are usually divided into two classes:—direct taxes, under which head are included taxes on land, and other real estate, and poll, or capitation taxes, or taxes on the polls or persons of individuals; indirect taxes, under which head are classed those, which are levied only upon articles of consumption, and, of course, of which every person pays only so much, as he consumes of the articles. The word "duties," is often used as synonymous with "customs," which are taxes levied upon goods and merchandise, which are exported or imported. In this sense, duties are equivalent to "imposts," although the latter word is often restrained to duties on goods and merchandise, which are imported from abroad. "Excises," is a word, generally used in contradistinction to "imposts," in its restricted sense; and is applied to internal or inland impositions, levied sometimes upon the consumption of a commodity, sometimes upon the retail sale of it, and sometimes upon the manufacture of it. Thus, a tax, levied upon goods imported from a foreign country, is generally called an "impost" duty;

133

and a tax, levied upon goods manufactured or sold in a country, is called an "excise" duty. The meanings of these words, therefore, often run into each other; and all of them are used in the Constitution, to avoid any ambiguity, as to any one of them being used in a general sense, or in a restricted sense, which might involve endless doubts as to the true extent of the constitutional power.

§157. The power of taxation is not, however, unlimited in its character. The taxes levied must be (as we have seen) either to pay the public debts, or to provide for the common defence and general welfare of the United States. They cannot be levied solely for foreign purposes, or in an aid of foreign nations, or for purposes not national in their objects or character. In the next place, all direct taxes (as we have also seen) are to be apportioned among the several States, in the same manner as Representatives, that is, according to the numbers of the population, to be ascertained in the particular mode pointed out in the Constitution. There is another clause of the Constitution, on the same subject, which declares, "That no capitation, or other direct tax, shall be laid, unless in proportion to the census, or enumeration, herein before directed to be taken." There do not seem to be any other cases, in which a direct tax can be laid according to the sense of the Constitution, except by a direct tax on land or other real estate, or a capitation or poll tax; for no other taxes seem capable of an apportionment among the States. All other taxes, that is, all "duties, imposts, and excises," are required to be uniform throughout the United States. The reason of the latter rule is to prevent Congress from giving any undue preference to the pursuits or interests of one State over those of any other. It might otherwise happen, that the agriculture, commerce, or manufactures of one State might be built up on the ruins of the interests of another; and, the combination of a few States in Congress might secure a monopoly of certain branches of trade and business exclusively to themselves.

§158. And, further, to enforce this uniformity, and to preserve the equal rights of all the States, it is declared, in a subsequent clause of the Constitution, that "No tax or duty shall be laid on articles exported from any State. No preference shall be given, by any regulation of commerce or revenue, to the ports of one State over those of another; nor shall vessels, bound to or from one State, be obliged to enter, clear, or pay duties in another."

§159. The obvious object of these provisions is, to prevent any possibility of applying the power to lay taxes, or regulate commerce, injuriously to the interests of any one State, so as to favor or aid another. If Congress were allowed to lay a duty on exports from any one State, it might unreasonably injure, or even destroy, the staple productions, or common articles of that State. The inequality of such a tax would be extreme. In some of the States, the whole of their means result from agricultural exports. In others, a great portion is derived from other sources; from external fisheries; from freights; and from the profits of commerce in its largest extent. The burden of such a tax would, of course, be very unequally distributed. The power is, therefore, wholly taken away to intermeddle with the subject of exports. On the other hand, preferences might be given to the ports of one State by regulations, either of commerce or of revenue, which might confer on them local facilities or privileges in regard to commerce, or to revenue. And such preferences might be equally fatal, if indirectly given under the milder form of requiring an entry, clearance, or payment of duties in the ports of any State, other than the ports of the State, to or from which the vessel was bound. The last clause, therefore, does not prohibit Congress from requiring an entry or clearance, or payment of duties at the custom-house on importations in any port of a State, to or from which the vessel is bound; but cuts off the right to require such acts to be done in other States, to which the vessel is not bound. In other words, it cuts off the power to require that circuity of voyage, which, under the British colonial system, was employed to interrupt the American commerce before the Revolution. No American vessel could then trade with Europe, unless through a circuitous voyage to and from a British port.

§160. But, as the power of taxation is not exclusively vested in the National Government, but may also be concurrently exercised by the State Governments, it became essential, in order fully to effectuate the same general purposes, and to prevent any State from securing undue preferences and monopolies in its own favor, to lay some restraints upon the exercise of this power by the States. Accordingly another clause in the Constitution declares—"No State shall, *without the consent of Congress,* lay any imposts or duties on imports, or exports, except what may be absolutely necessary for executing its inspection laws. And the net produce of all duties and imposts, laid by any State on imports and exports, shall be for the use of the treasury of the United States; and all such laws shall be subject to the revision of Congress. No State shall without the consent of Congress, lay any tonnage duty." A petty warfare of regulation among the States is thus prevented, which might otherwise rouse resentments, and create dissensions, dangerous to the peace and harmony of the Union. The exceptions in favor of inspection laws, to a limited extent, is for the purpose of enabling each State to improve the quality of articles, produced by the labor and industry of its own inhabitants; and thus to fit them better for exportation, as well as for domestic use. Yet, even here, the superintending power of Congress is reserved, lest, under color of such laws, attempts should be made to injure the interests of other States. The net produce of all such duties and imposts is to be for the use of the National treasury; and the laws themselves, by which they are imposed, are subject to the revision of Congress. Thus, the temptations on the part of any State to levy heavy inspection duties are materially diminished, and an effectual remedy is provided to meet any intentional, or accidental excess. Having thus brought together all the various, but scattered articles of the Constitution, on the subject of taxation, the subject may be dismissed with the single remark, that as no power is more likely, in its abuse, to be detrimental to the public welfare, so no one is guarded with more care, and adjusted with more anxious deference to local and sectional interests.

§161. Notwithstanding, however, all the solicitude manifested by the Constitution, on this subject, inasmuch as the power of taxation is concurrent in the National and State Governments, it is obvious, that many nice and delicate questions must perpetually arise (as indeed some have already arisen) as to the time and boundaries of the power and rights of each government. For, however true it may be, that in a direct conflict between the constitutional authority of the Union and that of a State, the former must be deemed paramount and superior in its obligatory force; yet the question when, and how far, such a conflict does in fact exist, must often involve many difficult and embarrassing inquiries, which do not admit of any universal solution.

CHAPTER XVI.

Power to Borrow Money, and Regulate Commerce.

§162. THE next power of Congress is, "to borrow money on the credit of the United States." This power, also, seems indispensable to the sovereignty and existence of the National Government; for otherwise, in times of great public dangers, or severe public calamities, it might be impossible to provide, adequately, for the public exigencies. In times of peace, it may not, ordinarily, be necessary for the expenditures of a nation to exceed its revenues. But the experience of all nations must convince us, that, in times of war, the burdens and expenses of a single year may more than equal the ordinary revenue of ten years. And, even in times of peace, there are occasions, in which loans may be the most facile, convenient, and economical means of supplying any extraordinary expenditure. The experience of the United States has already shown the importance of the power, both in peace and in war. Without this resource, neither the war of Independence, nor the more recent war with Great Britain could have been successfully carried on, or terminated. And the purchase of Louisiana was by the same means promptly provided for, without being felt by the nation, in its ordinary fiscal concerns.

§163. The next power of Congress is, "to regulate commerce with foreign nations, and among the several States, and with the Indian tribes." The want of this power to regulate commerce was, as has been already suggested, a leading defect of the Confederation. In the different States, the most opposite and conflicting regulations existed; each pursued its own real or supposed local interests; each was jealous of the rivalry of its neighbors; and each was successively driven to retaliatory measures, in order to satisfy public clamor, or to alleviate private distress. In the end, however, all their measures became utterly nugatory, or mischievous, engendering mutual hostilities, and prostrating all their commerce at the feet of foreign nations. It is hardly possible to exaggerate the oppressed and degraded state of domestic commerce, manufactures, and agriculture, at the time of the adoption of the Constitution. Our ships were almost driven from the ocean; our work-shops were nearly deserted; our mechanics were in a starving condition; and our agriculture was sunk to the lowest ebb. These were the natural results of the inability of the General Government to regulate commerce, so as to prevent the injurious monopolies and exclusions of foreign nations, and the conflicting, and often ruinous regulations of the different States. If duties were laid by one State, they were rendered ineffectual by the opposite policy of another. If one State gave a preference to its own ships or commerce, it was counteracted by another. If one State endeavored to foster its own manufactures by any measures of protection, that made it an object of jealousy to others; and brought upon it the severe retaliation of foreign governments. If one State was peculiarly favored in its agricultural products, that constituted an inducement with others to load them with some restrictions, which should redress the inequality. It was easy to foresee, that this state of things could not long exist, without bringing on a border warfare, and a deep-rooted hatred, among neighboring States, fatal to the Union, and, of course, fatal also to the liberty of every member of it.

§164. The power "to regulate foreign commerce," enabled the government at once to place the whole country upon an equality with foreign nations; to compel them to abandon their narrow and selfish policy towards us; and to protect our own commercial interests against their injurious competitions. The power to regulate commerce "among the several States," in like manner, annihilated the cause of domestic feuds and rivalries. It compelled every State to regard the interests of each, as the interests of all; and thus diffused over all the blessings of a free, active, and rapid exchange of commodities, upon the footing of perfect equality. The power to regulate commerce "with the Indian tribes," was equally necessary to the peace and safety of the frontier States. Experience had shown the utter impracticability of escaping from sudden wars, and invasions, on the part of these tribes; and the dangers were immeasurably increased by the want of uniformity of regulations and control in the intercourse with them. Indeed, in nothing has the profound wisdom of the framers of the Constitution been more displayed, than in the grant of this power to the Union. By means of it, the country has risen from poverty to opulence; from a state of narrow and scanty resources to an ample national revenue; from a feeble, and disheartening intercourse and competition with foreign nations, in agriculture, commerce, manufactures, and population, to a proud, and conscious independence in arts, in numbers, in skill, and in civil polity.

§165. In considering this clause of the Constitution, several important inquiries are presented. In the first place, what is the natural import of the terms; in the next place, how far the power is exclusive of that of the States; in the third place, to what purposes and for what objects the power may be constitutionally applied; and in the fourth place, what are the true nature and extent of the power to regulate commerce with the Indian tribes.

§166. In the first place, then, what is the constitutional meaning of the words, "to regulate commerce;" for the Constitution being (as has been aptly said) one of enumeration, and not of definition, it becomes necessary, in order to ascertain the extent of the power, to ascertain the meaning of the words. The power is to regulate; that is, to prescribe the rule, by which commerce is to be governed. The subject to be regulated is commerce. Is that limited to traffic, to buying and selling, or the interchange of commodities? Or does it comprehend navigation and intercourse? If the former construction is adopted, then a general term, applicable to many objects, is restricted to one of its significations. If the latter, then a general term is retained in its general sense. To adopt the former, without some guiding grounds furnished by the context, or the nature of the power, would be improper. The words being general, the sense must be general, also, and embrace all the subjects comprehended under them, unless there be some obvious mischief, or repugnance to other clauses, to limit them. In the present case, there is nothing to justify such a limitation. Commerce undoubtedly is traffic; but it is something more. It is intercourse. It describes the commercial intercourse between nations, and parts of nations, in all its branches; and is regulated by prescribing rules for carrying on that intercourse. The mind can scarcely conceive a system for regulating commerce between nations, which shall exclude all laws concerning navigation; which shall be silent on the admission of the vessels of one nation into the ports of another; and be confined to prescribing rules for the conduct of individuals in the actual employment of buying and selling, or barter. It may, therefore, be safely affirmed, that the terms of the Constitution have, at all times, been understood to include a power over navigation, as well as over trade, over intercourse, as well as over traffic. It adds no small strength to this interpretation, that the practice of all foreign countries, as well as of our own, has uniformly conformed to this view of the subject.

§167. The next inquiry is, whether this power to regulate commerce, is like that to lay taxes. The latter may well be concurrent, while the former is exclusive, resulting from the different nature of the two powers. The power of Congress in laying taxes is not necessarily, or naturally inconsistent with that of the States. Each may lay a tax on the same property, without interfering with the action of the other; for taxation is but taking small portions from the mass of property, which is susceptible of almost infinite division. In imposing taxes for State purposes, a State is not doing what Congress is empowered to do. Congress is not empowered to tax for those purposes, which are within the exclusive province of the States. When, then, each government exercises the power of taxation, neither is exercising the power of the other. But when a State proceeds to regulate commerce with foreign nations, or among the several States, it is exercising the very power, which is granted to Congress; and is doing the very thing, which Congress is authorized to do. There is no analogy, then, between the power of taxation, and the power of regulating commerce.

§168. Nor can any power be inferred in the States, to regulate commerce, from other clauses in the Constitution, or the acknowledged rights exercised by the States. The Constitution has prohibited the States from laying any impost or duty on imports or exports; but this does not admit, that the State might otherwise have exercised the power, as a regulation of commerce. The laying of such imposts and duties may be, and indeed often is, used, as a mere regulation of commerce, by governments possessing that power. But the laying of such imposts and duties is as certainly, and more usually, a right exercised as a part of the power to lay taxes; and with this latter power the States are clearly intrusted. So that the prohibition is an exception from the acknowledged power of the State to lay taxes, and not from the questionable power to regulate commerce. Indeed, the Constitution treats these as distinct and independent powers. The same remarks apply to a duty on tonnage.

§169. In the next place, to what extent, and for what objects and purposes, the power to regulate commerce may be constitutionally applied.

§170. And first, among the States. It is not doubted, that it extends to the regulation of navigation, and to the coasting trade and fisheries, within, as well as without any State, wherever it is connected with the commerce or intercourse with any other State, or with foreign nations. It extends to the regulation and government of seamen on board of American ships; and to conferring privileges upon ships built and owned in the United States, in domestic, as well as in foreign trade. It extends to quarantine laws, and pilotage laws, and wrecks of the sea. It extends, as well to the navigation of vessels engaged in carrying passengers, and whether steam vessels or of any other description, as to the navigation of vessels engaged in traffic and general coasting business. It extends to the laying of embargoes, as well on domestic, as on foreign voyages. It extends to the construction of lighthouses, the placing of buoys and beacons, the removal of obstructions to navigation in creeks, rivers, sounds, and bays, and the establishment of securities to navigation against the inroads of the ocean. It extends also to the designation of a particular port or ports of entry and delivery for the purposes of foreign commerce. These powers have been actually exerted by the National Government under a system of laws, many of which commenced with the early establishment of the Constitution; and they have continued unquestioned unto our day, if not to the utmost range of their reach, at least to that of their ordinary application.

§171. Many of the like powers have been applied in the regulation of foreign commerce. The commercial system of the United States has also been employed sometimes for the purpose of revenue; sometimes for the purpose of prohibition; sometimes for the purpose of retaliation and commercial reciprocity; sometimes to lay embargoes; sometimes to encourage domestic navigation, and the shipping and mercantile interest, by bounties, by discriminating duties, and by special preferences and privileges; and sometimes to regulate intercourse with a view to mere political objects, such as to repel aggressions, increase the pressure of war, or vindicate the rights of neutral sovereignty. In all these cases, the right and duty have been conceded to the National Government by the unequivocal voice of the people.

§172. It may be added, that Congress has also, from the earliest period of the government, applied the same power of regulating commerce for the purpose of encouraging and protecting domestic manufactures; and although this application of it has been recently contested, yet Congress has never abandoned the exercise of it for such a purpose. Indeed, if Congress does not possess the power to encourage domestic manufactures, by regulations of commerce, it is a power, that is utterly annihilated; for it is admitted, on all sides, that the States do not possess it. And America would then present the singular spectacle of a nation voluntarily depriving itself, in the exercise of its admitted rights of sovereignty, of all means of promoting some of its vital interests.

§173. In respect to trade with the Indian tribes. Antecedently to the American Revolution, the authority to regulate trade and intercourse with the Indian tribes, whether they were within, or without the boundaries of the Colonies, was understood to belong to the prerogative of the British crown. And after the American Revolution, the like power would naturally fall to the Federal Government, with a view to the general peace and interests of all the States. Two restrictions, however, upon the power, were, by express terms, incorporated into the Confederation, which occasioned endless embarrassments and doubts. The power of Congress was restrained to Indians, not members of any of the States; and was not to be exercised so as to violate or infringe the legislative right of any State, within its own limits. What description of Indians were to be deemed members of a State, was never settled under the Confederation; and was a question of frequent perplexity and contention in the federal councils. And how the trade with Indians, though not members of a State, yet residing within its legislative jurisdiction, was to be regulated by an external authority, without so far intruding on the internal rights of legislation, was absolutely incomprehensible. In this case, as in many other cases, the Articles of Confederation inconsiderately endeavored to accomplish impossibilities; to reconcile a partial sovereignty in the Union, with complete sovereignty in the States; to subvert a mathematical axiom, by taking away a part, and letting the whole remain. The Constitution has wisely disembarrassed the power of these two limitations; and thus has given to Congress, as the only safe and proper depositary, the exclusive power, which belonged to the Crown in the ante-revolutionary times; a power indispensable to the peace of the States, and to the just preservation of the rights and territory of the Indians.

CHAPTER XVII.

Naturalization, Bankruptcy, and Coinage of Money.

§174. THE next power of Congress is, "to establish a uniform rule of naturalization, and uniform laws on the subject of bankruptcies throughout the States." The power of naturalization is, with great propriety, confided to Congress, since, if left to the States, they might naturalize foreigners upon very different, and even upon opposite systems; and, as the citizens of all the States have common privileges in all, it would thus be in the power of any one State to defeat the wholesome policy of all the others in regard to this most important subject. Congress alone can have power to pass uniform laws, obligatory on all the States; and thus to adopt a system, which shall secure all of them against any dangerous results from the indiscriminate admission of foreigners to the right of citizenship upon their first landing on our shores. And, accordingly, this power is exclusive in Congress.

§175. The power to pass bankrupt laws is equally important, and proper to be intrusted to Congress, although it is greatly to be regretted, that it has not, except for a very brief period, been acted upon by Congress. Bankrupt and insolvent laws, when properly framed, have two great objects in view; first, to secure to honest but unfortunate debtors a discharge from debts, which they are unable to pay, and thus enable them to begin anew in the career of industry, without the discouraging fear, that it will be wholly useless; secondly, to secure to creditors a full surrender, and equal participation, of and in the effects of their debtors, when they have become bankrupt, or failed in business. On the one hand, such laws relieve the debtor from perpetual bondage to his creditors, in the shape, either of an unlimited imprisonment for his debts, or of an absolute right to appropriate all his future earnings. The latter course obviously destroys all encouragement to future enterprise and industry, on the part of the debtor; the former is, if possible, more harsh, severe, and indefensible; for it makes poverty, in itself sufficiently oppressive, the cause or occasion of penalties and punishments.

§176. It is obvious, that no single State is competent to pass a uniform system of bankruptcy, which shall operate throughout all of them. It can have no power to discharge debts, contracted in other States; or to bind creditors in other States. And it is hardly within the range of probability, that the same system should be universally adopted, and persevered in permanently, by all the States. In fact, before, as well as since the adoption of the Constitution, the States have had very different systems on the subject, exhibiting a policy as various and sometimes as opposite, as could well be imagined. The future will, in all human probability, be, as the past. And the utter inability of any State to discharge contracts made within its own territorial limits, before the passage of its own laws, or to discharge any debts whatever, contracted in other States, or due to the citizens thereof, must perpetually embarrass commercial dealings, discourage industry, and diminish private credit and confidence. The remedy is in the hands of Congress. It has been given for wise ends and has hitherto been strangely left without any efficient operation.

§177. The next power of Congress is, to "coin money, regulate the value thereof, and of foreign coins, and fix the standard of weights and measures." The object of the power over the coinage and currency of the country is, to produce uniformity in the value of money throughout the Union, and thus to save us from the embarrassments of a perpetually fluctuating and variable currency. If each State might coin money, as it pleased, there would be no security for any uniform coinage, or any uniform standard of value; and a great deal of base and false coin, would constantly be thrown into the market. The evils from this cause are abundantly felt among the small principalities of continental Europe. The power to fix the standard of weights and measures is a matter of great public convenience, although it has hitherto remained in a great measure dormant. The introduction of the decimal mode of calculation, in dollars and cents, instead of the old and awkward system of pounds, shillings, and pence, has been found of great public convenience, although it was at first somewhat unpopular. A similar system in weights and measures has been thought by many statesmen to have advantages equally great and universal. At all events, the power is safe in the hands of Congress, and may hereafter be acted upon, whenever either our foreign, or our domestic intercourse, shall imperiously require a new system.

§178. The next power of Congress is, "to provide for the punishment of counterfeiting the securities, and current coin of the United States." This is a natural, and, in a just view, an indispensable appendage to the power to borrow money, and to coin money. Without it, there would be no adequate means for the General Government to punish frauds or forgeries, detrimental to its own interests, and subversive of public and private confidence.

CHAPTER XVIII.

Post Office and Post Roads.—Patents for Inventions.

§179. THE next power of Congress, is to "establish post offices, and post roads." This power is peculiarly appropriate to the National Government, and would be at once unwieldly, dilatory, and irregular in the hands of the States, from the utter impracticability of adopting any uniform system of regulations for the whole continent, and from the inequality of the burdens, and benefits of any local system, among the several States, in proportion to their own expenditures. Under the auspices of the General Government, the post office has already become one of the most beneficent, and useful of our national establishments. It circulates intelligence, of a commercial, political, literary, and private nature, with incredible speed and regularity. It thus administers, in a very high degree, to the comfort, the interests, and the necessities of persons in every rank and station of life. It is not less effective, as an instrument of the government; enabling it, in times of peace and war, to send its orders, execute its measures, transmit its funds, and regulate its operations, with a promptitude and certainty, which are of incalculable importance, in point of economy, as well as of energy. The rapidity of its movements has been, in a general view, doubled within the last twenty years; and there were, at the close of the year 1838, twelve thousand five hundred and fifty-three post offices in the United States; and mails then travelled, in various directions and on various routes, more than one hundred and thirty-four thousand miles. The net amount of postage, in the same year, amounted to little short of three millions of dollars. It seems wholly unnecessary to vindicate the grant of a power, which has been thus demonstrated to be of the highest value to all the people of the Union.

§180. The next power of Congress is, "to promote the progress of science, and the useful arts, by securing, for limited times, to authors, and inventors, the exclusive right to their respective writings, and discoveries." The utility of this power has never been questioned. Indeed, if authors, or inventors, are to have any real property or interest in their writings, or discoveries, it is manifest, that the power of protection must be given to, and administered by, the General Government. A copy-right, or patent, granted by a single State, might be violated with impunity by every other; and, indeed, adverse titles might at the same time be set up in different States to the same timing, each of which, according to the laws of the State, in which it originated, might be equally valid. No class of men are more meritorious, or are better entitled to public patronage, than authors and inventors. They have rarely obtained, as the histories of their lives sufficiently establish, any due encouragement and reward for their ingenuity and public spirit. They have often languished in poverty, and died in neglect, while the world has derived immense wealth from their labors, and science and the arts have reaped unbounded advantages from their discoveries. They have but too often possessed a barren fame, and seen the fruits of their genre gathered by those, who have not blushed to purloin, what they have been unable to create. It is, indeed, but a poor reward, to secure to authors and inventors, for a limited period, only, an exclusive title to that, which is, in the noblest sense, their own property; and to require it ever afterwards to be dedicated to the public. But, such as the provision is, it is impossible to doubt its justice, or its policy, so far as it aims at their protection and encouragement.

§181. The power, in its terms, is confined to authors and inventors; and cannot be extended to the introducers of any new works or inventions. This has been thought, by some persons of high distinction, to be a defect in the Constitution. But perhaps the policy of further extending the right is questionable; and, at all events, the restriction has not hitherto operated as any discouragement of science or the arts. It has been doubted, whether Congress has authority to decide the fact, that a person is an author or inventor, in the sense of the Constitution, so as to preclude that question from judicial inquiry. But, at all events, such a construction ought never to be put upon the terms of any general act in favor of a particular inventor, unless it be inevitable.

§182. The next power of Congress is, "to constitute tribunals inferior to the Supreme Court." But this will hereafter properly come under review, in considering the structure and powers of the Judicial department.

CHAPTER XIX.

Punishment of Piracies and Felonies.—Declaration of War.

§183. THE next power of Congress is, "to define, and punish piracies and felonies, committed on the high seas, and offences against the law of nations." Piracy is commonly defined to be robbery, or forcible depredation upon the high seas with intent to steal. But "felony" is a term, not so exactly understood or defined. It is usually applied to designate capital offences, that is, offences punishable with death; but its true original meaning seems to be, to designate such offences as are by the common law punished by forfeiture of lands and goods. "Offences against the law of nations" are still less clearly defined; and therefore, as to these, as well as to felonies, the power to define, as well as to punish, is very properly given. As the United States is responsible to foreign governments for the conduct of its own citizens on the high seas, and as the power to punish offences committed there is also indispensable to the due protection and support of our navigation and commerce, and the States, separately, are incapable of affording adequate redress in such cases, the power is appropriately vested in the General Government.

§184. What the true meaning of the phrase "high seas," is,

within the intent of this clause, does not seem to be matter of any serious doubt. In order to understand it, resort must be had to the common law, in which, the definition of "high seas" is, that the high seas embrace not only all the waters of the ocean, which are out of sight of land, but also all waters on the seacoast below low-water mark, whether those waters be within the territorial sovereignty of a foreign nation or of a domestic State. It has accordingly been held, by our ablest law writers, that the main or high seas properly begin at low-water mark.

§185. The next power of Congress is, "to declare war, grant letters of marque and reprisal, and make rules concerning captures on land and water." That the power to declare war should belong exclusively to the National Government, would hardly seem matter of controversy. If it belonged to the States severally, it would be in the power of any one of them, at any time, to involve the whole Union in hostilities with a foreign country, not only against their interests, but against their judgement. Their very existence might thus be jeoparded without their consent, and their liberties sacrificed to private resentment, or popular prejudice. The power cannot, therefore, be safely deposited, except in the General Government; and, if in the General Government, it ought to belong to Congress, where all the States and all the people of the States are represented; and where a majority of both Houses must concur, to authorize the declaration. War, indeed, is, in its mildest form, so dreadful a calamity; it destroys so many lives, wastes so much property, and introduces so much moral desolation; that nothing but the strongest state of necessity can justify, or excuse it. In a republican government, it should never be resorted to, except as a last expedient to vindicate its rights; for military power and military ambition have but too often fatally triumphed over the liberties of the people.

§186. The power to declare war, if vested in the General Government, might have been vested in the President, or in the Senate, or in both, or in the House of Representatives alone. In monarchies, the power is ordinarily vested in the Executive. But certainly, in a republic, the chief magistrate ought not to be clothed with a power so summary, and, at the same time, so full of dangers to the public interest and the public safety. It would be to commit the liberties, as well as the rights of the people, to the ambition, or resentment, or caprice, or rashness of a single mind. If the power were confided to the Senate, either alone, or in connection with the Executive, it might be more safe in its exercise, and the less liable to abuse. Still, however, in such a case, the people, who were to bear the burdens, and meet the sacrifice and sufferings of such a calamity, would have no direct voice in the matter. Yet the taxes and the loans, which would be required to carry on the war, must be voted by their Representatives, or there would be an utter impossibility of urging it with success. If the Senate should be in favor of war, and the House of Representatives against it, an immediate conflict would arise between them, and in the distraction of the public councils, nothing but disaster or ruin would follow the nation. On the contrary, if the House of Representatives were called upon by the Constitution to join in the declaration of war, harmony in the public councils might fairly be presumed in carrying on all its operations; for it would be a war sustained by the authority of the voice of the people, as well as of the States. This reasoning was decisive in confiding the power to Congress.

§187. "Letters of marque and reprisal" are commissions, granted to private persons and ships, to make captures; and are usually granted in times of general war. The power to declare war would, of itself, carry the incidental power to grant letters of marque and reprisal, and to make rules concerning captures, in a general war. But such letters are also sometimes granted by nations, having no intention to enter into a general war, in order to redress a grievance to a private citizen, which the offending nation refuses to redress. In such a case, a commission is sometimes granted to the injured individual, to make a reprisal upon the property of the subjects of that nation to the extent of his injury. It thus creates an imperfect state of hostilities, not necessarily including a general warfare. Still,

157

however, it is a dangerous experiment; and the most usual, and wise course is, to resort to negotiations in such cases, and to wait until a favorable moment occurs to press the claim.

§188. If captures are to be made, as they necessarily must be, to give efficiency to a declaration of war, it follows, that the General Government ought to possess the power to make rules and regulations concerning them, thereby to restrain personal violence, intemperate cupidity, and degrading cruelty.

CHAPTER XX.

Power as to Army and Navy.

§189. THE next power of Congress is, "to raise and support armies; but no appropriation of money to that use shall be for a longer term than two years." The power to raise armies would seem to be an indispensable incident to the power to declare war, if the later is not to be a mere idle sound, or instrument of mischief. Under the Confederation, however, the two powers were separated; Congress was authorized to declare war; but it could not raise troops. It could only make requisitions upon the States to raise them. The experience of the whole country, during the Revolutionary War, established, to the satisfaction of every statesman, the utter inadequacy and impropriety of this system of requisition. It was equally at war with economy, efficiency, and safety. It gave birth to a competition between the States, which created a kind of auction of men. In order to furnish the quotas required of them, they outbid each other, till bounties grew to an enormous and insupportable size. On this account, many persons procrastinated their enlistment, or enlisted only for short periods. Hence, there were but slow and scanty levies of men in the most critical emergencies of our affairs; short enlistments at an unparalleled expense; and continual fluctuations in the troops, ruinous to their discipline, and subjecting the public safety frequently to the perilous crisis of a disbanded army. Hence also arose those oppressive expedients for raising men, which were occasionally practised, and which nothing, but the enthusiasm of liberty, could have induced the people to endure. The burden was also very unequally distributed. The States near the seat of war, influenced by motives of self-preservation, made efforts to furnish their quotas, which even exceeded their abilities, while those at a distance were exceedingly remiss in their exertions. In short, the army was frequently composed of three bodies of men; first raw recruits; secondly, persons, who were just about completing their term of service; and thirdly, of persons, who had served out half their term, and were quietly waiting for its determination. Under such circumstances, the wonder is not, that its military operations were tardy, irregular, and often unsuccessful; but, that it was ever able to make headway at all against an enemy, possessing a fine establishment, well appointed, well armed, well clothed, and well paid. The appointment, too, by the States, of all regimental officers, had a tendency to destroy all harmony and subordination, so necessary to the success of military life. The consequence was (as is well known) general inefficiency, want of economy, mischievous delays, and great inequality of burdens. This is, doubtless, the reason, why the power is expressly given to Congress. It insures promptitude and unity of action, and, at the same time, promotes economy and harmony of operations. Nor is it in war only, that the power to raise armies may be usefully applied. It is important to suppress domestic rebellions and insurrections, and to prevent foreign aggressions and invasions. A nation, which is prepared for war in times of peace, will, thereby, often escape the necessity of engaging in war. Its rights will be respected, and its wrongs redressed. Imbecility and want of preparation invite aggression, and protract controversy.

§190. But, inasmuch as the power to raise armies may be perverted in times of peace to improper purposes, a restriction is imposed upon the grant of appropriations by Congress for the maintenance of them. So that, at furthest, every two years, the propriety of retaining an existing army must regularly come before the Representatives of the people in Congress for consideration; and if no appropriation is made, the army is necessarily disbanded. Thus, the army may, at any time within two years, be in effect dissolved, by a majority of Congress, without the consent of the President, by a simple refusal to grant supplies. In point of fact, Congress has hitherto made the appropriations annual, as they have a constitutional right to do, if it is deemed expedient. The power, therefore, is surrounded by all reasonable restrictions, as to its exercise; and it has hitherto been used in a manner, which has conferred lasting benefits on the country.

§191. The next power of Congress is, "to provide, and maintain a navy." This power has the same general object, as that to raise armies. But, in its own nature, it is far more safe and, for a maritime nation, quite as indispensable. No nation was ever deprived of its liberty by its navy. The same cannot be said of its army. And a commercial nation would be utterly without its due share of sovereignty upon the ocean, its means of self-protection at home, and its power of efficient action abroad, without the possession of a navy. Yet this power, until a comparatively recent period, found little favor with some of our statesmen of no mean celebrity. It was not until the brilliant achievements of our little navy, during the late war, (1812-1814,) had shed a glory, as well as a protection, over our national flag in every sea, that the country became alive to its vast importance and efficiency. At present, it enjoys an extensive public favor, which, having been earned by the most gallant deeds, can scarcely fail of permanently engrafting it into the solid establishments of our national strength.

§192. The next power of Congress is, "to make rules, for the government and regulation of the land and naval forces." Upon the propriety of this power, as an incident to the preceding, it is unnecessary to enlarge. It is equally beyond the reach of cavil and complaint.

CHAPTER XXI.

Power over Militia.

§193. THE next power of Congress is, "to provide for calling forth the militia to execute the laws of the Union, suppress insurrections, and repel invasions." This is a natural incident to the duty, devolved on the General Government, of superintending the common defence, and providing for the general welfare in matters confided to it by the Constitution. There is but one of two alternatives, which can be resorted to in cases of insurrections, invasions, or violent oppositions to the execution of the laws; either to employ regular troops, or to employ the militia. In ordinary cases of riots and public disturbances, the magistracy of the country, with the assistance of the civil officers, and private individuals, may be sufficient to restore the public peace. But when force is contemplated by a discontented and lawless faction, it is manifest, that it must be met, and overthrown by force. Among a free people, there is a strong objection to the keeping up of a large standing army. But this will be indispensable, unless the power is delegated to command the services of the militia in such exigencies. The latter is, therefore, conferred on Congress, because it is the most safe, and the least obnoxious to popular jealousy. The employment of the militia is economical, and will generally be found to be efficient, in suppressing sudden and transitory insurrections, and invasions, and resistances of the laws.

§194. It is observable, that the power given to Congress over the militia is not limited as to the time of service, or as to the place of operation. And it is obvious, that to be effective, the power could not safely be limited in either respect; for it is impossible to foresee either the nature, or extent, or place, or duration, of the exigency, for which the militia might properly be called forth. It must be left, therefore, to the sound discretion of Congress, acting with a wise regard to the public interests and the convenience of military operations. If Congress had no authority to march the militia beyond the territorial boundaries of a particular State, either to execute the laws, or to suppress insurrections, or to repel invasions, the power over the militia might be perfectly nugatory for all the purposes of common safety, or common defence. Suppose there should be an invasion of Rhode Island by a public enemy, if the militia of the neighboring States could not be ordered into that State for military duty, it is obvious, that the militia would be utterly worthless for the general protection of the Union. Suppose a battle to be fought on the confines of two States, and the militia to stop at the boundary, and thus to lose all the advantages of mutual cooperation, and even of a victory almost achieved? In times of insurrection or invasion, it cannot admit of a reasonable doubt, that it would be both natural and proper, that the militia of the neighboring States should be marched into the suffering State to repel the invaders, or to suppress the insurgents. But it would rarely occur, if ever, that the militia of any one State would be required to march to a great distance from their homes, or for a long period of service, since it would be at once the most inconvenient, as well as the most expensive force, which could be employed upon distant expeditions. And yet an occasion might occur, when even such a service might be indispensable to the public safety; as it was in the late war with Great Britain (1814) when the militia of Tennessee and Kentucky were required to go to New Orleans; and there saved the country from the dreadful calamity of having the mouth of the Mississippi in the hands of the enemy.

§195. The next power of Congress is, "to provide for organizing, arming, and disciplining the militia, and for governing such part of them, as may be employed in the service of the United States; reserving to the States, respectively, the appointment of the officers, and the authority of training the militia, according to the discipline prescribed by Congress." And here, again, we have another instance of the distribution of powers, between the National and State Governments, over the same subject matter. Unless there is uniformity in the organization, arming, and disciplining of the militia, there can be little chance of any energy, or harmony of action, between the corps of militia of different States, when called into the public service. Uniformity can alone be prescribed by the General Government; and the power is accordingly given to it. On the other hand, as a complete control of the militia by the General Government would deprive the States of their natural means of military defence, even upon the most urgent occasions, and would leave them absolutely dependent upon the General Government, the power of the latter is limited to a few cases; and the former retain the appointment of all the officers, and also the authority to train the militia, according to the discipline prescribed by Congress. With these limitations, the authority of Congress would seem to be above all reasonable objections.

§196. Several questions, of great practical importance, have arisen under these clauses of the Constitution respecting the power of the National Government over the militia, which deserve mention in this place. Congress is authorized "*to provide* for calling forth the militia," in the particular exigencies above stated. And accordingly, by an act passed in 1795, under President Washington's administration, authority was given to the President to call forth the militia in case any of those exigencies occurred. The delegation of this power to the President would seem indispensable, since the exigency might occur in the recess of Congress; and by the Constitution, the

165

President is not only Commander-in-Chief of the army and navy, and of the militia, when called into service, but he is also (as we shall see) bound to see the laws duly executed. But the question has arisen, whether the President has the sole and exclusive authority to judge and decide, whether the exigency has arisen, or not; or, in other words, whether any subordinate officer of the militia, or any State magistrate, has a right to judge and decide for himself, whether the exigency has arisen, and whether, when called upon, he is bound to obey the requisitions of the President or not. This question was formerly a matter of heated controversy, and at last came before the Supreme Court of the United States for decision, where it was finally settled, upon full deliberation, that, from the necessity of the case, the President is the exclusive judge of the exigency; and that his decision was conclusive. The reasoning, which led to this conclusion, cannot be repeated in this work; but it deserves the attentive consideration of every statesman.

§197. Another question, of great practical importance, is, Who, in the personal absence of the President, is to command the militia called forth in the service of the National Government? Are the commanding officers of the militia of each State, so in service, to command their separate detachments during his absence, or has the President a right to delegate his authority to any superior military officer of the United States, or of the militia, to act as commander of the whole force during his absence? This question was also formerly a matter of great controversy; and perhaps is not now definitively settled. Practically, however, the National Government has constantly insisted upon the right of the President, in such cases, to appoint a person to act as his delegate in the command; and most of the States of the Union have acquiesced in this decision, as indispensable to any effective military operations.

CHAPTER XXII.

Seat of Government, and other Ceded Places.

§ 198. THE next power of Congress is, "to exercise exclusive legislation, in all cases whatsoever, over such District, not exceeding ten miles square, as may, by cession of particular States, and the acceptance of Congress, become the SEAT OF THE GOVERNMENT of the United States; and to exercise like authority over all places purchased by the consent of the Legislature of the State, in which the same shall be, for the erection of forts, magazines, arsenals, dockyards, and other needful buildings."

§ 199. A moment's consideration will establish the importance and necessity of this power. Without it, the National Government would have no adequate means to enforce its authority in the place, in which its public functionaries should be convened. They might be insulted, and their proceedings might be interrupted with impunity. And if the State should array itself in hostility to the proceedings of the National Government, the latter might be driven to seek another asylum, or be compelled to a humiliating submission to the State authorities. It never could be safe, to leave, in the possession of any one State, the exclusive power to decide, whether the functionaries of the National Government should have the moral or physical power to perform their duties. Nor let it be thought, that the evil is wholly imaginary. It actually occurred to the Continental Congress, at the very close of the Revolution, who were compelled to quit Philadelphia, and adjourn to Princeton, in order to escape from the violence of some insolent mutineers of the Continental army.

§200. It is under this clause, that the cession of the present District of Columbia was made, by the States of Maryland and Virginia, to the National Government; and the present seat of the National Government was established at the city of Washington, in 1800. That convenient spot was selected by the exalted patriot, whose name it bears, for this very purpose. And who, that loves his country, does not desire, that it may forever remain a monument of his wisdom, and the eternal capital of the republic?

§201. The other clause, as to cessions for forts, magazines, arsenals, dockyards, and other needful buildings, is dictated by a like policy. The public money expended on such places, the public property deposited there, the military, and other duties to be executed there, all require, that the sovereignty of the United States should have exclusive jurisdiction and control over them. It would be wholly improper, that such places, on which the security of the Union may materially depend, should be subjected to the authority of any single member of it. In order to guard against any possible abuse, the consent of the State Legislature is necessary to divest its own territorial jurisdiction; and, of course, that consent will never be given, unless the public good will be manifestly promoted by the cession.

§202. A great variety of cessions have been made by the States under this power. And generally there has been a reservation of the right to serve all State process, civil and criminal, upon persons found therein. This reservation has not been thought at all inconsistent with the provision of the Constitution; for the State process, in this respect, becomes the process of the United States, and the general power of exclusive legislation remains with Congress. Thus, these places are not capable of being made a sanctuary for fugitives, to exempt them from acts done within, and cognizable by, the States, to which the territory belonged; and, at the same time, Congress is enabled to accomplish the great objects of the power.

§203. The power of Congress to exercise exclusive jurisdiction over these ceded places is conferred on that body as the Legislature of the Union; and cannot be exercised in any other character. A law passed in pursuance of it is the supreme law of the land, and binding on all the States and cannot be defeated by them. The power to pass such a law carries with it all the incidental powers to give it complete and effectual execution; and such a law may be extended in its operation incidentally throughout the United States, if Congress thinks it necessary to do so. But if intended to have efficiency beyond the District, language must be used in the act expressive of such an intention; otherwise it will be deemed to be purely local.

§204. It follows from this review of the clause, that the States cannot take cognizance of any acts done in the ceded places after the cession; and, on the other hand, the inhabitants of those places cease to be inhabitants of the State, and can no longer exercise any civil or political rights under the laws of the State. But if there has been no cession by the State, of a particular place, although it has been constantly occupied and used, under purchase, or otherwise, by the United States, for a fort, arsenal, or other constitutional purpose, the State jurisdiction still remains complete and perfect.

§205. Upon a recent occasion, the nature and effect of the exclusive power of legislation, thus given by the Constitution in these ceded places, came under the consideration of the Supreme Court, and was much discussed. It was argued, that all such legislation by Congress was purely local, like that exercised by a territorial Legislature; and was not to be deemed legislation by Congress in the character of the Legislature of the Union. The object of the argument was to establish, that a law, made in or for such ceded places, had no extra-territorial force or obligation, it not being a law of the United States. The reasoning of the Court affirming, that such an act was a law of the

United States, and that Congress, in passing it, acted as the Legislature of the Union, can be best conveyed in their own language, and would be impaired by an abridgement, and therefore is omitted as incompatible with the design of the present work.

CHAPTER XXIII.

General Power to make Necessary and Proper Laws.

§206. THE next power of Congress is, "to make all laws, which shall be necessary and proper for carrying into execution the foregoing powers, and all other powers vested in this Constitution in the government of the United States, or in any department, or officer thereof."

§207. This clause is merely declaratory of a truth, which would have resulted by necessary implication from the act of establishing a National Government, and investing it with certain powers. If a power to do a thing is given, it includes the use of the means, necessary and proper, to execute it. If it includes any such means, it includes all such means; for none can, more correctly than others, be said exclusively to appertain to the power; and the choice must depend upon circumstances, to be judged of by Congress. What is a power, but the ability or faculty of doing a thing? What is the ability to do a thing, but the power of employing the *means* necessary to its execution? What is a legislative power, but a power of making laws? What are the means to execute a legislative power, but laws? What is the power, for instance, of laying and collecting taxes, but a legislative power, or a power to make laws to lay and collect taxes? What are the proper means of executing such a power, but necessary and proper laws? In truth, the constitutional operation of the government would be precisely the same, if the clause were obliterated, as if it were repeated in every article. It would otherwise result, that the power could never be exercised; that is, the end would be required, and yet no means allowed. This would be a perfect absurdity. It would be to create powers, and compel them to remain forever in a torpid, dormant, and paralytic state. It cannot, therefore, be denied, that the powers, given by the Constitution, imply the ordinary means of execution; for, without the substance of the power, the Constitution would be a dead letter. If it should be asked, why, then, was the clause inserted in the Constitution; the answer is, that it is peculiarly useful, in order to avoid any doubt, which ingenuity or jealousy might rise upon the subject. There was also a clause in the Articles of Confederation, which restrained the authority of Congress to powers *expressly* granted; and, therefore, it was highly expedient to make an explicit declaration, that that rule of interpretation, which had been the source of endless embarrassments under the Confederation, should no longer prevail. The Continental Congress had been compelled, in numerous instances, to disregard that limitation, in order to escape from the most absurd and distressing consequences. They had been driven to the dangerous experiment of violating the Confederation in order to preserve it.

§208. The plain import of the present clause is, that Congress shall have all the incidental and instrumental powers, necessary and proper to carry into execution the other express powers; not merely such as are indispensably necessary in the strictest sense, (for then the word "proper" ought to have been omitted,) but such also as are appropriate to the end required. Indeed, it would otherwise be difficult to give any rational interpretation to the clause; for it can scarcely be affirmed, that one means only exists to carry into effect any of the given powers; and if more than one should exist, then neither could be adopted, because neither could be shown to be indispensably necessary. The clause, in its just sense, then, does not enlarge any other power, specifically granted; nor is it the grant of any new power. It is merely a declaration, to remove all uncertainty, that every power is to be so interpreted, as to include suitable means to carry it into execution. The very controversies, which have since arisen, and the efforts, which have since been made, to narrow down the just interpretation of the clause, demonstrate its wisdom and propriety. The practice of the government, too, has been in conformity to this view of the matter. There is scarcely a law of Congress, which does not include the exercise of implied powers and means. This might be illustrated by abundant examples. Under the power "to establish post offices and post roads," Congress has proceeded to make contracts for the carriage of the mail, has punished offences against the establishment, and has made an infinite variety of subordinate provisions, not one of which is found expressly authorized in the Constitution. A still more striking case of implied power is, that the United States, as a government, has no express authority given to make any contracts; and yet it is plain, that the government could not go on for an hour without this implied power.

§209. There are many other cases, in which Congress has acted upon implied powers, some of which have given rise to much political discussion, and controversy; but it is not within the design of this work to examine those cases, or to express any opinion respecting them. It is proper, however, that the reader should be apprized, that among them, are the questions respecting the power of Congress to establish a national bank; to make national roads, canals, and other internal national improvements; to purchase cessions of foreign territory, (such, for example, as Louisiana and Florida;) to lay embargoes, without any fixed limitation of the time of their duration; and to prohibit intercourse or commerce with a foreign nation for an unlimited period.

§210. And here terminates the eighth section of the Constitution professing to enumerate the powers of Congress. But there are other clauses, delegating express powers, which, though detached from their natural connection in that instrument, should be here brought under review, in order to complete the enumeration.

CHAPTER XXIV.

Punishment of Treason.—State Records.

§211. THE third clause of the third article contains a constitutional definition of the crime of treason, (which will be reserved for a separate examination,) and then proceeds, in the same section, to provide,—"The Congress shall have power to declare the punishment of treason. But no attainder of treason shall work corruption of blood, or forfeiture, except during the life of the person attained." The punishment of treason by the common law, partakes, in a high degree, of those savage and malignant refinements in cruelty, which in former ages were the ordinary penalties attached to state offences. The offender is to be drawn to the gallows on a hurdle; hanged by the neck, and cut down alive; his entrails taken out, and burned, while he is yet alive; his head cut off; and his body quartered. Congress is intrusted with the power to fix the punishment, and has, with great wisdom and humanity, abolished these horrible accompaniments, and confined the punishment simply to death by hanging. The power to punish treason is exclusive in Congress; and the trial for the offence, as well as the award of the punishment, belongs, also, exclusively to the National tribunals, and cannot be exercised by any State tribunals.

§212. The other clause may require some explanation, to

those, who are not bred to the profession of the law. By the common law, one of the regular incidents to an *attainder* for treason, (that is, to a conviction and judgement in court against the offender,) is, that he forfeits all his estate, real and personal. His blood is also corrupted, that is, it loses all inheritable qualities, so that he can neither inherit any real estate himself, from any ancestor or relation by blood, nor can his heirs inherit any real estate from him, or through him, from any ancestor or relation by blood. So that, if the father should commit treason, and be attained of it in the life time of the grandfather, and the latter should then die, the grandson could not inherit any real estate from the grandfather, although both were perfectly innocent of the offence; for the father could communicate no inheritable blood to the grandson. Thus, innocent persons are made the victims of the misdeeds of their ancestors; and are punished, even to the remotest generations, by incapacities derived through them. The Constitution has abolished this corruption of blood, and general forfeiture; and confined the punishment exclusively to the offenders; thus adopting a rule founded in sound policy, and as humane, as it is just.

§213. The first section of the fourth article declares, "Full faith and credit shall be given in each State to the public acts, records, and judicial proceedings of every other State. And the Congress may, by general laws, prescribe the manner, in which such acts, records, and proceedings shall be proved, and the effect thereof."

§214. It is well known, that the acts, records, and judicial proceedings of foreign nations are not judicially taken notice of by our courts; that is, their genuineness, validity, and authority are not admitted as of course by our courts, as is the case with the acts, records, and judicial proceedings of the Legislature and judicial tribunals of the State; but they must be proved, like other facts, whenever they are brought into controversy in any suit. The nature and modes of such proof are different in different countries; and being wholly governed by the municipal law of each particular nation, must present many embarrassing questions. Independent of the *proof,* another not less serious difficulty is, as to the *effect* to be given to such acts, records, and proceedings, after they are duly authenticated. For example, what effect is to be given to the judgement of a court in one country, when it is sought to be enforced in another country? Is it to be held conclusive upon the parties, without further inquiry? Or, is it to be treated like common suits, and its justice and equity to be open to new proofs and new litigation? These are very serious questions, upon which different nations hold very different doctrines? Even in the American Colonies, before the Revolution, no uniform rules were adopted, in regard to judgements in other colonies. In some, they were held conclusive; in others, not. Some foreign nations hold the judgements of foreign courts between the parties, as of no validity or force out of the territory, where the judgements are pronounced; others hold such judgements to be only *prima facie* or presumptively valid and just, but open to be controverted and overthrown by any new proofs; and others, again, hold such judgements either absolutely, or under certain limitations and restrictions, to be binding and conclusive between the parties and their heirs and other representatives. Now, domestic judgements, that is, judgements rendered in the same State, are uniformly held, in all the tribunals of that State, to be conclusive between the parties and their heirs and representatives, so that they cannot be controverted, or their validity impeached, or new proofs offered to overthrow them in the ordinary administration of justice.

§215. We may readily perceive, upon a slight examination, how inconvenient it would be, to hold all the judgements rendered in one State to be controverted anew in any other state. Suppose a judgement in one State, after a trial, and verdict by a jury, upon a contract, or for a trespass, in the place where all the witnesses lived; and, afterwards, the defendent should remove into another State, and some of the material witnesses should die; or remove, so that their testimony could not be had; if the defendent were then called upon to satisfy the judgement in a new suit, and he might controvert anew all the facts, there could be no certainty of any just redress to the plaintiff. The Constitution, therefore, has wisely suppressed this source of heart-burning and mischief between the inhabitants of different States, by declaring, that *full faith* and *credit* shall be given to the acts, records, and judicial proceedings of every other State; and by authorizing Congress to prescribe the mode of authentication, and the effect of such authentication, when duly made. Congress has accordingly declared the mode, in which the records and judgements of the respective States shall be authenticated, and has further declared, that, when so authenticated, they shall have the same force and credit, and, of course, the same effect, in every other State, that they have in the State, where the records and judgements were originally made and rendered.

CHAPTER XXV.

Admission of New States.—Government of Territories.

§216. THE first clause of the fourth article declares, "New States may be admitted by the Congress into this Union. But no new State shall be formed or erected within the jurisdiction of any other State; nor any State be formed by the junction of two or more States, or parts of States, without the consent of the Legislatures of the States concerned, as well as of the Congress." It was early foreseen, from the extent of the territory of some States, that a division thereof into several States might become important and convenient to the inhabitants thereof, as well as add to the security of the Union. And it was also obvious, that new States would spring up in the then vacant western territory, which had been ceded to the Union, and that such new States could not long be retained in a state of dependence upon the National Government. It was indispensable, therefore, to make some suitable provisions for both these emergencies. On the one hand, the integrity of any of the States ought not to be severed without their own consent; for their sovereignty would, otherwise, be at the mere will of Congress. On the other hand, it was equally clear, that no State ought to be admitted into the Union without the consent of Congress; for, otherwise, the balance, equality, and harmony

179

of the existing States might be destroyed. Both of these objects are, therefore, united in the present clause. To admit a new State into the Union, the consent of Congress is necessary; to form a new State within the boundaries of an old one, the consent of the latter is also necessary. Under this clause, besides Vermont, three new States formed within the boundaries of the old States, viz., Kentucky, Tennessee, and Maine; and nine others, viz., Ohio, Indiana, Illinois, Mississippi, Alabama, Louisiana, Missouri, Arkansas, and Michigan, formed within the territories ceded to the United States, have been already admitted into the Union. Thus far, indeed, the power has been most propitious to the general welfare of the Union, and has realized the patriotic anticipation, that the parents would exult in the glory and prosperity of their children.

§217. The second clause of the same section is, "The Congress shall have power to dispose of, and make all needful rules and regulations respecting the territory, or other property, belonging to the United States. And nothing in this Constitution shall be so construed, as to prejudice any claims of the United States, or of any particular State." As the General Government possesses the right to acquire territory by cession and conquest, it would seem to follow, as a natural incident, that it should possess the power to govern and protect, what it had acquired. At the time of the adoption of the Constitution, it had acquired the vast region included in the Northwestern Territory; and its acquisitions have since been greatly enlarged by the purchase of Louisiana and Florida. The two latter Territories (Louisiana and Florida) subject to the treaty stipulations, under which they were acquired, are of course under the general regulation of Congress, so far as the power has not been or may not be parted with by erecting them into States. The Northwestern Territory has been peopled under the admirable Ordinance of the Continental Congress of the 13th of July, 1787, which we owe to the wise forecast and political wisdom of a man, whom New England can never fail to reverence.*

---

*The late Hon. Nathan Dane, of Beverly, Massachussetts.

§218. The main provisions of this Ordinance, which constitute the basis of the Constitutions and Governments of all the
States and Territories organized within the Northwestern Territory, deserve here to be stated, as the ordinance is equally remarkable for the beauty and exactness of its text, and for its
masterly display of the fundamental principles of civil and religious and political liberty. It begins, by providing a scheme for
the descent and distribution of estates equally among all the
children, and their representatives, or other relatives of the deceased in equal degree, making no distinction between the
whole and the half blood; and for the mode of disposing of
real estate by will, and by conveyances. It then proceeds to
provide for the organization of the territorial governments, according to their progress in population, confiding the whole
power to a Governor and Judges, in the first instance, subject
to the control of Congress. As soon as the Territory contains
five thousand inhabitants, it provides for the establishment of
a general Legislature, to consist of three branches, a Governor,
a Legislative Council, and a House of Representatives; with a
power to the Legislature to appoint a delegate to Congress. It
then proceeds to state certain fundamental articles of compact
between the original States, and the people and States in the
Territory, which are to remain unalterable, unless by common
consent. The first provides for the freedom of religious opinion and worship. The second provides for the right to the writ
of *habeas corpus;* for the trial by jury; for a proportionate representation in the Legislature; for judicial proceedings according to the course of the common law; for capital offences
being bailable; for fines being moderate, and punishments not
being cruel or unusual; for no man's being deprived of his liberty or property, but by the judgement of his peers, or the law
of the land; for full compensation for property taken, or services demanded, for the public exigencies; "and, for the just
preservation of rights and property, that no law ought ever to
be made, or have force in the said Territory, that shall, in any
manner whatever, *interfere with, or affect private contracts
or engagements, bona fide,* and without fraud, previously
formed." The third provides for the encouragement of reli-

gion, and education, and schools, and for good faith and due respect for the rights and property of the Indians. The fourth provides, that the Territory, and States formed therein, shall forever remain a part of the Confederacy, subject to the constitutional authority of Congress; that the inhabitants shall be liable to be taxed proportionately for the public expenses; that the Legislatures in the Territory shall never interfere with the primary disposal of the soil by Congress, nor with their regulations for securing the title to the soil to purchasers; that no tax shall be imposed on lands, the property of the United States; and non-resident proprietors shall not be taxed more than residents; that the navigable waters leading into the Mississippi and St. Lawrence, and the carrying places between the same, shall be common highways, and forever free. The fifth provides, that there shall be formed in the Territory not less than three, nor more than five States, with certain boundaries; and whenever any of the said States shall contain sixty thousand free inhabitants, such State shall (and may not before) be admitted, by its delegates, into Congress, on an equal footing with the original States in all respects whatever, and shall be at liberty to form a permanent Constitution and State government, provided it shall be republican, and in conformity to these articles of compact. The sixth and last provides, that there shall be neither slavery nor involuntary servitude in the said Territory, otherwise than in the punishment of crimes; but fugitives from other States, owing service therein, may be reclaimed. Such is a brief outline of this most important ordinance, the effects of which upon the destinies of the country have already been abundantly demonstrated in the Territory, by an almost unexampled prosperity and rapidity of population, by the formation of republican governments, and by an enlightened system of jurisprudence. Already five States, composing a part of that Territory, have been admitted into the Union; and others are fast advancing towards the same grade of political dignity.

§219. The proviso, reserving the claims of the Union, as well as of the several States, was adopted from abundant caution, to quiet public jealousies upon the subject of the consented titles, which were then asserted by some of the States to some parts of the Western Territory. Happily, these sources of alarm and irritation have long since been dried up.

§220. And here is closed our Review of the express powers conferred upon Congress. There are other incidental and implied powers, resulting from other provisions of the Constitution, which will naturally present themselves to the mind at our future examination of those provisions. At present, it may suffice to say, that, with reference to due energy in the General Government, to due protection of the national interests, and to due security to the Union, fewer powers could scarcely have been granted, without jeoparding the existence of the whole system. Without the power to lay and collect taxes, to provide for the common defence, and promote the general welfare, the whole system would have been vain and illusory. Without the power to borrow money upon sudden or unexpected emergencies, the National Government might have been embarrassed, and sometimes have been incapable of performing its own proper functions and duties. Without the power to declare war and raise armies, and provide a navy, the whole country would have been placed at the mercy of foreign nations, or of invading foes, who would trample upon our rights and liberties. Without the power exclusively to regulate commerce, the intercourse between the States would have been liable to constant jealousies, rivalries, and dissensions; and the intercourse with foreign nations would have been liable to mischievous interruptions, from secret hostilities, or open retaliatory restrictions. The other powers are principally auxiliary to these; and are dictated by an enlightened policy, a devotion to justice, and a regard to the permanence of the Union. The wish of every patriot must be, that the system thus formed may be perpetual, and that the powers thus conferred may be constantly used for the purposes, for which they were originally given, for the promotion of the true interests of all the States, and not for the gratification of party spirit, or the aggrandizement of rulers at the expense of the people.

CHAPTER XXVI.

Prohibitions on the United States.

§221. WE next come to the consideration of the prohibitions and limitations upon the powers of Congress, which are contained in the ninth section of the first article, passing by such, as have been already incidentally discussed.

§222. The first clause is, "The migration or importation of such persons, as any of the States now existing shall think proper to admit, shall not be prohibited by the Congress, prior to the year eighteen hundred and eight. But a tax or duty may be imposed upon such importation, not exceeding ten dollars for each person."

§223. This clause, as is manifest from its language, was designed solely to reserve to the Southern States, for a limited period, the right to import slaves. It is to the honor of America, that she should have set the first example of interdicting and abolishing the slave trade, in modern times. It is well known, that it constituted a grievance, of which some of the Colonies complained, before the Revolution, that the introduction of slaves was encouraged by the parent country, and that the prohibitory laws, passed by the Colonies, were negatived by the Crown. It was, doubtless, desirable, that the importation of slaves should have been at once interdicted throughout the Union. But it was indispensable to yield something to the prejudices, the wishes, and the supposed interests of the South. And it ought to be considered as a great point gained, in favor of humanity, that a period of twenty years should enable Congress to terminate, in America (as Congress in fact has terminated the African slave trade) a traffic, which has so long and so loudly upbraided the morals and justice of modern nations.

§224. The next clause is, "The privilege of the writ of *habeas corpus* shall not be suspended, unless when, in cases of rebellion or invasion, the public safety may require it." In order to understand the exact meaning of the terms here used, recourse must be had to the common law. The writ of *habeas corpus,* here spoken of, is a writ known to the common law, and used in all cases of confinement, or imprisonment of any party, in order to ascertain whether it is lawful or not. The writ commands the person, who detains the party, to produce his body, with the day and cause of his detention, before the Court or Judge, who issues the writ, to do, submit to, and receive, whatever the Court or Judge shall direct at the hearing. It is hence called the writ of *habeas corpus ad subjiciendum,* from the effective words of the writ, (when it was issued, as it originally was, in the Latin language) that you (the person, detaining the party) have the body *(habeas corpus)* to submit *(ad subjiciendum)* to the order of the Court or Judge. And if the cause of detention is found to be insufficient, or illegal, the party is immediately set at liberty by the order of the Court or Judge. It is justly, therefore, esteemed the great bulwark of personal liberty, and is grantable, as a matter of right, to the party imprisoned. But as it had often, for frivolous reasons of state, been suspended or denied in the parent country, to the grievous oppression of the subject, it is made a matter of constitutional right in all cases, except when the public safety may, in cases of rebellion or invasion, require it. The exception is reasonable, since cases of great urgency may arise, in which the suspension may be indispensable for the preservation of the liberties of the country against traitors and rebels.

§225. The next clause is, "No bill of attainder, or *ex post facto* law, shall be passed." A bill of attainder, in its technical sense, is an act passed by the legislature, convicting a person of some crime, for which it inflicts upon him, without any trial, the punishment of death. If it inflicts a milder punishment, it is usually called a bill of pains and penalties. Such acts are in the highest degree objectionable, and tyrannical, since they deprive the party of any regular trial by jury, and deprive him of his life, liberty, and property, without any legal proof of his guilt. In a republican government, such a proceeding is utterly inconsistent with first principles. It would be despotism in its worst form, by arming a popular Legislature with the power to destroy, at its will, the most virtuous and valuable citizens of the state.

§226. To the same class, belong *ex post facto* laws, that is, (in a literal interpretation of the phrase) laws made after the act is done. In a general sense, all retrospective laws are *ex post facto;* but the phrase is here used to designate laws to punish, as public offences, acts, which, at the time when they were done, were lawful, or were not public crimes, or, if crimes, which were not liable to so severe a punishment. It requires no reasoning to establish the wisdom of a prohibition, which puts a fixed restraint upon such harsh legislation. In truth, the existence of such a power in legislature is utterly incompatible with all just notions of the true ends and objects of a republican government.

§227. The next clause (not already commented on) is, "No money shall be drawn from the treasury, but in consequence of appropriations made by law. And a regular statement and account of the receipts and expenditures of all public money shall be published from time to time." The object of this clause is, to secure regularity, punctuality, fidelity, and responsibility, in the keeping and disbursement of the public money. No money can be drawn from the treasury by any officer, unless under appropriations made by some act of Congress. As all the taxes raised from the people, as well as the revenues arising from other sources, are to be applied to the discharge of the expenses, and debts, and other engagements of the government, it is highly proper, that Congress should possess the power to decide, how and when any money should be applied for these purposes. If it were otherwise, the Executive would possess an unbounded power over the public purse of the nation; and might apply all its monied resources at his pleasure. The power to control and direct the appropriations, constitutes a most useful and salutary check upon profusion and extravagance, as well as upon corrupt influence and public speculation. In arbitrary governments, the prince levies what money he pleases from his subjects, disposes of it, as he thinks proper, and is beyond responsibility or reproof. It is wise, in a republic, to interpose every restraint, by which the public treasure, the common fund of all, should be applied, with unshrinking honesty, to such objects, as legitimately belong to the common defence, and the general welfare. Congress is made the guardian of this treasure; and, to make its responsibility complete and perfect, a regular account of the receipts and expenditures is required to be published, that the people may know, what money is expended, for what purposes, and by what authority.

§228. The next clause is, "No title of nobility shall be granted by the United States; and no person, holding any office of profit or trust under them, shall, without the consent of the Congress, accept of any present, emolument, office, or title, of any kind whatever, from any king, prince, or foreign state." A perfect equality of rights, privileges, and rank, being contemplated by the Constitution among all citizens, there is a manifest propriety in prohibiting Congress from creating any titles of nobility. The other prohibition, as to presents, emoluments, offices, and titles from foreign governments, besides aiding the same general object, subserves a more important policy, founded on the just jealousy of foreign corruption and undue influence exerted upon our national officers. It seeks to destroy, in their origin, all the blandishments from foreign favors, and foreign titles, and all the temptations to a departure from official duty by receiving foreign rewards and emoluments. No officer of the United States can without guilt wear honors borrowed from foreign sovereigns, or touch for personal profit any foreign treasure.

CHAPTER XXVII.

Prohibitions on the States.

§229. SUCH are the prohibitions upon the government of the United States. And we next proceed to the prohibitions upon the States, which are not less important in themselves, or less necessary to the security of the Union. They are contained in the tenth section of the first article.

§230. The first clause is, "No State shall enter into any treaty, alliance, or confederation; grant letters of marque or reprisal; coin money; emit bills of credit; make any thing but gold or silver coin a tender in payment of debts; pass any bill of attainder, *ex post facto* law, or law impairing the obligation of contracts; or grant any title of nobility."

§231. The prohibition against a State's rendering into any treaty, alliance, or confederation, is indispensable to the preservation of the rights and powers of the National Government. A State might otherwise enter into engagements with foreign governments, utterly subversive of the policy of the National Government, or injurious to the rights and interests of the other States. One State might enter into a treaty or alliance with France, and another with England, and another with Spain, and another with Russia, each in its general objects inconsistent with the other; and thus, the seeds of discord might be spread over the whole Union.

§232. The prohibition to "grant letters of marque and reprisal" stands on the same ground. This power would hazard the peace of the Union by subjecting it to the passions, resentments, or policy of a single State. If any State might issue letters of marque or reprisal at its own mere pleasure, it might at once involve the whole Union in a public war; or bring on retaliatory measure by the foreign government, which might cripple the commerce, or destroy the vital interests of other States. The prohibition is, therefore, essential to the public safety.

§233. The prohibition to "coin money" is necessary to our domestic interests. The existence of the power in the States would defeat the salutory objects intended, by confiding the like power to the National Government. It would have a tendency to introduce a base and variable currency, perpetually liable to frauds, and embarrassing to the commercial intercourse of the States.

§234. The prohibition to "emit bills of credit." Bills of credit are a well-known denomination of paper money, issued by the Colonies before the Revolution. These bills of credit had no adequate funds appropriated to redeem them; and though on their face value they were often declared payable in gold and silver, they were in fact never so paid. The consequence was, that they became the common currency of the country, in a constantly depreciating state, ruinous to the commerce and credit, and disgraceful to the good faith of the country. The evils of the system were a most aggravated nature, and could not be cured, except by an entire prohibition of any future issues of paper money. And, indeed, the prohibition to coin money would be utterly nugatory, if the States might still issue a paper currency for the same purpose.

§235. But the inquiry here naturally occurs; What is the true meaning of the phrase "bills of credit" in the Constitution? In its enlarged, and perhaps in its literal sense, it may comprehend any instrument, by which a State engages to pay money at a future day (and, of course, for which it obtains a present credit) and thus it would include a certificate given for money borrowed. But the language of the Constitution itself, and the mischief to be prevented, which we know from the history of our country, equally limit the interpretation of the terms. The word "emit" is never employed in describing those contracts, by which a State binds itself to pay money at a future day for services actually recieved, or for money borrowed for present use. Nor are instruments, executed for such purposes, in common language denominated "bills of credit." To emit bills of credit, conveys to the mind the idea of issuing paper, intended to circulate through the community for ordinary purposes, as money, which paper is redeemable at a future day. This is the sense, in which the terms of the Constitution have been generally understood. The phrase (as we have seen) was well known, and generally used to indicate the paper currency, issued by the States during their colonial dependence. During the war of our Revolution, the paper currency issued by Congress was constantly denominated, in the acts of that body, bills of credit; and the like appellation was applied to similar currency issued by the States. The phrase had thus acquired a determinate and appropriate meaning. At the time of the adoption of the Constitution, bills of credit were universally understood to signify a paper medium intended to circulate between individuals, and between government and individuals, for the ordinary purposes of society. Such a medium has always been liable to considerable fluctuation. Its value is continually changing; and these changes, often great and sudden, expose individuals to immense losses, are the sources of ruinous speculations, and destroy all proper confidence between man and men. In no country, more than our own, had these truths been felt in all their force. In none, had more intense suffering, a more wide-spreading ruin accompanied the system. It was, therefore, the object of the prohibition to cut up the whole mischief by the roots, because it had been deeply felt throughout all the States, and had deeply affected the prosperity of all. The object of the prohibition was not to prohibit the thing, when it bore a particular name; but to prohibit the thing, whatever form or name it might assume. If the words are not merely empty sounds, the prohibition must comprehend the emission of any paper medium by a State government for the purposes of common circulation. It would be preposterous to suppose, that the Constitution meant solemnly to prohibit an issue under one denomination, leaving the power complete to issue the same thing under another. It can never be seriously contended, that the Constitution means to prohibit names, and not things; to deal with shadows, and to leave substances. What would be the consequence of such a construction? That a very important act, big with great and ruinous mischief, and on threat account forbidden by words the most appropriate for its description, might yet be performed by the substitution of a name. That the Constitution, even in one of its vital provisions, might be openly evaded by giving a new name to an old thing. Call the thing a bill of credit, and it is prohibited. Call the same thing a certificate, and it is constitutional.

§236. Connected with this, is the prohibition, No State shall "make any thing but gold and silver coin a tender in payment of debts." The history of the State laws on this subject, while we were Colonies, as well as during the Revolution, and afterwards before the adoption of the Constitution, is startling at once to our morals, to our patriotism, and to our sense of justice. In the intermediate period between the commencement of the Revolutionary War, and the adoption of the Constitution, the system had attained its most appalling character. Not only was paper money declared to be a tender in payment of debts; but other laws, having the same general object, and interfering with private debts, under the name of appraisement laws, installment laws, and suspension laws, thickened upon the statute book of many States in the Union, until all public confidence was lost, and all private evils, resulting from this source, can scarcely be comprehended in our day. But they were so enormous, that the whole country seemed involved in a general bankruptcy; and fraud and chicanery obtained an undisputed mastery. Nothing but an absolute prohibition, like that contained in the Constitution, could arrest the overwhelming flood; and it was accordingly hailed with the most sincere joy by all good citizens. It has given but that healthy and sound currency, and that solid private credit, which constitute the true foundation of our prosperity, industry, and enterprise.

§237. The prohibition, to "pass any bill of attainder, *ex post facto* law, or law impairing the obligation of contracts," requires scarcely any vindication or explanation, beyond what has been already given. The power to pass bills of attainder, and *ex post facto* laws, (the nature of which has been already sufficiently explained) is quite as unfit to be intrusted to the States, as to the General Government. It was exercised by the States during the Revolutionary War, in the shape of confiscation laws, to an extent, which, upon cool reflection, every sincere patriot must regret. Laws "impairing the obligation of contracts" are still more objectionable. They interfere with, and disturb, and destroy, private rights, solemnly secured by the plighted faith of the parties. They bring on the same ruinous effects, as paper tender laws, installment laws, and appraisement laws, which are but varieties of the same general noxious policy. And they have been truly described, as contrary to the first principles of the social compact and to every principle of sound legislation.

§238. Although the language of this clause, "law impairing the obligation of contracts," would seem, at first view, to be free from any real ambiguity; yet there is not perhaps a single clause of the Constitution, which has given rise to more acute and vehement controversy. What is a contract? What is the obligation of a contract? What is impairing a contract? To what classes of laws does the prohibition apply? To what extent does it reach, as to control prospective legislation on the subject of contracts? These and many other questions, of no small nicety and intricacy, have vexed the legislative halls, as well as the judicial tribunals, with an uncounted variety and frequency of litigation and speculation.

§239. In the first place, What is to be deemed a contract, in the constitutional sense of this clause? A contract is an agreement to do, or not to do, a particular thing; or (as was said on another occasion) a contract is a contract between two or more persons. A contract is either executory or executed. An executory contract is one, in which a party binds himself to do, or not to do, a particular thing. An executed contract is one, in which the object of the contract is performed. This differs in nothing from a grant; for a contract executed conveys a thing in possession; a contract executory conveys only a thing in action. Since, then, a grant is in fact a contract executed, the obligation of which continues; and since the Constitution uses the general term, *contract,* without distinguishing between those, which are executory, and those, which are executed; it must be construed to comprehend the former, as well as the latter. A State law, therefore, annulling conveyances between individuals, and declaring, that the grantors shall stand seized of their former estates, notwithstanding those grants, would be as repugnant to the Constitution, as a State law, discharging the vendors from the obligation of executing their contracts of sale by conveyances. It would be strange, indeed, if a contract to convey were secured by the Constitution, while an absolute conveyance remained unprotected. That the contract, while executory, was obligatory; but when executed, might be avoided.

§240. Contracts, too, are expressed, or implied. Express contracts are, where the terms of the agreement are openly avowed, and uttered at the time of the making of them. Implied contracts are such, as reason and justice dictate from the nature of the transaction, and which, therefore, the law presumes, that every man undertakes to perform. The Constitution makes no distinction between the one class of contracts and the other. It then equally embraces, and equally applies to both. Indeed, as by far the largest class of contracts in civil society, in the ordinary transactions of life, are implied, there would be very little object in securing the inviolability of express contracts, if those, which are implied, might be impaired by State legislation. The Constitution is not chargeable with such folly, or inconsistency. Every grant, in its own nature, amounts to an extinguishment of the right of the grantor, and implies a contract not to reassert it. A party is, therefore, always stopped by his own grant. How absurd would it be to provide, that an express covenant by a party, as a muniment attendant upon the estate, should bind him for ever, because executory, and resting in action; and yet, that he might reassert his title to the estate, and dispossess his grantee, because there was only an implied convenant not to reassert it.

§241. In the next place, What is the obligation of a contract? It seems agreed, that, when the obligation of contracts is spoken of in the Constitution, we are to understand, not the mere moral, but the legal obligation of contracts. The moral obligation of contracts is, so far as human society is concerned, of an imperfect kind, which the parties are left free to obey or not, as they please. It is addressed to the conscience of the parties, under the solemn admonitions of accountability to the Supreme Being. No human lawgiver can either impair, or reach it. The Constitution has not in contemplation any such obligations, but such only, as might be impaired by a State, if not prohibited. It is the civil obligation of contracts, which it is designed to reach, that is, the obligation, which is recognised by, and results from, the law of the State, in which it is made. If, therefore, a contract, when made, is by the law of the State declared to be illegal, or deemed to be a nullity, or a *naked pact,* or promise, it has no civil obligation; because the law, in such cases, forbids its having any binding efficacy, or force. It confers no legal right on the one party, and no correspondent legal duty on the other. There is no means allowed, or recognised to enforce it; for the maxim is, that from a mere naked promise no action arises. But when it does not fall within the predicament of being either illegal, or void, its obligatory force is coextensive with its stipulations.

§242. Nor is this obligatory force so much the result of the positive declarations of the municipal law, as of the general principles of natural, or (as it is sometimes called) universal, law. In a state of nature, independent of the obligations of positive law, contracts may be formed, and their obligatory force be complete. Between independent nations, treaties and compacts are formed, which are deemed universally obligatory;

and yet in no just sense can they be deemed dependent on municipal law. Nay, there may exist (abstractly speaking) a perfect obligation in contracts, where there is no known and and adequate means to enforce them. As, for instance, between independent nations, where their relative strength and power preclude the possibility, on the side of the weaker party, of enforcing them. So, in the same government, where a contract is made by a State with one of its own citizens, which yet its laws do not permit to be enforced by any action or suit. In this predicament are the United States, who are not suable on any contracts made by themselves; but no one doubts, that these are still obligatory on the United States. Yet their obligation is not recognised by any positive municipal law, in a great variety of cases. It depends altogether upon principles of public or universal law. Still, in these cases, there is a right in the one party to have the contract performed, and a duty on the other side to perform it. But, generally speaking, when we speak of the obligation of a contract, we include in the idea some known means acknowledged by the municipal law to enforce it. Where all such means are absolutely denied, the obligation of the contract is understood to be impaired, although it may not be completely annihilated. Rights may, indeed, exist, without any present adequate correspondent remedies between private persons. Thus, a State may refuse to allow imprisonment for debt; and the debtor may have no property. But still the right of the creditor remains; and he may enforce it against the future property of the debtor. So, a debtor may die without leaving any known estate, or without any known representative. In such cases, we should not say, that the right of the creditor was gone; but only, that there was nothing, on which it could presently operate. But suppose an administration should be appointed, and property in contingency should fall in, the right might then be enforced to the extent of the existing means.

§243. The civil obligation of a contract, then, although it can never arise, or exist, contrary to positive law, may arise or exist independently of it; and it may be, exist, notwithstanding there may be no present adequate remedy to enforce it. Wher-

ever the municipal law recognizes an absolute duty to perform
a contract, there the obligation to perform it is complete, although there may not be a perfect remedy.

§244. In the next place, What may properly be deemed impairing the obligation of contracts, in the sense of the Constitution? Is it perfectly clear, that any law, which enlarges,
abridges, or in any manner changes the intention of the parties, resulting from the stipulations in the contract, necessarily
impairs it. The manner or degree, in which this change is effected, can in no respect influence the conclusion; for,
whether the law affects the validity, the construction, the duration, the discharge, or the evidence of the contract, it impairs its obligation, although it may not do so, to the same
extent, in all the supposed cases. Any deviation from its terms,
by postponing, or accelerating the period of performance,
which it prescribes, or by imposing conditions not expressed
in the contract, or by dispensing with the performance of
those, which are a part of the contract, however minute, or ap-
parently immaterial in their effects upon it, impairs an obligation. *A fortiori,* a law, which makes the contract wholly
invalid, or extinguishes, or releases it, is a law impairing it. Nor
is this all. Although there is a distinction between the obligation of a contract, and a remedy upon it; yet if there are certain
remedies existing at the time, when it is made, all of which are
afterwards wholly extinguished by new laws, so that there remains no means of enforcing its obligation, and no redress for
its violation; such an abolition of all remedies, operating immediately, is also an impairing of the obligation of such contract. But every change and modification of the remedy does
not involve such a consequence. No one will doubt, that the
Legislature may vary the nature and extent of remedies, so always, that some substantive remedy be in fact left. Nor can it
be doubted, that the Legislature may prescribe the times and
modes, in which remedies may be pursued; and bar suits, not
brought within such periods, and not pursued in such modes.
Statutes of limitations are of this nature; and have never been
supposed to destroy the obligation of contracts, but to pre-

scribe the times, within which that obligation shall be enforced by a suit; and in default thereof, to deem it either satisfied, or abandoned. The obligation to perform a contract is coeval with the undertaking to perform it. It originates with the contract itself, and operates anterior to the time of performance. The remedy acts upon the broken contract, and enforces a preexisting obligation. And a State Legislature may discharge a party from imprisonment upon a judgement in a civil case of contract, without infringing the Constitution; for this is but a modification of the remedy, and does not impair the obligation of the contract. So, if a party should be in jail, and give a bond for prison liberties, and to remain a true prisoner, until lawfully discharged, a subsequent discharge by an act of Legislature would not impair the contract, for it would be a lawful discharge in the sense of the bond.

§245. These general considerations naturally conduct us to some more difficult inquiries growing out of them; and upon which there has been a very great diversity of judicial opinion. The great object of the framers of the Constitution undoubtedly was, to secure the inviolability of contracts. This principle was to be protected in whatever form it might be assailed. No enumeration was attempted to be made of the modes, by which contracts might be impaired. It would have been unwise to have made such an enumeration, since it might have been defective; and the intention was to prohibit every mode or device for such purpose. The prohibition was universal.

§246. The question has arisen, and has been most elaborately discussed, how far the States may constitutionally pass an insolvent law, which shall discharge the obligation of contracts. It is not doubted, that the States may pass insolvent laws, which shall discharge the person, or operate in the nature of a *cessio bonorum,* or a surrender of all the debtor's property, provided such laws do not discharge, or intermeddle with, the obligation of contracts. Nor is it denied, that insolvent laws, which discharge the obligation of contracts, made antecedently to their passage, are unconstitutional. But the question is, how far the States may constitutionally pass insolvent laws, which shall operate upon, and discharge contracts, which are made subsequently to their passage. After the most ample argument, it has at length been settled, by a majority of the Supreme Court, that the States may constitutionally pass such laws operating upon *future* contracts, although not upon *past.*

§247. The remaining prohibition is, to "grant any title of nobility," which is supported by the same reasoning as that already suggested, in considering the like prohibition upon the National Government.

§248. The next clause, omitting the prohibition (already cited) to lay any imposts or duties on imports or exports, is, "No State shall, without the consent of Congress, lay any duty on tonnage; keep troops, or ships of war, in time of peace; enter into any agreement or compact with another State, or with a foreign power; or engage in war unless actually invaded, or in such imminent danger, as will not admit of delay." That part, which respects tonnage duties, has been already considered. To allow the States to keep troops, or ships of war, in time of peace, might be hazardous to the public peace or safety, or compel the National Government to keep up an expensive corresponding force. To allow the States to enter into agreements with each other, or with foreign nations, might lead to mischievous combinations, injurious to the general interests, and bind them into confederacies of a geological or sectional character. To allow the States to engage in war, unless compelled to do so in self-defence and upon sudden emergencies, would be (as has been already stated) to put the peace and safety of all the States in the power and discretion of any one of them. But an absolute prohibition of all these powers might, in certain exigencies, be inexpedient, and even mischievous; and, therefore, Congress may, by its consent, authorize the exercise of any of them, whenever, in its judgement, the public good shall require it.

§249. We have thus passed through the positive prohibitions introduced upon the powers of the States. It will be observed, that they divide themselves into two classes; those, which are political in their character, as an exercise of sovereignty; and those, which more especially regard the private rights of individuals. In the latter, the prohibition is absolute and universal. In the former, it is sometimes absolute, and sometimes subjected to the consent of Congress. It will, at once, be perceived, how full of difficulty and delicacy the task was, to reconcile the jealous tenancy of the States over their own sovereignty, with the permanent security of the National Government, and the inviolability of private rights. If everything has not been accomplished, which a wise forecast might have deemed proper for the preservation of our national rights and liberties in all political events, much has been done to guard us against the most obvious evils, and to secure a wholesome administration of private justice. To have attempted more, would probably have endangered the whole fabric; and thus might have perpetuated the dominion of misrule and imbecility.

§250. It has been already seen, and it will hereafter more fully appear, that there are implied, as well as express, prohibitions in the Constitution upon the power of the States. Among the former, one clearly is, that no State can control, or abridge, or interfere with the exercise of any authority under the National Government. And it may be added, that State laws, as, for instance, State statutes of limitations, and State insolvent laws, have no operation upon the rights or contracts of the United States.

§251. And here end our commentaries upon the first article of the Constitution, embracing the organization and powers of the Legislative department of the government, and the prohibitions upon the State and National Governments. If we here pause, but for a moment, we cannot be struck with the reflection, how admirable this division and distribution of legislative powers between the State and National Governments is adapted to preserve of the liberty, and to promote the happiness of the people of the United States. To the General Government are assigned all those powers, which relate to the common interests of all the States, as comprising one confederated nation; while to each State is reserved all those powers, which may affect, or promote its own domestic interests, its peace, its prosperity, its policy, and its local institutions. At the same time, such limitations and restraints are imposed upon each government, as experience has demonstrated to be wise to control any public functionaries, or as are indispensible to secure the harmonious operation of the Union.

CHAPTER XXVIII.

The Executive Department.

§252. WE next come to the second article of the Constitution, which prescribes the structure, organization, and powers of the Executive department. What is the best constitution for the executive department, and what are the powers, with which it should be intrusted, are problems among the most important, and probably the most difficult to be satisfactorily solved, of all, which are involved in the theory of free governments. No man, who has ever studied the subject with profound attention, has risen from the labor without an increased and almost overwhelming sense of its intricate relations, and perplexing doubts. No man, who has ever deeply read the human history, and especially the history of republics, but has been struck with the consciousness, how little has been hitherto done to establish a safe depositary of power in any hands, and how often, in the hands of one, or a few, or many,—of an hereditary monarch, or an elective chief, or a national council, the executive power has brought ruin upon the state, or sunk under the oppressive burden of its own imbecility. Perhaps our own history has not, as yet, established that we shall wholly escape all the dangers; and that here will not be found, as has been the case in other nations, the vulnerable part of the republic.

§253. The first clause of the first section is, "The executive power shall be vested in a President of the United States of America. He shall hold his office during the term of four years; and, together with the Vice President, chosen for the same term, be elected as follows."

§254. In considering this clause, three practical questions may arise: (1) whether there should be any executive department; (2) whether it should be composed of more than one person; (3) and what should be the duration of the term of office. Upon the first question, little need now be said, to establish the propriety of an executive department. It is founded upon a maxim admitted in all our State Constitutions, that the legislative, executive, and judicial departments ought to be kept separate, and the power of one ought not to be exercised by either of the others. The want of an executive department was felt as a great defect under the Confederation.

§255. In the next place, in what manner should the executive department be organized? It may, in general terms, be answered,—In such a manner as best to secure energy in the Executive, and safety to the people. A feeble Executive implies a feeble execution of the government; and a feeble execution is but another phrase for a bad execution. Unity in the Executive is favorable to energy, promptitude, and responsibility. A division of the power among several persons impairs each of these qualities; and introduces discord, intrigue dilatoriness, and not unfrequently, personal rivalries, incompatible with the public good. On the other hand, a single Executive is quite as safe for the people. His responsibility is more direct and efficient, as his measures cannot be disguised, or shifted upon others; and any abuse of authority can be more clearly seen, and carefully watched, than when it is shared by numbers.

§256. In the next place, the duration of the term of office of the Executive. It should be long enough to enable a chief magistrate to carry fairly through a system of government, according to the laws; and to stimulate him to personal firmness in the execution of his duties. If the term is very short, he will feel very little of the just pride of office; from the precariousness of its tenure. He will act more with reference to immediate and temporary popularity, than to permanent fame. His measures will tend to insure his own reelection, (if he desires it,) rather than to promote the good of the country. He will bestow offices upon mean dependents, or fawning courtiers, rather than upon persons of solid honor and distinction. He will fear to encounter opposition by a lofty course; and his wishes for office, equally with his fears, will debase his fortitude, weaken his integrity, and enhance his irresolution.

§257. On the other hand, the period should not be so long, as to impair the proper dependence of the Executive upon the people for encouragement and support; or to enable him to persist in a course of measures, deeply injurious to the public interests, or subversive of the public faith. His administration should be known to come under the review of the people at short periods; so that its merits may be decided, and its errors be corrected by the sober exercise of the electoral vote by the people.

§258. For all of these purposes, the period, actually assigned for the duration of office of the President, by the Constitution, seems adequate and satisfactory. It is four years, a period intermediate between the term of office of the Representatives, and that of the Senators. By this arrangement, too, the whole organization of the legislative department is not dissolved at the same moment. A part of the functionaries are constantly going out of office, and as constantly renewed, while a sufficient number remain, to carry on the same general system with intelligence and steadiness. The President is not precluded from being reeligible to office; and thus with a just estimate of the true dignity and true duties of his office, he may confer lasting benefits on his country, as well as acquire for himself the enviable fame of a statesman and patriot.

§259. The like term of office is fixed for the Vice President; and in case of the vacancy of the office of President, he is to succeed to the same duties and powers. In the original scheme of the government, the Vice President was an equal candidate for the office of President. But that provision has been altered (as we shall presently see) by an amendment of the Constitution. As President of the Senate, it seems desirable, that the Vice President should have the experience of at least four years service, to perfect him in the forms of business, and secure to him due distinction, and weight of character.

§260. The next clause provides for the mode of choice of the President and Vice President. "Each state shall appoint, in such a manner as the Legislature thereof may direct, a number of Electors, equal to the whole number of Senators and Representatives, to which the State may be entitled in the Congress. But no Senator or Representative, or person holding an office of trust or profit under the United States, shall be appointed an Elector."

§261. Various modes were suggested as to the choice of these high officers; first, the choice was proposed to be made by the National Legislature; secondly, by the State Legislatures; thirdly, by the people at large; fourthly, by the people in districts; and lastly, by Electors. Upon consideration of the whole subject, the last was deemed the most eligible course, as it would secure the united action and wisdom of a select body of distinguished citizens in the choice, and would be attended with less excitement, and more deliberation, than a mere popular election. Such a body would also have this preference over any mere Legislature, that it would not be chosen for the ordinary functions of legislation, but singly and solely for this duty. It was supposed from these circumstances, that the choice would be more free and independent, more wise and cautious, more satisfactory, and more unbiased by party spirit, than in either of the other modes. The State Legislatures would still have an agency in the choice, by prescribing the mode, in which the Electors should be chosen, whether it should be by the people at large, or in districts, or by the Legislature itself. For the purpose of excluding all undue influence in the electoral colleges, the Senators and Representatives in Congress, and all officers under the National Government are disqualified from being Electors.

§262. The remaining clause regulates the conduct of the Electors, in giving and certifying their votes; the manner of ascertaining and counting the votes in Congress; and the mode of choice, in case there is no choice made by the Electors. The original clause was as follows:—"The Electors shall meet in their respective States, and vote by ballot for two persons, of whom one, at least, shall not be an inhabitant of the same State with themselves. And they shall make a list of all the persons voted for, and of the number of votes for each; which list they shall sign and certify, and transmit, sealed, to the seat of the government of the United States, directed to the President of the Senate. The President of the Senate shall, in the presence of the Senate and House of Representatives, open all the certificates, and the votes shall then be counted. The person having the greatest number of votes shall be the President, if such number be a majority of the whole number of electors appointed; and if there be more than one who has such a majority, and has an equal number of votes, then the House of Representatives shall immediately choose by ballot one of them for President; and if no person has a majority, then, from the five highest on the list, the said House shall in like manner choose the President. But in choosing the President the votes shall be taken by States, the representation from each state having one vote; a quorum for this purpose shall consist of a member or members from two thirds of the States, and a majority of all the States shall be necessary to a choice. In every case, after the choice of the President, the person having the greatest number of votes of the Electors shall be the Vice President. But if there should remain two or more who have equal votes, the Senate shall choose from them by ballot the Vice President."

§263. This clause is now repealed, (whether wisely or not, has been a matter of grave question among statesmen,) and the following substituted in its stead:—"The Electors shall meet in their respective States, and vote by ballot for President and Vice President, one of whom, at least, shall not be an inhabitant of the same state with themselves. They shall name in their ballots the person voted for as President, and in distinct ballots the person voted for as Vice President. And they shall make distinct lists of all persons voted for as President, and of all persons voted for as Vice President, and of the number of votes for each; which lists they shall sign and certify, and transmit sealed to the seat of government of the United States, directed to the President of the Senate. The President of the Senate shall, in the presence of the Senate and House of Representatives, open all the certificates; and the votes shall then be counted. The person, having the greatest number of votes for President, shall be the President, if such number be a majority of the whole number of Electors appointed; and if no person having such majority, then, from the persons having the highest numbers, not exceeding three, on the list of those voted for as President, the House of Representatives shall choose immediately, by ballot, the President. But in choosing the President, the votes shall be taken by States, the Representatives from each State having one vote; a quorum for this purpose shall consist of a member or members from two thirds of the States; and a majority of all the States shall be necessary to a choice. And if the House of Representatives shall not choose a President, whenever the right of choice shall devolve upon them, before the fourth day of March next following, then the Vice President shall act as President, as in the case of the death, or other constitutional disability of the President. The person, having the greatest number of votes as Vice President, shall be the Vice President, if such number be a majority of the whole number of Electors appointed. And if no person having a majority, then, from the two highest numbers on the list, the Senate shall choose the Vice President. A quorum for this purpose shall consist of two thirds of the whole number of Senators, and a majority of the whole number shall be necessary to a choice. But no person, constitutionally ineligible to the office of President, shall be eligible to that of Vice President of the United States."

§264. The principal differences between the original plan, and this amendment to the Constitution, are the following: First, by the original plan, two persons were voted for as President; and after the President was chosen, the person, having the greatest number of votes of the Electors was to be Vice President; but if two or more had equal votes, the Senate was to choose the Vice President from them by ballot. By the present plan, the votes for President and Vice President are distinct. Secondly, by the original plan, in case of no choice of President by the Electors, the choice was to be made by the House of Representatives, from the five highest on the list. It is now reduced to three. Thirdly, by the original plan, the Vice President need not have a majority of all the electoral votes, but only a greater number than any other person. It is now necessary, that he should have a majority of all the votes. Fourthly, by the original plan, the choice of Vice President could not be made until after a choice of President. It now can be made by the Senate, as soon as it is ascertained, that there is no choice by the Electors. Fifthly, no provision was made for the case of no choice of President by the House of Representatives, before the fourth day of March next. It is now provided that the Vice President in such a case shall act as President.

§265. A few words, only, will be necessary, to explain the main provisions, respecting the choice of these high functionaries, since the adoption of this amendment, as an elaborate examination of the subject would occupy too much space. In the first place, the Electors, as well as the House of Representatives, are to vote by ballot, and not *vivâ voce,* or by oral declaration. The object of this provision, is, to secure the Electors from all undue influence, and undue odium for their vote, as it was supposed, that perfect secrecy could be maintained. In the next place, both candidates cannot be an inhabitant of the same State, as Electors. The object of this clause is to suppress local partialities and combinations. In the next place, the votes are to be certified by the Electors themselves, in order to insure the genuineness of the vouchers. In the next place, they are to be sealed, and opened and counted only in the presence of the Senate and House of Representatives, in order to prevent any frauds or alterations in their transmission. In the next place, a majority of all the electoral votes is, in the first instance, required for a choice, and not a mere plurality; thus enabling the people, in case there is no choice, to exercise through their Representatives a sound discretion, in selecting from the three highest candidates. It might otherwise happen, if there were many candidates, that a person, having a very small number of votes over any one of the others, might succeed against the wishes of a great majority of the people. In the next place, the House of Representatives are to vote by States, each having one vote in the choice. The choice is, as we have seen, in the first instance to be by the people of each State, according to the number of their Senators and Representatives. But if no choice is thus made, then the choice devolves on the House of Representatives, and each State is to have an equal voice in the election, and to have but a single vote, whatever may be the number of its Representatives. Thus, the primary election is in effect surrendered to the large States; and if that fails, then it is surrendered to the small States. So that an important motive is thus suggested for union among the large States in the first instance; and for union among the small States in the last resort.

§266. There probably is no part of the plan of the framers of the Constitution, which, practically speaking, has so little realized the expectations of its friends, as that which regards the choice of President. They undoubtedly intended, that the Electors should be left free to make the choice according to their own judgement of the relative merits and qualifications of the candidates for this high office; and that they should be under no pledge to any popular favorite, and should be guided by no sectional influences. In both respects, the event has disappointed all these expectations. The Electors are now almost universally pledged to support a particular candidate, before they receive their own appointment; and they do little more than register the previous decrees, made by public and private meetings of the citizens of their own State. The President is in no just sense the unbiased choice of the people, or of the States. He is commonly the representative of a party, and not of the Union; and the danger, therefore is, that the office may hereafter be filled by those, who will gratify the private resentments, or prejudices, or selfish objects of their particular partisans, rather than by those, who will study to fulfill the high destiny contemplated by the Constitution, and be the impartial patrons, supporters, and friends of the great interests of the whole country.

§267. It is observable, that the mode, in which the electoral vote of each state is to be given, is confided to the State Legislature. The mode of choice has never been uniform since the Constitution was adopted. In some States, the choice is by the people by a general ticket; in others, by the people in electoral districts; and in others, by the immediate choice of the State Legislature. This want of uniformity has been deemed as a serious defect by many statesmen; but, hitherto, it has remained unredressed by any constitutional amendment.

§268. The next clause is, "The Congress may determine the time of choosing the Electors, and the day, on which they shall give their votes; which day shall be the same throughout the United States." This measure is undoubtedly the result of sound policy. A fixed period, at which all the electoral votes shall be given on the same day, has a tendency to repress political intrigues and speculations, by rendering a combination among all the electoral colleges, as to their votes, more difficult, if not unavailing.This object would still be more certainly obtained, by fixing the choice of the electors themselves on the same day, and at so short a period, before they gave their votes, as to render any general negotiations and arrangements among them nearly impracticable. Practically speaking, however, this provision, as well as the preceding, has had far less influence than was expected; for the votes of the Electors are now, in consequence of their pledges, almost as well known before, as after, their votes are counted.

§269. The next clause respects the qualifications of the President; and the qualifications of the Vice President are (as we have seen) to be the same. "No person except a natural born citizen, or a citizen of the United States at the time of the adoption of this Constitution, shall be eligible to the office of President. Neither shall any person be eligible to the office, who shall not have attained to the age of thirty-five years, and been fourteen years a resident within the United States."

§270. Considering the nature of the duties, the extent of the information, and the solid wisdom and experience, required in the Executive department, no one can reasonably doubt the propriety of some qualification of the age of the President.

That, which is selected, is the middle age of life, by which period, the character and talents of individuals are generally known, and fairly developed; the passions of youth have become moderated; and the faculties are fast advancing to their highest state of maturity. An earlier period could scarcely have afforded sufficient pledges of talents, wisdom, and virtue, adequate to the dignity and importance of the office.

§271. The other qualifications respect citizenship and inhabitancy. It is not too much to say, that no one, but a native citizen, ought ordinarily to be intrusted with an office so vital to the safety and liberties of the people. But an exception was, from a deep sense of gratitude, made in favor of those distinguished men, who, though not natives, had, with such exalted patriotism, and such personal sacrifices, united their lives and fortunes with ours during the Revolution. But even a native citizen might, from long absence, and voluntary residence abroad, become alienated from, or indifferent to his country; and, therefore, a residence for fourteen years within the United States is made indispensable, as a qualification to the office. This, of course, does not exclude persons, who are temporarily abroad in the public service, or on their private affairs, and who have not intentionally given up their domicile here.

§272. The next clause is, "In case of the removal of the President from office, or of his death, resignation, or inability to discharge the powers and duties of the said office, the same shall devolve on the Vice President. And the Congress may by law provide for the case of the removal, death, resignation, or inability of the President and Vice President; declaring what officer shall act accordingly, until the disability be removed, or a President shall be elected." The propriety of this power is manifest. It provides for cases, which may occur in the progress of the government; and it prevents in such cases a total suspension of the executive functions, which would be injurious, and might even be fatal to the interests of the country.

§273. What shall be the proper proof of the resignation of the President or Vice President, or of their refusal to accept the office, is left open by the Constitution. But Congress, with great wisdom and foresight, has provided, that the only evidence of a refusal to accept the office, or of a resignation of the office, shall be an instrument in writing, declaring the same, subscribed by the party and delivered into the office of the Secretary of State. No provision has as yet been made for the case of the inability of the President or Vice President to perform the duties of his office, nor has any mode of proof been prescribed, to ascertain the fact of inability, or what shall be deemed an inability.

§274. The next clause provides for the compensation of the President. "The President shall, at stated times, receive for his services a compensation, which shall neither be increased nor diminished, during the period for which he shall have been elected; and he shall not receive, within that period, any other emolument from the United States, or any of them."

§275. The propriety of granting to the President a suitable compensation, cannot well be doubted. The Constitution would, otherwise, exclude all persons of moderate fortune from the office; or expose them to gross temptations, to sacrifices of duty, and perhaps to direct corruption. The compensation should be adequate to the just expenditures of the office. If the Legislature should possess a discretionary authority to increase or diminish it at their pleasure, the President would become a humble dependent upon their bounty, or a mean suppliant for their favor. It would give them a complete command of his independence, and perhaps of his integrity. And on the other hand, if the actual incumbent could procure an augmentation of it during his official term to any extent he might desire, he might be induced, from mere avarice, to seek this as his highest reward, and undermine the virtue of the Congress, in order to accomplish it. The prohibition equally forbids any increase or diminution. And, to exclude all other exterior influences, it equally denies to him any emoluments arising from any other sources, State or National. He is thus secured, in a great measure, against all sinister foreign influences. And he must be lost to all just sense of the high duties of his station, if he does not conduct himself with an exclusive devotion to the good of the whole people, unmindful at once of the blandishments of courtiers, who seek to deceive him, and of partisans, who aim to govern him, and thus to accomplish their own selfish purposes.

§276. The next clause is, "Before he enters on the execution of his office, he shall take the following oath or affirmation: I do solemnly swear (or affirm) that I will faithfully execute the office of the President of the United States, and will, to the best of my ability, preserve, protect, and defend, the Constitution of the United States." There is little need of commentary here. No man can doubt the propriety of placing the President under the sanction of an oath of office, to preserve, protect, and defend, the Constitution, who would require an oath or solemn affirmation on any other occasion. If a judge, or a juryman, or a witness, ought to take a solemn oath or affirmation, to bind his conscience, surely a President, holding in his hands the destiny of the nation, ought so to do. Let it not be deemed a vain or idle form. In all these things, God will bring us into judgement. A President, who shall dare to violate the obligations of his solemn oath or affirmation of office, may escape human censure, nay, may even receive applause from the giddy multitude. But he will be compelled to learn, that there is a watchful Providence, that cannot be deceived; and a Righteous Being, the searcher of all hearts, who will render unto all men according to their deserts. Considerations of this sort will necessarily make a conscientious man more scrupulous in the discharge of his duty; and will even make a man of looser principles pause, when he is about to enter upon a deliberate violation of his official oath.

CHAPTER XXIX

Powers and Duties of the President

§277. WE next come to the consideration of the powers and duties of the President. The first clause of the second section is, "The President shall be commander-in-chief of the army and navy of the United States, and of the militia of the several States, when called into the actual service of the United States. He may require the opinion in writing of the principal officer in each of the executive departments, upon any subject relating to the duties of their respective offices; and he shall have power to grant reprieves and pardons for offenses against the United States, except in cases of impeachment."

§278. The command, direction, and application, of the public forces, to execute the laws, maintain peace, resist invasion, and carry on war, are powers obviously belonging to the executive department, and require the exercise of qualifications, which cannot properly be presumed to exist in any other department of the government. Promptitude of action, unity of design, and harmony of operations, are in such cases indispensable to success. Timidity, indecision, obstinacy, pride, and sluggishness, must mingle, in a greater or less degree, in all numerous bodies, and render their councils inert and imbecile, and their military operations slow and uncertain. There is, then, true wisdom and policy in confiding the command of the army and navy to the President, since it will insure activity, responsibility, and firmness, in public emergencies.

§279. The President is also authorized to require the opinions of the Heads of Departments, in writing, on subjects relative to their official duties. This, perhaps, might have been deemed an incidental right to his general authority. But it was desirable to make it a matter of constitutional right, so as to enforce responsibility in critical times.

§280. To the President, also, is confided the power "to grant reprieves and pardons." Without this power, no government could be deemed to be suitably organized for the purposes of administering human justice. The criminal code of every country must necessarily partake, in some of its punishments, of a high degree of severity; and it is not possible to fix the exact degree of punishment, for every kind of offence, under every variety of circumstances. There are so many things, which may extenuate, as well as inflame the atrocity of crimes, and so many infirmities, which belong to human nature in general, which may furnish excuses, or mitigations for the commission of them, that any code, which did not provide for any pardoning or mitigating power, would be universally deemed cruel, unjust, and indefensible. It would introduce the very evils, which it would seek to avoid, by inducing the community to connive at an escape from punishment, in all cases, where the latter would be disproportionate to the offence. The power of pardon and reprieve is better vested in a single person, than in a numerous body. It brings home a closer responsibility; it can be more promptly applied; and, by cutting off delays, it will, on the one hand, conduce to certainty of punishment, and, on the other hand, enable the Executive, at critical moments, to apply it as a means of detecting, or of suppressing gross offences. But if the power of pardon extended to impeachments, it is obvious, that the latter might become wholly inefficient, as a protection against political offences. The party accused might be acting under the authority of the President, or be one of his corrupt favorites. It is, therefore, wisely excepted from his general authority.

§281. The next clause respects the power to make treaties and appointments to office. "He (the President) shall have power, by and with the advice and consent of the Senate, to make treaties, provided two thirds of the Senators present concur. And he shall nominate, and, by and with the advice and consent of the Senate, shall appoint, ambassadors, other public ministers and consuls, judges of the Supreme Court, and all other officers of the United States, whose appointments are not herein otherwise provided for, and which shall be established by law. But the Congress may by law vest the appointment of such inferior officers, as they think proper, in the President alone, in the Courts of Law, or in the Heads of Departments."

§282. The power to make treaties is general, and, of course, it embraces treaties for peace, or war; for commerce, or cessions of territory; for alliance, or succors; for indemnity for injuries, or payment of debts; for the recognition or establishment of principles of public law; and for any other purposes, which the policy, necessities, or interests of independent nations may dictate. Such a power is so large, and so capable of abuse, that it ought not to be confided to any one man, nor even to a mere majority of any public body, in a republican government. There should be some higher pledge for the sound policy or necessity of a treaty. It should receive the sanction of such a number of public functionaries, as would furnish a sufficient guaranty of such policy or necessity. Two thirds of the Senate, therefore, are required to give validity to a treaty. It would seem to be perfectly safe in such a body, under such circumstances, representing, as it does, all the States of the Union. The House of Representatives would not have been so eligible a body, because it is more numerous, more popular in its structure, most short in its duration, more unfit to act upon sudden emergencies, more under the control of a few States; and, from its organization, it may fairly be presumed to have less experience in public affairs, and less knowledge of foreign relations, than the Senate.

§283. The power of appointment, one of the most important and delicate in a republican government, is next provided for. Upon its fair and honest exercise, must, in a great measure, depend the vigor, the public virtue, and even the safety, of the government. If it shall ever be wielded by any Executive, exclusively to gratify his own ambition or resentments, to satisfy his own personal favorites, or to carry his own political measure, and, still more, if it shall ever interfere with the freedom of elections by the people, or suppress the honest expression of opinion and judgement by voters, it will become one of the most dangerous and corrupt engines to destroy private independence and public liberty, which can assail the republic. It should, therefore, be watched in every free government with uncommon vigilance, as it may, otherwise, soon become as secret, as it will be irresistible, in its mischievous operations. If the time shall ever arrive, when no citizen can obtain any appointment to office, unless he submits to sacrifice all personal independence and opinion, and to become the mere slave of those, who can confer it, it is not difficult to foresee, that the power of appointment will then become the fittest instrument of artful men to accomplish the worst purposes. The framers of the Constitution were aware of this danger, and have sedulously interposed certain guards to check, if not wholly to prevent, the abuse of the power. The advice and consent of the Senate is required to the appointment of ambassadors, other public ministers, consuls, judges of the Supreme Court, and other high officers.

§284. The mode of appointment of inferior officers is left in good measure to the discretion of Congress; and the power may be vested by them in the President, in the Courts of Law, or in the Heads of Departments. The propriety of this grant of discretionary power, in certain cases, cannot well be doubted. But it is very questionable, if Congress has not permitted its exercise, in some departments of the government, to an extent, which may be highly alarming, and even incompatible with the sound policy and interests of the government. Some departments possess only the unenviable power of appointing their own clerks; whilst others possess a power of patronage, which almost rivals that of the President himself; and the exercise of it is left, in a great measure, without the check of the constitutional advice or consent of the Senate.

§285. It is observable, that the Constitution makes no mention of any power of removal of any officer by the President, or by any other body. As, however, the tenure of office is not provided for in the Constitution, except in the judicial department, (where it is during good behavior,) the natural inference is, that all other officers are to hold their offices during pleasure, or during such period, as Congress shall prescribe. But if the power of removal exists, in cases where the term of officer is not thus limited by Congress, the question is, in whom does it reside? Does it reside in the President alone? Or does it reside in the body intrusted with the particular appointment? It was maintained, with great earnestness and ability, by some of the ablest statesmen, who assisted in framing the Constitution, that it belonged to the latter; and that, in all cases where the advice and consent of the Senate are necessary to an appointment, the same advice and consent are also necessary to a removal from office. In short, they maintained, with great force of argument and reasoning, that the power of removal was but an incident to the power of appointment, and that, consequently, the removal could only take place by the appointing power, and was consummated only by a new appointment. It is singular enough, that in the first Congress, jealous, as it was, of executive power, a different doctrine was maintained, viz., that it is an incident to the executive department. This doctrine arose (it has been said) partly from a just deference to the great man (Washington) then in the office of President, and partly from a belief, that a removal from office without just cause would be an impeachable offense in the President; and, therefore, that there could be no danger of its exercise, except in flagrant cases of malversation, or incapacity of the officer. This latter doctrine has ever since prevailed in practice; and the President is accordingly now permitted to exercise the power of removal, without any restraint from the Senate, although the Constitution, in the enumeration of his powers, is wholly silent on the subject. If we connect this power of removal, thus practically expounded, with another power, which is given in the succeeding clause, to fill up vacancies in the recess of the Senate, the chief guards, intended by the Constitution, over the power of appointment, may become utterly nugatory. A President of high ambition and feeble principles may remove all officers, and make new appointments, in the recess of the Senate; and if his choice should not be confirmed by the Senate, he may reappoint the same persons in the recess, and thus set at defiance the salutary check of the Senate in all such cases.

§286. The clause to which we have alluded is, "The President shall have power to fill up all vacancies, that may happen during the recess of the Senate, by granting commissions, which shall expire at the end of their next session." This is a provision almost indispensable to secure a due performance of public duties by officers of the government, during the recess of the Senate; and as the appointments are but temporary, the temptation to any abuse of the power would seem to be sufficiently guarded, if it might not draw in its train the dangerous consequences, which have been before stated.

§287. The third section of the second article enumerates the duties of the President. "He shall from time to time give to the Congress information of the state of the Union, and recommend to their consideration such measures, as he shall judge necessary and expedient. He may, on extraordinary occasions, convene both Houses, or either of them; and in case of disagreement between them, with respect to the time of adjournment, he may adjourn them to such time, as he shall think proper. He shall receive ambassadors, and other public ministers. He shall take care, that the laws be faithfully executed; and shall commission all the officers of the United States."

§288. The duty of giving information by the President to Congress, of the state of the Union, and of recommending measures, would seem almost too clear to require any express provision. But it is not without its use. It fixes the responsibility on the President; and, on the other hand, it disables Congress from taking any objection, that he is impertinently interfering with their appropriate duties. His knowledge of public affairs may be important to them; and the people ought consequently to have a right to demand it. His recommendation of measure may give Congress the benefit of his large experience; and, at all events, may compel them to a just discharge of their legislative powers. So that, in this way, each department may be brought more fully before the public, both as to what each does, and what each omits to do, and each will share the responsibility accordingly.

§289. The power to convene Congress on extraordinary occasions is found on the wisest policy. Sudden emergencies may arise in the recess of Congress, and be wholly beyond any previous foresight, yet indispensable to be met with promptitude and vigor. The power to adjourn Congress, in cases of disagreement between the two Houses, is a quiet way of disposing of a practical difficulty in cases of irritation or obstinate difference of opinion between them.

§290. The power to receive ambassadors and other public ministers, is a very important and delicate function; and far more so, than it seems to have been deemed even by the framers of the Constitution. In times of profound tranquillity throughout the world, it may properly be confided to the Executive alone. But it is not so clear, that the Senate ought not, in cases of revolutions in foreign governments, to partake of the functions, by their advice and consent. The refusal to receive an ambassador or minister, is sometimes a source of discontent to foreign nations, any may even provoke public hostilities. But in cases of revolution, or the separation of a kingdom into two or more distinct governments, the acknowledgement of an ambassador or minister, of either party, is often treated as an interference in the contest, and may lead to an open rupture. There would therefore seem to be a peculiar propriety, in all such cases, to require greater caution on the part of the Executive, by interposing some check upon his own unlimited discretion. Our own times have furnished abundant examples of the critical nature of the trust; but it has hitherto been exercised with such sound judgement, that the power has been felt to be practically safe, and eminently useful.

§291. Another duty of the President is, "to take care that the laws be *faithfully executed.*" And by the laws we are here to understand, not merely the acts of Congress, but all the obligations of treaties, and all the requisitions of the Constitution, as the latter are, equally with the former, the "supreme law of the land." The great object of the establishment of the executive department is, to accomplish, in this enlarged sense, a faithful execution of the laws. Without it, be the form of government whatever it may, it will be utterly worthless for confidence, or defence, for the redress of grievances, or the protection of rights, for the happiness and good order of citizens, or for the public and political liberties of the people.

§292. But we are not to understand, that this clause confers on the President any new and substantial power to cause the laws to be faithfully executed, by any means, which he shall see fit to adopt, although not prescribed by the Constitution, or by the acts of Congress. That would be to clothe him with an absolute despotic power over the lives, the property, and the rights of the whole people. A tyrannical President might, under a pretence of this sort, punish for a crime, without any trial by jury, or usurp the functions of other departments of the government. The true interpretation of the clause is, that the President is to use all such means as the Constitution and laws have placed at his disposal, to enforce the due execution of the laws. As, for example, if crimes are committed, he is to direct a prosecution by the proper public officers, and see, that the offenders are brought to justice. If treaties are violated by foreign nations, he is to make suitable demands for a due enforcement of them; but he cannot employ the public force, or make war, to accomplish the purpose. If public officers refuse or neglect to perform their appropriate duties, he is bound to remove them, and appoint others who will honestly and faithfully perform them.

§293. The remaining duty is, "to commission all the officers of the United States." The President cannot lawfully refuse, or neglect it in any case, where it is required by law. It is not designed, as some have incorrectly supposed, to give him a control over all appointments; but to give to the officers a perfect voucher of their right to office. In this view, it is highly important, as it introduces uniformity and regularity into all the departments of the government, and furnishes an indisputable evidence of a rightful appointment.

§294. The remaining section of this article contains an enumeration of the persons, who shall be liable to be removed from office by impeachment, and for what offences. It is, "The President, Vice President, and all civil officers of the United States, shall be removed from office, on impeachment for, and conviction of, treason, bribery, or other high crimes and misdemeanors." The true objects and interpretation of this clause have been already sufficiently considered.

§295. There are other incidental powers, belonging to the executive department, which are necessarily implied from the nature of the functions, which are confided to it. Among these, must necessarily be included the power to perform them, without any obstruction or impediment whatsoever. The President cannot, therefore, be liable to arrest, imprisonment, or detention, while he is in the discharge of the duties of his office; and for this purpose his person must be deemed, in civil cases at least, to possess an official inviolability. In the exercise of his political powers, he is to use his own discretion, and is accountable only to his country, and to his own conscience. His decision, in relation to these powers, is subject to no control; and his discretion, when exercised, is conclusive. But he has no authority to control other officers of the government, in relation to the duties imposed upon them by law, in cases not touching his own political powers.

§296. Thus is closed the examination of the rights, powers, and duties of the Executive department. Unless my judgement has been unduly biased, I think it will be found impossible to withhold from this part of the Constitution a tribute of profound respect, if not of the liveliest admiration. All, that seems desirable in order to gratify the hopes, secure the reverence, and sustain the dignity the nation, is, that it should always be occupied by a man of elevated talents, of ripe virtues, of incorruptible integrity, and of tried patriotism; one, who shall forget his own interests, and remember, that he represents not a party, but the whole nation; one, whose fame may be rested with posterity, not upon the false eulogies of favorites, but upon the solid merit of having preserved the glory, and enhanced the prosperity of the country.

CHAPTER XXX

The Judicial Department.

§297. HAVING finished our examination of the structure and organization of the Legislative and Executive Departments, we next come to an examination of the remaining coordinate department, the JUDICIARY. No one, who has duly reflected, can doubt, that the existence of such a department, with powers coextensive with those of the Legislative and Executive departments, is indispensable to the safety of a free government. Where there is no Judiciary department to interpret, pronounce, and execute the laws, to decide controversies, to punish offences, and to enforce rights, the government must either perish from its own weakness, or the other departments of government must usurp powers for the purpose of commanding obedience, to the utter extinction of civil and political liberty. The will of those who govern, must, under such circumstances, become absolute and despotic, and it is wholly immaterial, whether absolute power be vested in a single tyrant, or in an assembly of tyrants. No remark is better founded in human experience than that of Montesquieu, that "there is no liberty, if the judiciary be not separated from the legislative and executive powers." It is no less true, that personal security and private property depend entirely upon the wisdom, integrity, and stability of courts of justice. How, otherwise, are the innocent to be protected against unjust accusations, or the injured to obtain redress for their wrongs? If that government can be truly said to be despotic and intolerable, in which the law is vague and uncertain; it cannot but be rendered still more oppressive and more mischievous, when the actual administration of justice is dependent upon caprice, or favor, upon the will of rulers, or the influence of popularity. When power becomes right, it is of little consequence, whether decisions rest upon corruption, or weakness, upon the accidents of chance, or upon deliberate wrong. In every well-organized government, therefore, with reference to the security both of public rights and private rights, it is indispensable, that there should be a judicial department, to ascertain, and decide, rights, to punish crimes, to administer justice, and to protect the innocent from injury and usurpation.

§298. In the National Government, the judicial power is equally as important, as it is in the States. The want of it was a vital defect in the Confederation; and led to the most serious embarrassments during the brief existence of that ill-adjusted instrument. Without it, the laws of the Union would be perpetually in danger of being contravened by the laws of the States. The National Government would be reduced to a servile dependence upon the latter for the due execution of its powers; and we should have reacted over the same solemn mockery, which began in the neglect, and ended in the ruin of the Confederation. Power without adequate means to enforce it, is like a body in a state of suspended animation. For all practical purposes, it is, as if its faculties were extinguished. A single State might, under such circumstances, at its mere pleasure, suspend the whole operations of the Union.

§299. Two ends, of paramount importance, and fundamental to a free government, are to be attained by a National Judiciary. The first is, a due execution of the powers of the government; the second is, a uniformity of interpretation and operation of those powers, and of the laws made in pursuance of them. The power of interpreting the laws, necessarily involves the power to decide, whether they are conformable to the Constitution, or not; and in a conflict between the laws, State or National, and the Constitution, no one can doubt, that the latter is, and ought to be, of paramount obligation and force. And, accordingly, it has always been deemed a function indispensable to the safety and liberty of the people, that courts of justice should have a right to declare void such laws, as violate the Constitution. The framers of the Constitution, having these great principles in view, unanimously adopted two fundamental resolutions on this subject; first, that a National Judiciary ought to be established; and secondly, that it ought to possess powers coextensive with those of the legislative department.

§300. The third article of the Constitution shows the manner, in which these great principles are carried into effect. The first section is, "The judicial power of the United States shall be vested in one Supreme Court, and in such inferior courts, as the Congress may from time to time ordain and establish. The judges, both of the supreme and inferior courts, shall hold their offices during good behavior; and shall at stated times receive for their services a compensation, which shall not be diminished during their continuance in office." The establishment of a Supreme Court is positively required; the establishment of inferior courts is left to the discretion of Congress. Unless a Supreme Court were established, there would be no adequate means to insure uniformity in the interpretation and operations of the Constitution and laws. Inferior tribunals, whether State, or National, might construe them in very different manners; and, thus their full obligation might be admitted in one State, and denied in another State. The existence of a Supreme Court is, therefore, at all times indispensable for the purposes of public justice; and it is accordingly made the imperative and absolute duty of Congress to establish such a Court. But the establishment of inferior courts may not, in all cases, and under all circumstances, be as indispensable. And, at all events, the nature and extent of the organization and jurisdiction of these inferior courts, may properly vary, at different times, to suit the public convenience and exigencies. The power, therefore, to establish these courts, as well as prescribe their organization and jurisdiction, is confided to the discretion of Congress.

§301. The next consideration is, the mode of appointment, and tenure of office, of the judges. We have already seen, that the judges of the Supreme Court are to be appointed by the President, by and with the advice and consent of the Senate. The appointment of inferior judges is not expressly provided for. But it has either been left to the discretion of Congress, or silently belongs to the President, by and with the advice and consent of the Senate, under the clause already considered, authorizing him to appoint all other officers, whose appointments are not otherwise, in the Constitution, provided for.

§302. The tenure of office of the judges, both of the Supreme and the inferior courts, is during good behavior. This tenure of office seems indispensable to a due degree of independence and firmness on their part, in the discharge of the duties of their office; and to a due security to the people for their fidelity and impartiality, in administering private rights, and preserving the public liberties. Such was the opinion of the framers of the Constitution, who unanimously agreed to this tenure of office. Let us briefly consider some of the reasoning, by which it is supported.

§303. In the first place, factions and parties are quite as common in republics, as in monarchies; and the same safeguards are as indispensable in the former, as in the latter, against the encroachments of party spirit, and the tyranny of faction. Laws, however wholesome or necessary, are sometimes the objects of temporary aversion, of popular odium, and even of popular resistance. Nothing is more easy in republics, than for demagogues, under artful pretences, to stir up combinations against the regular exercise of authority, in order to advance their own selfish projects. The independence and impartiality of upright magistrates often interpose barriers to the success of their schemes, which make them the secret enemies of any regular and independent administration of justice. If, under such circumstances, the tenure of office of the judges were for a short period, they could easily intimidate them in the discharge of their duties, or, by rendering them odious, easily displace them. And thus the minority in the state, whose sole reliance for protection, in all free governments, must be upon the Judiciary, would be deprived of their natural protectors.

§304. In the next place, the independence of the Judiciary is indispensable, to secure the people against the unintentional, as well as the intentional usurpations of authority, in the Executive and Legislative departments. It has been observed, with great sagacity, that power is perpetually stealing from the many to the few; and that there is a perpetual tendency in the Legislative and Executive departments to absorb all power. If the judges are appointed at short intervals, either by the Legislative or by the Executive authority, they will naturally, and almost necessarily, become mere dependents upon the appointing power. If they have a desire to obtain, or to hold office, they will at all times evince a desire to follow, and obey the will of the predominant power in the state. Public justice will be administered with a faltering and feeble hand. The Judiciary will under such circumstances seek little but the possession of office, and the approbation of those who value, because they can control it. It will be apt to decree, what best suits the opinions of the day; and to forget, that the precepts of the law rest on eternal foundations, and are not to be changed at the arbitrary will of the judges. The rulers and the citizens will not stand upon an equal ground in litigations. The favorites of the day will overcome by their power, or seduce by their influence. And thus the fundamental maxim of a republic, that it ought to be a Government of laws, and not of men, will be silently disproved, or openly abandoned.

§305. In the next place, all these considerations acquire still more cogency and force, when applied to constitutional questions. These questions may arise, not merely between citizen and citizen, but between State and State, and between the United States and the States. Can it be supposed, for a moment, that men, who hold their offices for two, or four, or even six years, would be generally found firm enough to resist the will of those, who have appointed them, and can so soon displace them? If they are to administer the Constitution, according to its true spirit and principles, to support the weak against the strong, the humble against the powerful, the few against the many; how can they be expected to possess the requisite independence and impartiality, unless they hold their offices by a tenure beyond the reach of the power of the Legislature and Executive? He is ill read in the history of human experience, who does not foresee, as well as provide for, such exigencies. In republics, the other departments of the government may sometimes, if not frequently, be found combined in hostility against the Judiciary; and even the people, for a while, under the influence of party spirit and turbulent factions, may be ready to abandon the judges to their fate. Few men possess the firmness to resist the torrent of popular opinion, or popular prejudice. Still fewer are content to sacrifice present ease and popular favor, in order to earn the slow rewards of a conscientious discharge of their duty. If we would preserve the Constitution from internal, as well as from external perils, from the influences of the great, and the corruptions of the selfish and ambitious, we must place around it every guard, which experience has shown will encourage good men in their integrity, and will awe bad men in their intrigues. If the Constitution ever perishes, it will be, when the Judiciary shall have become feeble and inert, and either unwilling or unable to perform the solemn duties imposed upon it by the original structure of the Government. Hitherto, no attempts have been made to alter the Constitution, in respect to the tenure of office. The views of the framers of it have, in all the vicissitudes of party, still been supported by the general approbation of the people. And, if any changes shall hereafter be proposed, which shall diminish the just authority of this, as an independent department, they will only be matters of regret, so far as they may take away any checks to the exercise of arbitrary power by either of the other Departments of the Government.

§306. But the tenure of office during good behavior, would

be of little consequence, if Congress possessed an unlimited power over the compensation of judges. It has been well remarked, that, in the course of human affairs, a power over a man's subsistence is a power over his will. If Congress could diminish at pleasure the salaries of the judges, they could reduce it to a mere pittance, and thus might sink them into an abject dependence. The Constitution has, therefore, wisely provided, that the compensation of the judges shall not be diminished during their continuance in office, and shall be paid at stated times.

§307. It is almost unnecessary to add, that, although the Constitution has thus sedulously endeavored, from motives of public good, to place the independence of the Judiciary upon a solid basis; yet, the judges are not beyond the reach of the law. They hold their offices during good behavior only; and for misconduct, they may be removed from office upon impeachment. Thus, personal responsibility is brought home to them; and, like all other public functionaries, they are also bound by an oath to obey the laws, and support the Constitution.

CHAPTER XXXI.

POWERS AND JURISDICTION OF THE JUDICIARY.

§308. THE next, the second section of the third article, contains an exposition of the jurisdiction appertaining to the National Judiciary. "The judicial power shall extend to all cases in law and equity, arising under this Constitution, the laws of the United States, and treaties made, or which shall be made, under their authority; to all cases affecting ambassadors, other public ministers, and consuls; to all cases of admiralty and maritime jurisdiction; to controversies, to which the United States shall be a party; to controversies between two or more States; between a State and citizens of another State; between citizens of different States; between citizens of the same State, claiming lands under grants of different States; and between a State, or the citizens thereof, and foreign states, citizens, or subjects."

§309. In a work like the present, it is impossible to present a full exposition of the reasons for conferring the different portions of this jurisdiction, all having the same general object, the promotion of harmony, good order, and justice at home, and the preservation of peace and commercial intercourse abroad. In a general summary, it may be said, that the jurisdiction extends to cases arising under the Constitution,

233

laws, and treaties, of the United States, because the judicial power ought to be coextensive with the legislative and executive powers, in order to ensure uniformity of interpretation and operation of the Constitution, laws, and treaties, and the means of enforcing rights, duties, and remedies, arising under them. It extends to cases affecting ambassadors, public ministers, and consuls, because they are officers of foreign nations, entitled by the law of nations to the protection of our Government; and any misconduct towards them might lead to private retaliations, or open hostilities, on the part of the offended Government. It extends to cases of admiralty and maritime jurisdiction, because such cases grow out of, and are intimately connected with, foreign commerce and navigation, with offences committed on the ocean, and with the right of making captures, and carrying on the operations of war. It extends to controversies, to which the United States is a party, because the Government ought to possess a right to resort to National courts, to decide all controversies and contracts, to which it is a party. It extends to controversies between two or more States, in order to furnish a peaceable and impartial tribunal, to decide cases, where different States claim conflicting rights, in order to prevent gross irritations, and border warfare. It extends to controversies between a State and the citizens of another State; because a State ought not to be the sole judge of its own rights, as against the citizens of other States. It extends to controversies between citizens of different States; because these controversies may embrace questions, upon which the tribunals of neither State could be presumed to be perfectly impartial, from the peculiar public interests involved in them. It extends to controversies between citizens of the same State, claiming lands under grants of different States; because a similar doubt of impartiality may arise. It extends to controversies between a State, or its citizens, and foreign States, citizens, or subjects; because foreign States and citizens have a right to demand an impartial tribunal for the decision of cases, to which they are a party; and want of confidence in the tribunals of one party may be fatal to the public tranquility, or at least, may create a discouraging sense of injustice. Even this cursory view cannot fail to satisfy reasonable minds of the importance of the powers of the National Judiciary to the tranquility and sovereignty of the States, and to the preservation of the rights and liberties of the people.

§310. But the subject is so important, and has so often become matter of political discussion, and constitutional inquiry, that it deserves to be examined more at large in this place. We shall, therefore, proceed to examine each of these cases, in which jurisdiction is conferred, in the order, in which it stands, in order more fully to comprehend the particular reasons, on which it is founded.

§311. And first: The judicial power extends to all cases in law and equity, arising under the Constitution, the laws, and the treaties, of the United States. And, by cases in this clause, we are to understand criminal, as well as civil, cases.

§312. The propriety of the delegation of jurisdiction, in "cases arising under the Constitution," rests on the obvious consideration, that there ought always to be some constitutional method of giving effect to constitutional provisions. What, for instance, would avail restrictions on the authority of the State Legislatures, without some constitutional mode of enforcing the observance of them? The States are, by the Constitution, prohibited from doing a variety of things; some of which are incompatible with the interests of the Union; others, with its peace and safety; others, with the principles of good government. The imposition of duties on imported articles, the declaration of war, and the emission of paper money, are examples of each kind. No man of sense will believe, that such prohibitions would be scrupulously regarded, without some effectual power in the Government to restrain, or correct the infractions of them. The power must be either a direct negative on the State laws, or an authority in the National courts to overrule such, as shall manifestly be in contravention to the Constitution. The latter course was thought by the convention to be preferable to the former; and it is, without question, by far the most acceptable to the States.

§313. The same reasoning applies, with equal force, to "cases arising under the laws of the United States." In fact, the necessity of uniformity, in the interpretation of these laws, would of itself settle every doubt, that could be raised on the subject. "Thirteen independent courts of final jurisdiction over the same causes, (it was said,) is a Hydra in government, from which nothing but contradiction and confusion can proceed." The number is now increased to twenty-six.

§314. There is still more cogency, if it be possible, in the reasoning, as applied to "cases arising under treaties made, or which shall be made, under the authority of the United States." Without this power, there would be perpetual danger of collision, and even of war, with foreign powers, and an utter incapacity to fulfil the ordinary obligations of treaties. The want of this power was (as we have seen) a most mischievous defect in the Confederation; and subjected the country, not only to violations of its plighted faith, but to the gross, and almost proverbial, imputation of punic insincerity.

§315. It is observable, that the language is, that "the judicial power shall extend to all cases *in law and equity,*" arising under the Constitution, laws, and treaties, of the United States. What is to be understood by "cases in law and equity," in this clause? Plainly, cases at the common law, as contradistinguished from cases in equity, according to the known distinction in the jurisprudence of England, which our ancestors brought with them upon their emigration, and with which all the American States were familiarly acquainted. Here, then, at least the Constitution of the United States appeals to, and adopts, the common law, to the extent of making it a rule in the pursuit of remedial justice in the courts of the Union. If the remedy must be in law, or in equity, according to the course of proceedings at the common law, in cases arising under the Constitution, laws, and treaties of the United States, it would seem irresistibly to follow, that the principles of decision, by which these remedies must be administered, must be derived from the same source. Hitherto, such has been the uniform interpretation and mode of administering justice, in civil suits, in the courts of the United States, in this class of cases.

§316. Another inquiry may be, what constitutes a *case*, within the meaning of this clause. It is clear, that the Judicial department is authorized to exercise jurisdiction to the full extent of the Constitution, laws and treaties, of the United States, whenever any question respecting them shall assume such a form, that the judicial power is capable of acting upon it. When it has assumed such a form, it then becomes a case; and then, and not till then, the judicial power attaches to it. A case, then, in the sense of this clause of the Constitution, arises, when some subject, touching the Constitution, laws, or treaties, of the United States, is submitted to the court by a party, who asserts his rights in the form prescribed by law. In other words, a case is a suit in law or equity, instituted according to the regular course of judicial proceedings; and, when it involves any question arising under the Constitution, laws, or treaties, of the United States, it is within the judicial power confided to the Union.

§317. Cases arising under the Constitution, as contradistinguished from those, arising under the laws of the United States, are such as arise from the powers conferred, or privileges granted, or rights claimed, or protection secured, or prohibitions contained, in the Constitution itself, independent of any particular statute enactment. Many cases of this sort may easily be enumerated. Thus, if a citizen of one State should be denied the privileges of a citizen in another State; if a State should coin money, or make paper money a tender; if a person, tried for a crime against the United States, should be denied a trial by jury, or a trial in the State, where the crime is charged to be committed; if a person, held to labor, or service, in one State, under the laws thereof, should escape into another, and there should be a refusal to deliver him up to the party, to whom such service or labor may be due, in these, and many other cases, the question, to be judicially decided, would be a case arising under the Constitution. On the other hand, cases arising under the laws of the United States, are such as grow out of the legislation of Congress, within the scope of their constitutional authority, whether they constitute the right, or privilege, or claim, or protection, or defence, of the party, in whole or in part, by whom they are asserted. The same reasoning applies to cases arising under treaties. Indeed, wherever, in a judicial proceeding, any question arises, touching the validity of a treaty, or statute, or authority, exercised under the United States, or touching the construction of any clause of the Constitution, or any statute, or treaty, of the United States; or touching the validity of any statute, or authority exercised under any State, on the ground of repugnancy to the Constitution, laws, or treaties, of the United States, it has been invariably held to be a case, to which the judicial power of the United States extends.

§318. It has sometimes been suggested, that a case, to be within the purview of this clause, must be one, in which a party comes into court to demand something conferred on him by the Constitution, or a law, or a treaty, of the United States. But this construction is clearly too narrow. A case in law or equity consists of the right of the one party, as well as of the other, and may truly be said to arise under the Constitution, or a law, or a treaty, of the United States, whenever its correct decision depends on the construction of either. This is manifestly the construction given to the clause by Congress, by the *25th* section of the Judiciary act, (which was almost contemporaneous with the Constitution,) and there is no reason to doubt its solidity or correctness. Indeed, the main object of this clause would be defeated by any narrower construction; since the power was conferred for the purpose, in an especial manner, of producing a uniformity of construction of the Constitution, laws, and treaties, of the United States.

§319. Cases may also arise under laws of the United States by implication, as well as by express enactment; so that due redress may be administered by the judicial power of the United States. It is not unusual for a legislative act to involve consequences, which are not expressed. An officer, for example, is ordered to arrest an individual. It is not necessary, nor is it usual, to say, that he shall not be punished for obeying this order. His security is implied in the order itself. It is no unusual thing for an act of Congress to imply, without expressing, this very exemption from State control. The collectors of the revenue, the carriers of the mail, the mint establishment, and all those institutions, which are public in their nature, are examples in point. It has never been doubted, that all, who are employed in them, are protected, while in the line of their duty; and yet this protection is not expressed in any act of congress. It is incidental to, and is implied in, the several acts, by which those institutions are created; and it is secured to the individuals, employed in them, by the judicial power alone; that is, the judicial power is the instrument employed by the Government in administering this security.

§320. It has also been asked, and may again be asked, why the words, "cases in equity," are found in this clause? What equitable causes can grow out of the Constitution, laws, and treaties, of the United States? To this, the general answer seems at once clear and satisfactory. There is hardly a subject of litigation between individuals, which may not involve those ingredients of *fraud, accident, trust,* or *hardship,* which would render the matter an object of equitable, rather than of legal, jurisdiction, as the distinction is known and established in several of the States. It is the peculiar province, for instance, of a court of equity, to relieve against what are called hard bargains. These are contracts, in which, though there may have been no direct fraud or deceit, sufficient to invalidate them in a court of law; yet there may have been some undue and unconscionable advantage taken of the necessities, or misfortunes, of one of the parties, which a court of equity would not tolerate. In such cases, where foreigners were concerned on either side, it would be impossible for the Federal judicatories to do justice, without an equitable, as well as a legal jurisdiction. Agreements to convey lands, claimed under the grants of different States, may afford another example of the necessity of an equitable jurisdiction in the Federal courts. This reasoning may not be so palpable in those States, where the formal and technical distinction between LAW and EQUITY is not maintained, as in other States, where it is exemplified by every day's practice.

§321. The next clause, extends the judicial power "to all cases affecting ambassadors, other public ministers, and consuls." The propriety of this delegation of power to the National Judiciary will scarcely be questioned by any persons, who have duly reflected upon the subject. There are various grades of public ministers, from ambassadors, (which is the highest grade,) down to common resident ministers, whose rank, and diplomatic precedence, and authority, are well known, and well ascertained, in the law and usages of nations. But whatever may be their relative rank and grade, public ministers of every class are the immediate representatives of their sovereigns. As such representatives, they owe no subjection to any laws, but those of their own country, any more than their sovereign; and their actions are not generally deemed subject to the control of the private law of that State, wherein they are appointed to reside. He, that is subject to the coercion of laws, is necessarily dependent on that power, by whom those laws were made. But public ministers ought, in order to perform their duties to their own sovereign, to be independent of every power, except that by which they are sent; and, of consequence, ought not to be subject to the mere municipal law of that nation, wherein they are to exercise their functions. The rights, the powers, the duties, and the privileges, of public ministers, are, therefore, to be determined, not by any municipal constitutions, but by the law of nature and nations, which is equally obligatory upon all sovereigns, and all states. What these rights, powers, duties, and privileges are, are inquiries properly belonging to a treatise on the law of nations, and need not be discussed here. But it is obvious, that every question, in which these rights, powers, duties, and privileges are involved, is so intimately connected with the public peace, and policy, and diplomacy, of the nation, and touches the dignity and interest of the sovereigns of the ministers concerned so deeply, that it would be unsafe, that they should be submitted to any other, than the highest judicature of the nation.

§322. Consuls, indeed, have not in strictness a diplomatic character. They are deemed to be mere commercial agents: and, therefore, partake of the ordinary character of such agents; and are subject to the municipal laws of the countries, where they reside. Yet, as they are the public agents of the nation, to which they belong and are often entrusted with the performance of very delicate functions of state, and as they might be greatly embarrassed by being subject to the ordinary jurisdiction of inferior tribunals, State and National, it was thought highly expedient to extend the original jurisdiction of the Supreme Court to them also. The propriety of vesting jurisdiction, in such cases, in some of the National courts, seems hardly to have been questioned by the most zealous opponents of the Constitution. And in cases *against* ambassadors, and other foreign ministers, and consuls, the jurisdiction has been deemed exclusive.

§323. The next clause extends the judicial power "to all cases of admiralty and maritime jurisdiction."

§324. The admiralty and maritime jurisdiction, (and the word, "maritime," was doubtless added to guard against any narrow interpretation of the preceding word, "admiralty,") conferred by the Constitution, embraces two great classes of cases; one dependent upon locality, and the other upon the nature of the contract. The first, respects acts, or injuries, done upon the high sea, where all nations claim a common right and common jurisdiction; or acts, or injuries, done upon the coast of the sea; or, at farthest, acts and injuries done within the ebb and flow of the tide. The second, respects contracts, claims, and services purely maritime, and touching rights and duties appertaining to commerce and navigation. The former is again divisible into two great branches, one embracing captures, and questions of prize arising by the rights of war; the other embracing acts, torts, and injuries, strictly of civil cognizance, independent of belligerent operations.

241

§325. By the law of nations, the cognizance of all captures, *jure belli*, or, as it is more familiarly phrased, of all questions of prize, and their incidents, belongs exclusively to the courts of the country, to which the captors belong, and from whom they derive their authority to make the capture. No neutral nation has any right to inquire into, or to decide upon, the validity of such capture, even though it should concern property belonging to its own citizens or subjects, unless its own sovereign or territorial rights are violated; but the sole and exclusive jurisdiction belongs to the courts of the capturing belligerent. And this jurisdiction, by the common consent of nations, is vested exclusively in courts of admiralty, possessing an original, or appellate jurisdiction. The courts of common law are bound to abstain from any decision of questions of this sort, whether they arise directly or indirectly in judgement. The remedy for illegal acts of capture is, by the institution of proper prize proceedings in the prize courts of the captors. If justice be there denied, the nation itself becomes responsible to the parties aggrieved; and if every remedy is refused, it then becomes a subject for the consideration of the nation, to which the parties aggrieved belong, which may vindicate their rights, either by a peaceful appeal to negotiation, or by a resort to arms.

§326. It is obvious, upon the slightest consideration, that the cognizance of all questions of prize, made under the authority of the United States, ought to belong exclusively to the National courts. How, otherwise, can the legality of the captures be satisfactorily ascertained, or deliberately vindicated? It seems not only a natural, but a necessary, appendage to the power of war, and of negotiation with foreign nations. It would otherwise follow, that the peace of the whole nation might be put at hazard, at any time, by the misconduct of one of its members. It could neither restore, upon an illegal capture; nor, in many cases, afford any adequate redress for the wrong; nor punish the aggressor. It would be powerless and palsied. It could not perform, or compel the performance, of the duties required by the law of nations. It would be a sovereign, without any solid attribute of sovereignty; and move in chains, only to betray its own imbecility. Even under the confederation, the power to decide upon questions of capture and prize was exclusively conferred, in the last resort, upon the National court of appeals. But, like all other powers conferred by that instrument, it was totally disregarded, wherever it interfered with State policy, or with extensive popular interests. We have seen, that the sentences of the National prize court of appeals were treated as mere nullities; and were incapable of being enforced, until after the establishment of the present Constitution. The same reasoning, which conducts us to the conclusion, that the National courts ought to have jurisdiction of this class of admiralty cases, conducts us equally to the conclusion, that, to be effectual for the administration of international justice, it ought to be exclusive. And, accordingly, it has been constantly held, that this jurisdiction is exclusive in the courts of the United States.

§327. The other branch of admiralty jurisdiction, dependent upon locality, respects civil acts, torts, and injuries done on the sea, or, in certain cases, on waters of the sea, where the tide ebbs and flows, without any claim of exercising the rights of war. Such are cases of assaults, and other personal injuries; cases of collision, or running of ships against each other; cases of spoliation and damage, (as they are technically called,) such as illegal seizures, or depredations upon property; cases of illegal dispossession, or withholding possession from the owners of ships, commonly called possessory suits; cases of seizures under municipal authority for supposed breaches of revenue, or other prohibitory laws; and cases of salvage for meritorious services performed, in saving property, whether derelict, or wrecked, or captured, or otherwise in imminent hazard from extraordinary perils.

§328. It is obvious, that this class of cases has, or may have, an intimate relation to the rights and duties of foreigners, in navigation and maritime commerce. It may materially affect our intercourse with foreign states; and may raise many questions of international law, not merely touching private claims, but national sovereignty, and national reciprocity. Thus, for instance, if a collision should take place at sea between an American and a foreign ship, many important questions of public law might be connected with its just decision; for it is obvious, that it could not be governed by the mere municipal law of either country. So, if a case of recapture, or other salvage service, performed to a foreign ship, should occur, it must be decided by the general principles of maritime law, and the doctrines of national reciprocity. Where a recapture is made of a friendly ship from the hands of its enemy, the general doctrine now established is, to restore it upon salvage, if the foreign country, to which it belongs, adopts a reciprocal rule; or to condemn it to the recaptors, if the like rule is adopted in the foreign country. And, in other cases of salvage, the doctrines of international and maritime law come into full activity, rather than those of any mere municipal code. There is, therefore, a peculiar fitness in appropriating this class of cases to the National tribunals; since they will be more likely to be there decided upon large and comprehensive principles, and to receive a more uniform adjudication; and thus to become more satisfactory to foreigners.

§329. The remaining class respects contracts, claims, and services purely maritime. Among these, are the claims of material-men and others, for repairs and outfits of ships belonging to foreign nations, or to other States, bottomry bonds, for moneys lent on ships in foreign ports, to relieve their distresses, and enable them to complete their voyages; surveys of vessels damaged by perils of the seas; pilotage on the high seas; and suits for mariners' wages. These, indeed, often arise in the course of the commerce and navigation of the United States; and seem emphatically to belong, as incidents, to the power to regulate commerce. But they may also affect the commerce and navigation of foreign nations. Repairs may be done, and supplies be furnished, to foreign ships; money may be lent on foreign bottoms; pilotage and mariners' wages may become due in voyages in foreign employment; and in such cases, the general maritime law enables the courts of admiralty to administer a wholesome and prompt justice. Indeed, in many of these cases, as the courts of admiralty entertain suits *in rem,* (that is, upon the thing,) as well as *in personam,* (that is, upon the person) they are often the only courts, in which an effectual redress can be afforded, especially when it is desirable to enforce a specific maritime lien, or claim, in the nature of a pledge.

§330. So that we see, that the admiralty jurisdiction naturally connects itself, on the one hand, with our diplomatic relations and duties to foreign nations, and their subjects; and, on the other hand, with the great interests of navigation and commerce, foreign and domestic. There is, then, a peculiar wisdom in giving to the National Government a jurisdiction of this sort, which cannot be wielded, except for the general good; and which multiplies the securities for the public peace abroad, and gives to commerce and navigation the most encouraging support at home. It may be added, that, in many of the cases included in these latter classes, the same reasons do not exist, as in cases of prize, for an exclusive jurisdiction; and, therefore, whenever the common law is competent to give a remedy in the State courts, they may retain their accustomed concurrent jurisdiction in the administration of it.

§331. We have been thus far considering the admiralty and maritime jurisdiction in civil cases only. But it also embraces all public offences, committed on the high seas, and in creeks, haven, basins, and bays, within the ebb and flow of the tide; at least, in such as are out of the body of any county of a State. In these places, the jurisdiction of the courts of admiralty over offences is exclusive; for that of the courts of common law is limited to such offences, as are committed within the body of some county. And on the seacoast, there is an alternate, or divided jurisdiction of the courts of common law, and admiralty, in places between high and low water mark; the former having jurisdiction when, and as far as the tide is out, and the latter when, and as far as the tide is in, or to high water mark. This criminal jurisdiction of the admiralty is therefore exclusively vested in the National Government; and may be exercised over such crimes and offences, as Congress may, from time to time, delegate to the cognizance of the National courts. The propriety of vesting this criminal jurisdiction in the National Government depends upon the same reasoning, and is established by the same general considerations, as have been already suggested in regard to civil cases. It is essentially connected with the due regulation, and protection of our commerce and navigation on the high seas, and with our rights and duties in regard to foreign nations, and their subjects, in the exercise of common sovereignty on the ocean. The States, as such, are not known in our intercourse with foreign nations, and are not recognized as common sovereigns on the ocean. And if they were permitted to exercise criminal or civil jurisdiction thereon, there would be endless embarrassments, arising from the conflict of their laws, and the most serious dangers of perpetual controversies with foreign nations. In short, the peace of the Union would be constantly put at hazard by acts, over which it had no control; and by assertions of right, which it might wholly disclaim.

§332. The next clause extends the judicial power "to controversies, to which the United States shall be a party." It scarcely seems possible to raise a reasonable doubt, as to the propriety of giving to the National courts jurisdiction of cases, in which the United States is a party. It would be a perfect novelty in the history of national jurisprudence, as well as of public law, that a sovereign had no authority to sue in his own courts. Unless this power were given to the United States, the enforcement of all its rights, powers, contracts, and privileges, in its sovereign capacity, would be at the mercy of the States. They must be enforced, if at all, in the state tribunals. And there would not only not be any compulsory power over those courts to perform such functions; but there would not be any means of producing uniformity in their decisions. A sovereign, without the means of enforcing civil rights, or compelling the performance, either civilly or criminally, of public duties, on the part of the citizens, would be a most extraordinary anomaly. It would prostrate the Union at the feet of the States. It

would compel the National Government to become a suppli-
cant for justice before the judicature of those, who were by
other parts of the Constitution placed in subordination to it.

§333. The next clause extends the judicial power "to controversies between two or more States; between a State and the
citizens of another State; between citizens of different States,
claiming lands under grants of different States; and between a
State, or the citizens thereof, and foreign States, citizens, or
subjects." Of these, we will speak in their order. And, first,
"Controversies between two or more States." This power
seems to be essential to the preservation of the peace of the
Union. History gives a horrid picture of the dissensions and
private wars, which distracted and desolated Germany, prior to
the institution of the imperial chamber by Maximilian, towards
the close of the fifteenth century; and informs us, at the same
time, of the vast influence of that institution, in appeasing the
disorders, and establishing the tranquility, of the empire. This
was a court invested with authority to decide finally all differences among the members of the Germanic body. But we need
not go for illustrations to the history of other countries. Our
own has presented, in past times, abundant proofs of the irri-
tating effects resulting from territorial disputes, and interfering
claims of boundary between the States. And there are yet controversies of this sort, which have brought on a border warfare, at once dangerous to public repose, and incompatible
with the public interests.

§334. Under the Confederation, authority was given to the
National Government, to hear and determine, (in the manner
pointed out in the article,) in the last report, on appeal, all disputes and differences between two or more States concerning
boundary, jurisdiction, or any other cause whatsoever. Before
the adoption of this instrument, as well as afterwards, very ir-
ritating and vexatious controversies existed between several of
the States, in respect to soil, jurisdiction, and boundary; and
threatened the most serious public mischiefs. Some of these
controversies were heard and determined by the court of commissioners, appointed by Congress. But, notwithstanding

these adjudications, the conflict was maintained in some cases, until after the establishment of the present Constitution.

§335. Before the Revolution, controversies between the colonies, concerning the extent of their rights of soil, territory, jurisdiction, and boundary, under their respective characters, were heard and determined before the King in council, who exercised original jurisdiction therein, upon the principles of feudal sovereignty. This jurisdiction was often practically asserted, as in the case of the dispute between Massachusetts and New Hampshire, decided by the Privy Council, in 1679; and in the case of the dispute between New Hampshire and New York, in 1764. Lord Hardwicke recognized this appellate jurisdiction in the most deliberate manner, in the great case of *William Penn* v. *Lord Baltimore*. The same necessity, which gave rise to it in our colonial state, must continue to operate through all future time. Some tribunal, exercising such authority, is essential to prevent an appeal to the sword, and a dissolution of the government. That it ought to be established under the National, rather than under the State, Government; or, to speak more properly, that it can be safety established under the former only, would seem to be a position self-evident, and requiring no reasoning to support it. It may justly be presumed, that under the National Government, in all controversies of this sort, the decision will be impartially made, according to the principles of justice; and all the usual and most effectual precautions are taken to secure this impartiality, by confiding it to the highest judicial tribunal.

§336. Next: "Controversies between a State and the citizens of another State." There are other sources, besides interfering claims of boundary, from which bickerings and animosities may spring up among the members of the Union. The past experience of the Country has furnished some melancholy instances of this truth. Under the Confederation, laws, of a character utterly indefensible in point of justice and principle, were passed in some of the States, affecting the rights of citizens of other States. And though the Constitution establishes particular guards against the repetition of those instances, which have hitherto made their appearance; yet it is warrantable to apprehend, that the spirit, which produced them, will assume new shapes, that could not be foreseen, not specifically provided against. Whatever practices may have a tendency to district the harmony of the States, are proper objects of national superintendence and control. It may be esteemed the basis of the Union, that 'the citizens of each State shall be entitled to all the privileges and immunities of citizens of the several States.' And if it be a just principle, that every government ought to possess the means of executing its own provisions by its own authority, it will follow, that, in order to the inviolable maintenance of that equality of privileges and immunities, to which the citizens of the Union will be entitled, the National Judiciary ought to preside in all cases, in which one State, or its citizens, are opposed to another State, or its citizens. To secure the full effect of so fundamental a provision against all evasion and subterfuge, it is necessary, that its interpretation should be committed to that tribunal, which, having no local attachments, will be likely to be impartial between the different States and their citizens, and which, owing its official existence to the Union, will never be likely to feel any bias inauspicious to the principles, on which it is founded. It may be added, that the reasonableness of the agency of the National courts in cases, in which the State tribunals cannot be supposed to be impartial, speaks for it. No man ought certainly to be a judge in his own case, or in any cause, in respect to which he has the least interest or bias. This principle had no inconsiderable weight in designating the national courts, as the proper tribunals for the determination of controversies between different States and their citizens.

§337. And here a most important question of a constitutional nature was formerly litigated; and that is, whether the jurisdiction, given by the Constitution, in cases, in which a State is a party, extended to suits brought *against* a State, as well as *by* it, or was exclusively confined to the latter. It is obvious, that, if a suit could be brought, by any citizen of one State against another State, upon any contract, or matter of property, the State would be constantly subjected to judicial action, to enforce private rights against it in its sovereign capacity. Accordingly, at a very early period, numerous suits were brought against particular States by their creditors, to enforce the payment of debts, or other claims. The question was made, and most elaborately considered, in the celebrated case of *Chisholm* v. *Georgia;* and the majority of the Supreme Court held, that the judicial power, under the Constitution, applied equally to suits brought *by,* and suits brought *against* a State. All the learned judges, on that occasion, delivered opinions, containing the grounds of their respective judgements. It is not my intention to go over these grounds, although they are stated with great ability and legal learning, and exhibit a very thorough mastery of the whole subject. The decision created general alarm among the States; and an amendment was proposed, and ratified by the States, by which the power was entirely taken away, so far as it regards suits brought *against* a State. It is in the following words: "The judicial power of the United States shall not be construed to extend to any suit in law, or equity, commenced or prosecuted *against* one of the United States, *by* citizens of another State, or *by* citizens, or subjects of any foreign State." This amendment was construed to include suits then pending, as well as suits to be commended thereafter; and, accordingly, all the suits then pending were dismissed, without any further adjudication.

§338. Since this amendment has been made, a question of equal importance has arisen; and that is, whether the amendment applies to original suits only, brought against a State, leaving the appellate jurisdiction of the Supreme Court in its full vigor over all constitutional questions arising in the progress of any suit brought by a State, in any State court, against any private citizen or alien. But this question will more properly come under review, when we are considering the nature and extent of the appellate jurisdiction of the Supreme Court. At present, it is only necessary to state, that it has been solemnly adjudged, that the amendment applies only to original suits against a State; and does not touch the appellate jurisdiction of the Supreme Court to re-examine, on an appeal or writ or error, a judgement or decree rendered in any State court, in a suit brought originally *by* a State against any private person.

§339. Another inquiry, suggested by the original clause, as well as by the amendment, is, when a State is properly to be deemed a party to a suit, so as to avail itself of, or to exempt itself from, the operation of the jurisdiction conferred by the Constitution. To such an inquiry, the proper answer is, that a State, in the sense of the Constitution, is a party only, when it is on the record as such; and it sues, or is sued in its political capacity. It is not sufficient, that it may have an interest in a suit between other persons, or that its rights, powers, privileges, or duties, may come therein incidentally in question. It must be in terms a plaintiff or defendant, so that the judgement, or decree, may be binding upon it, as it is in common suits, binding upon parties and privies. The point arose in an early stage of the government, in a suit between private persons, where one party asserted the land in controversy to be in Connecticut, and the other in New York; and the court held, that neither State could be considered as a party. It has been again discussed in some late cases; and the doctrine now firmly established is, that a State is not a party in the sense of the Constitution, unless it appears on the record, as such, either as plaintiff or defendant. It is not sufficient, that it may have an interest in the cause, or that the parties before the Court are sued for acts done, as agents of the State. In short, the very immunity of a State from being made a party, constitutes, or may constitute, a solid ground, why the suit should be maintained against other parties, who act as its agents, or claim under its title; although otherwise, as the principal, it might be fit, that the State should be made a party upon the common principles of a court of equity.

§340. The same principle applies to cases, where a State has an interest in a corporation; as, when it is a stockholder in an incorporated bank, the corporation is still suable, although the State, as such, is exempted from any action. The State does not, by becoming a corporator, identify itself with the corporation.

The bank, in such a case, is not the State, although the State holds an interest in it. Nor will it make a difference in the case, that the State has the sole interest in the corporation, if in fact it creates other persons corporators. An analogous case will be found in the authority, given by an act of Congress to the postmaster-general, to bring suits in his official capacity. In such suits, the United States are not understood to be a party, although the suits solely regard their interests. The postmaster-general does not, in such cases, sue under the clause giving jurisdiction, "in controversies, to which the United States shall be a party;" but under the clause extending the jurisdiction to cases arising under the laws of a United States.

§341. It may, then, be laid down, as a rule, which admits of no exception, that, in all cases under the Constitution of the United States, where jurisdiction depends upon the party, it is the party named on the record. Consequently the amendment, above referred to, which restrains the jurisdiction granted by the Constitution over suits against States, is of necessity limited to those suits, in which a State is a party on the record. The amendment has its full effect, if the Constitution is construed, as it would have been construed, had the jurisdiction never been extended to suits brought against a State by the citizens of another State, or by aliens.

§342. Next: "Controversies between citizens of different States." Although the necessity of this power may not stand upon grounds quite as strong, as some of the preceding, there are high motives of state policy and public justice, by which it can be clearly vindicated. There are many cases, in which such a power may be indispensable, or in the highest degree expedient, to carry into effect some of the privileges and immunities conferred, and some of the prohibitions upon States expressly declared, in the Constitution. For example: It is declared, that "the citizens of each State shall be entitled to all the privileges and immunities of citizens of the several States." Suppose an attempt is made to evade, or withhold these privileges and immunities, would it not be right to allow the party aggrieved an opportunity of claiming them, in a contest with a citizen of the State, before a tribunal, at once national and impartial? Suppose a State should pass a tender law, or law impairing the obligation of private contracts, or should, in the course of its legislation, grant unconstitutional preferences to its own citizens, is it not clear, that the jurisdiction to enforce the obligations of the Constitution, in such cases, ought to be confided to the national tribunals? These cases are not purely imaginary. They have actually occurred; and may again occur under peculiar circumstances, in the course of State legislation. What was the fact under the Confederation? Each state was obliged to acquiesce in the degree of justice, which another State might choose to yield to its citizens. There was not only danger of animosities growing up from this source; but, in point of fact, there did grow up retaliatory legislation, to meet such real or imagined grievances.

§343. Nothing can conduce more to general harmony and confidence among all the States, than a consciousness, that controversies are not exclusively to be decided by the State tribunals; but may, at the election of the party, be brought before the National tribunals. Besides; it cannot escape observation, that the judges in different States hold their offices by a very different tenure. Some hold during good behavior; some for a term of years; some for a single year; some are irremovable, except upon impeachment; and others may be removed upon address of the Legislature. Under such circumstances, it cannot but be presumed, that there may arise a course of State policy, or State legislation, exceedingly injurious to the interests of the citizens of other States, both as to real and to personal property. It would require an uncommon exercise of candor or credulity to affirm, that, in cases of this sort, all the State tribunals would be wholly without State prejudice, or State feelings; or, that they would be as earnest in resisting the encroachments of State authority upon the just rights, and interests of the citizens of other States, as a tribunal differently constituted, and wholly independent of State authority. And, if justice should be as fairly and as firmly administered in the former, as in the latter, still the mischiefs would be most serious, if the public opinion did not indulge such a belief. Justice, in cases of this sort, should not only be above all reproach, but above all suspicion. The sources of State irritations and State jealousies are sufficiently numerous, without leaving open one so copious and constant, as the belief, or the dread, of wrong in the administration of State justice. Besides; if the public confidence should continue to follow the State tribunals, (as in many cases it doubtless will,) the provision will become inert and harmless; for, as the party will have his election of the forum, he will not be inclined to desert the State courts, unless for some sound reason, founded either in the nature of his cause, or in the influence of State prejudices. On the other hand, there can be no real danger of injustice on the other side in the decisions of the National tribunals; because the cause must still be decided upon the true principles of the local law, and not by any foreign jurisprudence. There is another circumstance of no small importance, as a matter of policy, and that is, the tendency of such a power to increase the confidence and credit between the commercial and agricultural States. No man can be insensible to the value, in promoting credit, on the belief of there being a prompt, efficient, and impartial administration of justice in enforcing contracts.

§344. The next inquiry, growing out of this part of the clause, is, who are to be deemed citizens of different States, within the meaning of it. Are all persons born within a State to be always deemed citizens of that State, notwithstanding any change of domicil? Or does their citizenship change with their change of domicil? The answer to this inquiry is equally plain and satisfactory. The Constitution having declared, that the citizens of each State shall be entitled to all privileges and immunities of citizens in the several States, every person, who is a citizen of one State, and removes into another, with the intention of taking up his residence and inhabitancy there, becomes *ipso facto* a citizen of the State, where he resides; and he then ceases to be a citizen of the State, from which he has removed his residence. Of course, when he gives up his new residence, or domicil, and returns to his native, or other State residence

254

or domicil, he reacquires the character of the latter. What circumstances shall constitute such a change of residence or domicil, is an inquiry, more properly belonging to a treatise upon public or municipal law, than to commentaries upon constitutional law. In general, however, it may be said, that a removal from one State into another, with an intention of residence, or with a design of becoming an inhabitant, constitutes a chance of domicil, and of course a change of citizenship. But a person, who is a native citizen of one State, never ceases to be a citizen thereof, until he has acquired a new citizenship elsewhere. Residence in a foreign country has no operation upon his character, as a citizen, although it may, for purposes of trade and commerce, impress him with the character of the country. To change allegiance is one thing; to change inhabitancy is quite another thing. The right and the power are not coextensive in each case. Every citizen of a State is *ipso facto* a citizen of the United States.

§345. And a person, who is a naturalized citizen of the United States, by a like residence in any state in the Union, becomes *ipso facto* a citizen of that State. So a citizen of a Territory of the Union, by a like residence, acquires the character of the State, where he resides. But a naturalized citizen of the United States, or a citizen of a Territory, is not a citizen of a State, entitled to sue in the courts of the United States, in virtue of that character, while he resides in any such Territory, nor until he has acquired a residence or domicil in the particular State.

§346. A corporation, as such, is not a citizen of a State, in the sense of the Constitution. But, if all the members of the corporation are citizens, their character will confer jurisdiction; for then it is substantially a suit by citizens, suing in their corporate name. And a citizen of a State is entitled to sue, as such, notwithstanding he is a trustee for others, or sues in *autre droit,* as it is technically called, that it, as representative of another. Thus, a citizen may sue, who is a trustee at law, for the benefit of the person entitled to the trust. And an administrator, and an executor, may sue for the benefit of the estate, which they represent; for, in each of these cases, it is their personal suit. But if citizens, who are parties to a suit, are merely nominally so; as, for instance, if magistrates are officially required to allow suits to be brought in their names for the use or benefit of a citizen or alien, the latter are deemed the substantial parties entitled to sue.

§347. Next: "Controversies between citizens of the same State, claiming lands under grants of different States." This clause was not in the first draft of the Constitution, but was added without any known objection to its propriety. It is the only instance, in which the Constitution directly contemplates the cognizance of disputes between citizens of the same State; but certainly not the only one, in which they may indirectly, upon Constitutional questions, have the benefit of the judicial power of the Union. It has been already remarked, that the reasonableness of the agency of the National courts, in cases in which the State tribunals cannot be supposed to be impartial, speaks for itself. No man ought certainly to be a judge in his own cause, or in any cause, in respect to which he has the least interest or bias. This principle has no inconsiderable weight in designating the National courts, as the proper tribunals for the determination of controversies between different States and their citizens. And it ought to have the same operation, in regard to some cases between citizens of the same State. Claims to land under grants of different States, founded upon adverse pretensions of boundary, are of this description. The courts of neither of the granting States could be expected to be unbiased. The laws may even have prejudged the question, and tied the courts down to decisions in favor of the grants of the State, to which they belonged. Where this has not been done, it would be natural, that the judges, as men, should feel a strong predilection for the claims of their own government. And, at all events, the providing of a tribunal, having no possible interest on the one side, more than the other, would have a most salutary tendency in quieting the jealousies, and disarming the resentments of the State, whose grant should be held invalid. This jurisdiction attaches not only to grants made by different

States, which were never united; but also to grants made by different States, which were originally united under one jurisdiction, if made since the separation, although the origin of the title may be traced back to an antecedent period.

§348. Next: "Controversies between a State, or the citizens thereof, and foreign states, citizens, or subjects." This provision has been vindicated in the following brief, but powerful manner. The peace of the whole ought not to be left at the disposal of a part. The Union will undoubtedly be answerable to foreign powers for the conduct of its members. And the responsibility for any injury ought ever to be accompanied with the faculty of preventing it. As the denial or perversion of justice, by the sentences of courts, is with reason classed among the just causes of war, it will follow, that the National Judiciary ought to have cognizance of all causes, in which the citizens of other countries are concerned. This is not less essential to the preservation of the public faith, than to the security of the public tranquility. A distinction may perhaps be imagined between cases arising upon treaties and the laws of nations, and those, which may stand merely on the footing of the municipal law. The former kind may be supposed proper for the National jurisdiction; the latter for that of the States. But it is at least problematical, whether an unjust sentence against a foreigner, where the subject of controversy was wholly relative to the *lex loci,* as it is called, that is, to the local law, would not, if unredressed, be an aggression upon his sovereign, as well as one, which violated the stipulations of a treaty, or the general law of nations. And a still greater objection to the distinction would result from the immense difficulty, if not impossibility, of a practical discrimination between the cases of one complexion, and those of the other. So great a proportion of the controversies, in which foreigners are parties, involve national questions, that it is by far the most safe and most expedient, to refer all those, in which they are concerned, to the National tribunals.

§349. In addition to these suggestions, it may be remarked, that it is of great national importance to advance public, as well as private credit, in our intercourse with foreign nations and their subjects. Nothing can be more beneficial in this respect, than to create an impartial tribunal, to which they may have resort upon all occasions, when it may be necessary to ascertain, or enforce their rights. Besides; it is not wholly immaterial, that the law, to be administered in cases of foreigners, is often very distinct from the mere municipal code of a State, and dependent upon the law merchant, or the more enlarged consideration of international rights and duties, in a case of conflict of the foreign and domestic laws. And it may fairly be presumed, that the National tribunals will, from the nature of their ordinary functions, become better acquainted with the general principles, which regulate subjects of this nature, than other courts, however enlightened, which are rarely required to discuss them.

§350. In regard to controversies between an American state and a foreign state, it is obvious, that the suit must, on one side at least, be wholly voluntary. No foreign state can be compelled to become a party, plaintiff or defendant in any of our tribunals. If, therefore, it chooses to consent to the institution of any suit, it is its consent alone, which can give effect to the jurisdiction of the court. It is certainly desirable, to furnish some peaceable mode of appeal in cases, where any controversy may exist between an American state and a foreign state, sufficiently important to require the grievance to be redressed by any other mode, than through the instrumentality of negotiations.

§351. The inquiry may here be made, who are to be deemed aliens, entitled to sue in the courts of the United States. The general answer is, any person, who is not a citizen of the United States. A foreigner, who is naturalized, is no longer entitled to the character of an alien. And when an alien is the substantial party, it matters not, whether he is a suitor in his own right; or whether he acts, as a trustee, or a personal representative; or whether he is compellable, by the local law, to sue through some official organ. A foreign corporation, established in a foreign country, all of those members are aliens, is entitled to sue in the same manner, that an alien may personally sue in the courts of the Union. It is not sufficient to vest the jurisdiction, that an alien is a party to the suit, unless the other party be a citizen. British subjects, born before the American Revolution, are to be deemed aliens; and may sue American citizens, born before the Revolution, as well as those born since that period. The Revolution severed the ties of allegiance; and made the inhabitants of each country aliens to each other. In relation to aliens, however, it should be stated, that they have a right to sue only, while peace exists between their country and our own. For, if a war breaks out, and they thereby become alien enemies, their right to sue is suspended, until the return of peace.

§352. We have now furnished our review of all the classes of cases, to which the judicial power of the United States extends; and this review will (we trust) amply establish the reasonableness, the sound policy, and in many cases, the indispensable necessity, of confining this jurisdiction on the National Government. The next inquiry naturally presented, is in what mode this jurisdiction is to be exercised, and in what courts it is to be vested. The next clause of the third article, answers the inquiry. It is as follows: "In all cases affecting ambassadors, other public ministers, and consults, and those, in which a State shall be a party, the Supreme Court shall have original jurisdiction. In all the other cases before mentioned, the Supreme Court shall have appellate jurisdiction, both as to law and fact, with such exceptions, and under such regulations, as the Congress shall make."

§353. By *original* jurisdiction, is here meant, that the party may commence his suit directly, and in the first instance, in the Supreme Court; *by appellate* jurisdiction is meant, a right to revise the decision or judgement, made by some other court, in which the suit has been instituted. For reasons of the highest public policy, original jurisdiction is given to the Supreme Court in cases, in which foreign nations and the States are concerned, as more appropriate to their dignity, and, under all circumstances, more fit to receive the decision of the highest tribunals. Other cases may conveniently be left to the inferior tribunals, and be brought by appeal for revision before the Supreme Court, if either party should require it, leaving to Congress the authority to regulate the right of appeal, in the exercise of a sound discretion.

§354. There are some additional suggestions upon this clause, which may, perhaps, be useful to that class of readers who desire to comprehend the full force and operation of this clause, in its various practical hearings.*

§355. The first remark, rising out of this clause, is, that, as the judicial power of the United States extends to all the cases enumerated in the Constitution, it may extend to all such cases, in any form, in which judicial power may be exercised. It may, therefore, extend to them in the shape of original, or of appellate jurisdiction, or of both; for there is nothing in the nature of the cases, which binds to the exercise of the one in preference to the other. But it is clear, from the language of the Constitution, that, in one form or the other, it is absolutely obligatory upon Congress, to vest all the jurisdiction in the National courts, in that class of cases, at least, where it has declared, that it shall extend to *"all cases."*

§356. In the next place, the jurisdiction, which is by the Constitution to be exercised by the Supreme Court in an *original* form, is very limited, and extends only to cases affecting ambassadors, and other public ministers, and consuls, and cases, where a State is a party. And Congress cannot constitutionally confer on it any other, or further original jurisdiction. This is one of the appropriate illustrations of the rule, that the affirmation of a power in particular cases, excludes it in all others. The clause itself would otherwise be wholly inoperative and nugatory. If it had been been intended to leave it to the discretion of Congress, to apportion the judicial power between the Supreme and inferior courts, according to the will of that body, it would have been useless to have proceeded fur-

---

*The following sections of this chapter can be omitted by those, whose studies may not enable them fully to understand this complicated subject.

ther, than to define the judicial power, and the tribunals, in which it should be vested. Affirmative words often, in their operation, imply a negative of other objects, than those affirmed; and in this case, a negative, or exclusive sense, must be given to the words, or they have no operation at all. If the solicitude of the Convention, respecting our peace with foreign powers, might induce a provision to be made, that the Supreme Court should have original jurisdiction in cases, which might be supposed to affect them; yet the clause would have proceeded no further, than to provide for such cases, unless some further restriction upon the powers of Congress had been intended. The direction, that the Supreme Court shall have appellate jurisdiction, in all cases, with such exceptions, as Congress shall make, will be no restriction, unless the words are to be deemed exclusive of original jurisdiction. And accordingly, the doctrine is firmly established, that the Supreme Court cannot constitutionally exercise any original jurisdiction, except in the enumerated cases. If Congress should confer it, it would be a mere nullity.

§357. But, although the Supreme Court cannot exercise original jurisdiction, in any cases, except those specially enumerated, it is certainly competent for Congress to vest, in any inferior courts of the United States, original jurisdiction of all other cases, not thus specially assigned to the Supreme Court; for there is nothing in the Constitution, which excludes such inferior courts from the exercise of such original jurisdiction. Original jurisdiction, so far as the Constitution gives a rule, is coextensive with the judicial power; and except, so far as the Constitution has made any distribution of it among the courts of the United States, it remains to be exercised in an original, or an appellate form, or in both, as Congress may, in their wisdom, deem fit. Now, the Constitution has made no distribution, except of the original and appellate jurisdiction of the Supreme Court. It has nowhere insinuated, that the inferior tribunals shall have no original jurisdiction. It has nowhere affirmed, that they shall have appellate jurisdiction. Both are left unrestricted and undefined. Of course, as the judicial power is to be vested in the Supreme and inferior courts of the Union, both are under the entire control and regulation of Congress.

§358. Another question, of a very different nature, is, whether the Supreme Court can exercise appellate jurisdiction in the class of cases, of which original jurisdiction is delegated to it by the Constitution; in other words, whether the original jurisdiction excludes the appellate; and so, on the other hand, whether the latter implies a negative of the former. It has been said, that the very distinction, taken in the Constitution, between original and appellate jurisdiction, presupposes, that, where the one can be exercised, the other cannot. For example, since the original jurisdiction extends to cases, where a State is a party, this is the proper form, in which such cases are to be brought before the Supreme Court; and, therefore, a case, where a State is a party, cannot be brought before the Court, in the exercise of its appellate jurisdiction; for the affirmative here, as well as in the cases of original jurisdiction, includes a negative of the cases not enumerated.

§359. If the correctness of this reasoning were admitted, it would establish no more, than that the Supreme Court could not exercise appellate jurisdiction in cases, where a State is a party. But it would by no means establish the doctrine, that the judicial power of the United States did not extend, in an appellate form, to such cases. The exercise of appellate jurisdiction is far from being limited, by the terms of the Constitution, to the Supreme Court. There can be no doubt, that Congress may create a succession of inferior tribunals, in each of which it may vest appellate, as well as original jurisdiction. This results from the very nature of the delegation of the judicial power in the Constitution. It is delegated in the most general terms; and may, therefore, be exercised under the authority of Congress, under every variety of form of original and of appellate jurisdiction. There is nothing in the instrument, which restrains or limits the power; and it must, consequently, subsist in the utmost latitude, of which it is in its nature susceptible. The result, then, would be, that, if the appellate jurisdiction over cases, to which a State is a party, could not, according to the terms of the Constitution, be exercised by the Supreme Court, it might be exercised exclusively by an inferior tribunal. The soundness of any reasoning, which would lead us to such a conclusion, may well be questioned.

§360. But the reasoning itself is not well founded. It proceeds upon the ground, that, because the character of the *party* alone, in some instances, entitled the Supreme Court to maintain original jurisdiction, without any reference to the nature of the case, therefore, the character of the *case,* which in other instances is made the very foundation of appellate jurisdiction, cannot attach. Now, that is the very point of controversy. It is not only not admitted, but it is solemnly denied. The argument might just as well, and with quite as much force, be pressed in the opposite direction. It might be said, that the appellate jurisdiction is expressly extended by the Constitution to all cases in law and equity, arising under the Constitution, laws, and treaties of the United States, and, therefore, in no such cases could the Supreme Court exercise original jurisdiction, even though a State were a party.

§361. The next inquiry is, whether the eleventh amendment to the Constitution has effected any change of the jurisdiction, thus confided to the judicial power of the United States. The words of the amendment, are, "The judicial power of the United States shall not be construed or prosecuted against one of the States, by citizens of another State, or by citizens or subjects of any foreign state." It is a part of our history, that, at the adoption of the Constitution, all the States were greatly indebted; and the apprehension, that these debts might be prosecuted in the National courts, formed a very serious objection to that instrument. Suits were instituted; and the Supreme Court maintained its jurisdiction. The alarm was general; and, to quiet the apprehensions, that were so extensively entertained, this amendment was proposed in Congress, and adopted by the State Legislatures. That its motive was not to maintain the sovereignty of a State from the degradation, supposed to attend a compulsory appearance before the tribunal of the Nation, may be inferred from the terms of the amendment. It does not comprehend controversies between two or more States, or between a State and a foreign state. The jurisdiction of the Court still extends to these cases; and in these, a State may still be sued. We must ascertain the amendment, then, to some other cause, than the dignity of a State. There is no difficulty in finding this cause. Those, who were inhibited from commencing a suit against a State, or from prosecuting one, which might be commended before the adoption of the amendment, were persons, who might probably be its creditors. There was not much reason to fear, that foreign or sister States would be creditors to any considerable amount; and there was reason to retain the jurisdiction of the Court in those cases, because it might be essential to the preservation of peace. The amendment, therefore, extended to suits commenced, or prosecuted by individuals, but not to those brought by States.

§362. The first impression, made on the mind by this amendment, is, that it was intended for those cases, and for those only, in which some demand against a State is made by an individual in the courts of the Union. If we consider the cause, to which it is to be traced, we are conducted to the same conclusion. A general interest might well be felt, in leaving to a State the full power of consulting its convenience in the adjustment of its debts, or of other claims upon it; but no interest could be felt in so changing the relations between the whole and its parts, as to strip the Government of the means of protecting, by the instrumentality of its courts, the Constitution and laws from active violation.

§363. This amendment, then, was designed to prevent any suit being originally commended *by* any private person against a State; but it was not designed to control or interfere with the appellate jurisdiction of the Supreme Court, in cases to which that appellate jurisdiction extended before the amendment. A case, therefore, originally commenced *by* a State *against* a private person in any other Court, which involved any question arising under the Constitution, laws, or treaties, of the United

States, might still be revised by the Supreme Court, upon an appeal, or writ of error, as the case might require.

§364. Another inquiry, touching the appellate jurisdiction of the Supreme Court, of a still more general character, is, whether it extends only to the inferior courts of the Union, constituted by Congress, or reaches to cases decided in the State courts. This question has been made on several occasions; and it has been most deliberately and solemnly decided by the Supreme Court, that it reaches the latter cases.

§365. We have already seen, that appellate jurisdiction is given by the Constitution to the Supreme Court, in all cases, where it has not original jurisdiction; subject, however, to such exceptions and regulations, as Congress may prescribe. It is, therefore, capable of embracing every case enumerated in the Constitution, which is not exclusively to be decided by way of original jurisdiction. But the exercise of appellate jurisdiction is far from being limited, by the terms of the Constitution, to the Supreme Court. There can be no doubt, that Congress may create a succession of inferior tribunals, in each of which it may vest appellate, as well as original jurisdiction. The judicial power is delegated by the Constitution in the most general terms, and may, therefore, be exercised by Congress, under every variety of form of appellate, or of original jurisdition. And as there is nothing in the Constitution, which restrains, or limits this power, it must, therefore, in all these cases, subsist in the utmost latitude, of which, in its own nature, it is susceptible.

§366. If the Constitution is meant to limit the appellate jurisdiction to cases pending in the courts of the United States, it would necessarily follow, that the jurisdiction of these courts would, in all the cases enumerated in the Constitution, be exclusive of State tribunals. How, otherwise, could the jurisdiction extend to *all cases* arising under the Constitution, laws, and treaties, of the United States, or, to *all cases* of admiralty and maritime jurisdiction? If some of these cases might be entertained by State tribunals, and no appellate jurisdiction, as to them, should exist, then the appellate power would not extend to *all,* but to *some,* cases. If State tribunals might exercise concurrent jurisdiction over all, or some of the other classes of cases in the Constitution, without control, then the appellate jurisdiction of the United States might, as to such cases, have no real existence, contrary to the manifest intent of the Constitution. Under such circumstances, to give effect to the judicial power, it must be construed to be exclusive; and this, not only when the very question should arise directly; but when it should arise incidentally, in cases pending in State courts. This construction would abridge the jurisdiction of such courts far more, than has been ever contemplated in any act of Congress.

§367. But it is plain, that the framers of the Constitution did contemplate, that cases within the judicial cognizance of the United States, not only might, but would arise in the State courts, in the exercise of their ordinary jurisdiction. With this view, the sixth article declares, that, "This Constitution, and the laws of the United States, which shall be made in pursuance thereof, and all treaties made, or which shall be made, under the authority of the United States, shall be the supreme law of the land, and the judges, in every State, shall be bound thereby, any thing, in the Constitution or laws of any State, to the contrary notwithstanding." It is obvious, that this obligation is imperative upon the State judges in their official, and not merely in their private capacities. From the very nature of their judicial duties, they would be called upon to pronounce the law, applicable to the case in judgment. They were not to decide, merely according to the laws, or Constitution, of the State, but according to the Constitution, laws, and treaties, of the United States,—"the supreme law of the land."

§368. A moment's consideration will show us the necessity and propriety of this provision, in cases, where the jurisdiction of the State courts is unquestionable. Suppose a contract, for the payment of money, is made between citizens of the same State, and performance thereof is sought in the courts of that State; no person can doubt, that the jurisdiction completely and exclusively attaches, in the first instance, to such courts. Suppose at the trial, the defendant sets up, in his defence, a tender under a State law, making paper money a good tender, or a State law, impairing the obligation of such contract, which law, if binding, would defeat the suit. The constitution of the United States has declared, that no State shall make any thing but gold or silver coin a tender in payment of debts, or pass a law impairing the obligation of contracts. If Congress shall not have passed a law, providing for the removal of such a suit to the courts of the United States, must not the State court proceed to hear, and determine it? Can a mere plea in defence be, of itself, a bar to further proceedings, so as to prohibit an inquiry into its truth, or legal propriety, when no other tribunal exists, to which judicial cognizance of such cases is confided? Suppose an indictment for a crime in a State court, and the defendant should allege in his defence, that the crime was created by an *ex post facto* act of the State, must not the State court, in the exercise of a jurisdiction, which has already rightfully attached, have a right to pronounce on the validity, and sufficiency of the defence? It would be extremely difficult, upon any legal principles, to give a negative answer to these inquiries. Innumerable instances of the same sort might be stated in illustration of the position; and unless the State courts could sustain jurisdiction in such cases, this clause of the sixth article would be without meaning or effect; and public mischiefs, of a most enormous magnitude, would inevitably ensue.

§369. It must, therefore; be conceded, that the Constitution not only contemplated, but meant to provide for, cases within the scope of the judicial power of the United States, which might yet be brought before State tribunals. It was foreseen, that, in the exercise of their ordinary jurisdiction, State courts would, incidentally, take cognizance of cases arising under the Constitution, the laws, and treaties, of the United States. Yet, to all these cases the judicial power, by the very terms of the Constitution, is to extend. It cannot extend, by original jurisdiction, if that has already rightfully and exclusively attached in the State courts, which (as has been already shown) may occur; it must, therefore, extend by appellate jurisdiction, or not at all. It would seem to follow, that the appellate power of the United States must, in such cases, extend to State tribunals; and, if in such cases, there is no reason, why it should not equally attach upon all others within the purview of the Constitution.

§370. It is manifest, that the Constitution has proceeded upon a theory of its own, and given and withheld powers according to the judgement of the American people, by whom it was adopted. We can only construe its powers, and cannot here inquire into the policy, or principles, which induced the grant of them. The Constitution has presumed, (whether rightly or wrongly, we do not here inquire,) that the State attachments, State prejudices, State jealousies, and State interests, might sometimes obstruct, or control, the regular administration of justice. Hence, in controversies between States; between citizens of different States; between citizens, claiming grants under different States; between a State and its citizens, or foreigners; and between citizens and foreigners; it enables the parties, under the authority of Congress, to have the controversies heard, tried, and determined, before the National tribunals. No other reason, than that, which has been stated, can be assigned, why some, at least, of these cases should not have been left to the cognizance of the State courts. In respect to the other enumerated cases,—cases arising under the Constitution, laws, and treaties, of the United States; cases affecting ambassadors, and other public ministers; and cases of admiralty and maritime jurisdiction,—reasons of a higher and more extensive nature, touching the safety, peace, and sovereignty, of the Nation, might well justify a grant of exclusive jurisdiction.

§371. This is not all. A motive of another kind, perfectly compatible with the most sincere respect for State tribunals, might induce the grant of appellate power over their decisions. That motive is the importance, and even necessity, of *uniformity* of decisions throughout the whole United States, upon all subjects within the purview of the Constitution.

Judges of equal learning and integrity, in different States, might differently interpret a statute, or a treaty, of the United States, or even the Constitution itself. If there were no revising authority to control these jarring and discordant judgements, and harmonize them into uniformity, the laws, the treaties, and the Constitution, of the United States, would be different in different States; and might, perhaps, never have precisely the same construction, obligation, or efficacy, in any two States. The public mischiefs, which would attend such a state of things, would be truly deplorable; and I cannot believe, that they could have escaped the enlightened Convention, which formed the Constitution. What, indeed, might then have been only prophecy has now become fact; and the appellate jurisdiction must continue to be the only adequate remedy for such evils.

§372. There is an additional consideration, which is entitled to great weight. The Constitution of the United States was designed for the common and equal benefit of all the people of the United States. The judicial power was granted for the same benign and salutary purpose. It was not to be exercised exclusively for the benefit of parties, who might be plaintiffs, and would elect the National forum; but also for the protection of defendants, who might be entitled to try their rights, or assert their privileges, before the same forum. Yet, if the appellate jurisdiction does not extend to such cases, it will follow, that, as the plaintiff may always elect the State courts, the defendant may be deprived of all the security, which the Constitution intended in aid of his rights. Such a state of things can, in no respect, be considered as giving equal rights.

§373. Strong as this conclusion stands upon the general language of the Constitution, it may still derive support from other sources. It is an historical fact, that this exposition of the Constitution, extending its appellate power to State court, was, previous to its adoption, uniformly and publicly avowed by its friends, and admitted by its enemies, as the basis of their respective reasonings, both in and out of the State conventions. It is an historical fact, that, at the time, when the Judiciary Act was submitted to the deliberations of the first Congress, composed, as it was, not only of men of great learning and ability, but of men, who had acted a principal part in framing, supporting, or opposing, that Constitution, the same exposition was explicitly declared, and admitted by the friends, and by the opponents of that system. It is an historical fact, that the Supreme Court of the United States has, from time to time, sustained this appellate jurisdiction, in a great variety of cases, brought from the tribunals of many of the most important States in the Union; and that no State tribunal ever breathed a judicial doubt on the subject, or declined to obey the mandate of the Supreme Court, until a comparatively recent period. This weight of contemporaneous exposition, by all parties, this acquiescence of enlightened State courts, and these judicial decisions of the Supreme Court, through so long a period, places the doctrine upon a foundation of authority, which cannot be shaken, without delivering over the subject to perpetual, an irremediable doubts.

§374. It would be difficult, and perhaps not desirable, to lay down any general rules in relation to the cases, in which the judicial power of the courts of the United State is exclusive of the State courts, or in which it may be made so by Congress, until they shall be settled by some positive adjudication of the Supreme Court. That there are some cases, in which that power is exclusive, cannot well be doubted; that there are others, in which it may be made so by Congress, admits of as little doubt; and that, in other cases, it is concurrent in the State courts, at least until Congress shall have passed some act, excluding the concurrent jurisdiction, will scarcely be denied. It seems to be admitted, that the jurisdiction of the courts of the United States is, or at least may be, made exclusive in all cases arising under the Constitution, laws, and treaties, of the United States; in all cases affecting ambassadors, other public ministers, and consuls; in all cases of admiralty and maritime jurisdiction, (which are exclusive in their character;) in controversies, to which the United States shall be a party; in controversies between two or more States; in controversies between a State and citizens of another State; and in controversies between a State and foreign States, citizens, or subjects. And it is only in those cases, where, previous to the constitution, State tribunals possessed jurisdiction, independent of National authority, that they can now constitutionally exercise a concurrent jurisdiction.

§375. In the exercise of the jurisdiction confided respectively to the State courts, and those courts of the United States, (where the latter have not appellate jurisdiction), it is plain, that neither can have any right to interfere with, or control, the operations of the other. It has accordingly been settled, that no State court can issue an injunction upon any judgement in a court of the United States; the latter having an exclusive authority over its own judgements and proceedings. Nor can any State court, or any State legislature, annul the judgements of the courts of the United States, or destroy the rights acquired under them; nor in any manner deprive the Supreme Court of its appellate jurisdiction; nor in any manner interfere with, or control, the process (whether mesne or final) of the courts of the United States; nor prescribe the rules or forms of proceeding; nor affect a process in the courts of the United States; nor issue a mandamus to an officer of the United States, or compel him to perform duties, devolved on him by the laws of the United States. And, although writs of *habeas corpus* have been issued by State judges, and State courts, in cases where the party has been in custody, under the authority of process of the courts of the United States, there has been considerable diversity of opinion, whether such an exercise of authority is constitutional; and it yet remains to be decided, whether it can be maintained.

§376. On the other hand, the National courts have no authority (in cases not within the appellate jurisdiction of the United States) to issue injunctions to judgements in the State courts; or in any other matter to interfere with their jurisdiction or proceedings.

§377. Having disposed of these points, we may again recur to the language of the Constitution, for the purpose of some further illustrations. The language is, that "the Supreme Court shall have appellate jurisdiction, both as to law and fact, with some exceptions, and under such regulations, as the Congress shall make."

§378. In the first place, it may not be without use to ascertain, what is here meant by an appellate jurisdiction; and what is the mode, in which it may be exercised. The essential criterion of appellate jurisdiction is, that it revises and corrects the proceedings in a cause already instituted, and does not create that cause. In reference to judicial tribunals, an appellate jurisdiction, therefore, necessarily implies, that the subject matter has been already instituted in, and acted upon by, some other court, whose judgement or proceedings are to be revised. This appellate jurisdiction may be exercised in a variety of forms, and indeed any form, which the Legislature may choose to prescribe; but, still, the substance must exist, before the form can be applied to it. To operate at all, then, under the Constitution of the United States, it is not sufficient, that there has been a decision by some officer, or Department, of the United States; but it must be by one clothed with judicial authority, and acting in a judicial capacity. A power, therefore, conferred by Congress on the Supreme Court, to issue a mandamus to public officers of the United States generally, is not warranted by the Constitution; for it is, in effect, under such circumstances, an exercise of original jurisdiction. But where the object is to revise a judicial proceeding, the mode is wholly immaterial; and a writ of *habeas corpus,* or of mandamus, a writ of error, or an appeal, may be used, as the Legislature may prescribe.

§379. The most usual modes of exercising appellate jurisdiction, at least, those, which are most known in the United States, are, by writ of error, or by an appeal, or by some process of removal of a suit from an inferior tribunal. An appeal is a process of civil law origin, and removes a cause entirely, subjecting the fact, as well as the law, to a review and a re-trial. A writ of error is a process of common law origin; and it removes nothing for re-examination, but the law. The former mode is usually adopted in cases of equity and admiralty jurisdiction; the latter, in suits at common law tried by a jury.

§380. It is observable, that the language of the Constitution is, that "the Supreme Court shall have appellate jurisdiction, *both as to law and fact.*" This provision was a subject of no small alarm and misconstruction at the time of the adoption of the Constitution, as it was supposed to confer on the Supreme Court, in the exercise of its appellate jurisdiction, the power to review the decision of a jury in mere matters of fact; and thus, in effect, to destroy the validity of their verdict, and to reduce to a mere form, the right of a trial by jury in civil cases. The objection was at once seized hold of by the enemies of the Constitution; and it was pressed with an urgency and zeal, which were well nigh preventing its ambiguity of the language, to justify an interpretation, that such a review might constitutionally be within the reach of the appellate power, if Congress should choose to carry it to that extreme latitude. But, practically speaking, there was not the slightest danger, that Congress would ever adopt such a course, even if it were within their constitutional authority; since it would be at variance with all the habits, feelings, and institutions, of the whole country. At least, it might be affirmed, that Congress would scarcely take such a step, until the people were prepared to surrender all the great securities of their civil, as well as of their political rights and liberties; and in such an event, the retaining of the trial by jury would be a mere mockery. The real object of the provision was, to retain the power of reviewing the fact, as well as the law, in cases of equity, and of admiralty, and maritime jurisdiction. And the manner, in which it is expressed, was probably occasioned by the desire to avoid the introduction of the subject of a trial by jury, in civil cases, upon which the Convention were greatly divided in opinion.

§381. These views, however reasonable they may seem to considerate minds, did not wholly satisfy the popular opinion; and as the objection had a vast influence under public opinion, and amendments were proposed by various State conventions on the subject, Congress, at its first session, under the guidance of the friends of the Constitution, proposed an amendment, which was ratified by the people, and is now incorporated into the Constitution. It is in these words: "In suits at common law, where the value in controversy shall exceed twenty dollars, the right of a trial by jury shall be preserved. And no fact, tried by jury, shall be otherwise re-examined in any court of the United States, than according to the rules of the common law." This amendment completely struck down the objection; and has secured the right of a trial by jury, in civil cases, in the fullest latitude of the common law. It is a most important and valuable amendment; and places upon the high ground of constitutional right, the inestimable privilege of a trial by jury in civil cases, a privilege scarcely inferior to that in criminal cases, which is conceded by all persons to be essential to political and civil liberty.

§382. The appellate jurisdiction is to be, "with such exceptions, and under such regulations, as the Congress shall prescribe." But, here, a question is presented upon the construction of the Constitution, whether the appellate jurisdiction attaches to the Supreme Court, subject to be withdrawn and modified by Congress; or, whether an act of Congress is necessary to confer the jurisdiction upon the court. If the former be the true construction, then the entire appellate jurisdiction, if Congress should make no exceptions or regulations, would attach, by force of the terms, to the Supreme Court. If the latter, then, notwithstanding the imperative language of the Constitution, the Supreme Court is lifeless, until Congress has conferred power on it. And if Congress may confer power, they may repeal it. So that the whole efficiency of the judicial power is left by the Constitution wholly unprotected and inert, if Congress shall refrain to act. There is certainly very strong ground to maintain, that the language of the Constitution meant to confer the appellate jurisdiction absolutely on the Supreme Court, independent of any action by Congress; and to require this action to divest or regulate it. The language, as to the original jurisdiction of the Supreme Court, admits of no doubt. It confers it without any action of Congress. Why should not the same language, as to the appellate jurisdiction, have the same interpretation? It leaves the power of Congress complete, to make exceptions and regulations; but it leaves nothing to their inaction. This construction was asserted in argument at an early period of the Constitution, and it has since been deliberately confirmed by the Supreme Court.

§383. The functions of the judges of the courts of the United States are strictly and exclusively judicial. They cannot, therefore, be called upon to advise the President in any Executive measures; or to give extra judicial interpretations of law; or to act as commissioners in cases of pensions, or other like proceedings.

CHAPTER XXXII.

Trial by Jury, and its Incidents.—Definition of Treason.

§384. THE next clause of the second section of the third article is, "The trial of all crimes, except in cases of impeachment, shall be by jury; and such trial shall be held in the State, where the said crimes shall have been committed. But when not committed within any State, the trial shall be at such place or places, as the Congress may by law have directed." It seems hardly necessary, in this place, to expatiate upon the antiquity, or importance, of the trial by jury in criminal cases. It was, from very early times, insisted on by our ancestors in the parent country, as the great bulwark of their civil and political liberties, and watched with an unceasing jealousy and solicitude. The right constitutes a fundamental article of Magna Charta, in which it is declared, "that no man shall be arrested, nor imprisoned, nor banished, nor deprived of life, &c., but by the judgement of his peers, or by the law of the land." The judgement of his peers here alluded to, and commonly called, in the quaint language of former times, a trial *per pais,* or trial by the country, is the trial by a jury, who are called the peers of the party accused, being of the like condition and equality in the state. When our more immediate ancestors removed to America, they brought this great privilege with them, as their birthright and inheritance, as a part of that admirable common law, which had fenced round, and interposed barriers on every side against the approaches of arbitrary power. It is now incorporated into all our State Constitutions as a fundamental right; and the Constitution of the United States would have been justly obnoxious to the most conclusive objection, if it had not recognised and confirmed it, in the most solemn terms.

§385. The great object of a trial by jury, in criminal cases, is to guard against a spirit of oppression and tyranny, on the part of rulers, and against a spirit of violence and vindictiveness, on the part of the people. Indeed, it is often more important to guard against the latter, than the former. The sympathies of all mankind are enlisted against the revenge and fury of a single despot; and every attempt will be made to screen his victims from punishment. But it is difficult to escape from the vengeance of an indignant people, roused into hatred by unfounded calumnies, or stimulated to cruelty by political enmity, and party jealousy. The appeal for safety, under such circumstances, can scarcely be made by the innocent, in any other manner, than by the strict control of a court of justice, and the firm and impartial verdict of a jury, sworn to do right, and guided solely by legal evidence, and a sense of duty.

§386. It is observable, that the trial of all crimes is not only to be by jury, but to be held in the State, where they are committed. The object of this clause is, to secure the party accused from being dragged to a trial in some distant State, far away from his friends, and witnesses, and neighborhood; and thus subjected to the verdict of mere strangers, who may feel no common sympathy, or who may even cherish animosities, or prejudices, against him. Besides this, a trial in a distant State or Territory might subject the party to the most oppressive expenses, or perhaps even to the inability of procuring the proper witnesses to establish his innocence. There is little danger, indeed, that Congress would ever exert its power in so oppressive and unjustifiable a manner. But upon a subject, so vital to the security of the citizen, it was fit to leave as little as possible to mere discretion. By the common law, the trial of all crimes is required to be in the county, where they are committed. Nay, it originally carried its jealousy still farther, and required, that the jury itself should come from the vicinage of the place, where the crime was alleged to be committed. This was certainly a precaution, which, however justifiable in an early and barbarous state of society, is little commendable in its more advanced stages. It has been justly remarked, that in such cases, to summon a jury, laboring under local prejudices, is laying a snare for their consciences; and, though they should have virtue and vigor of mind sufficient to keep them upright, the parties will grow suspicious, and indulge many doubts of the impartiality of the trial. It was doubtless by analogy to this rule of the common law, that all criminal trials are required to be in the State, where the crimes are committed. But, as crimes may be committed on the high seas, and elsewhere, out of the territorial jurisdiction of a State, it was indispensable, that, in such cases, Congress should be enabled to provide the place of trial. But even here we may perceive, from the language used, that the trial is to be in the place, which Congress may *have* directed; not in one, which they shall direct after the commission of the offence.

§387. In order to secure this great palladium of liberty, the trial by jury, in criminal cases, from all possibility of abuse, certain amendments have since been made to the Constitution, which add greatly to the original constitutional barriers against persecution and oppression. They are as follows: "No person shall be held to answer for a capital, or otherwise infamous crime, unless on a presentment or indictment of a grand jury, except in cases arising in the land or naval forces, or in the militia, when in actual service, in time of war, or public danger. Nor shall any person be subject for the same offence to be twice put in jeopardy of life or limb; nor shall be compelled, in any criminal case, to be a witness against himself; nor be deprived of life, liberty, or property, without due process of law; nor shall private property be taken for public use, without just compensation in all criminal prosecutions, the accused shall enjoy the right to a speedy and public trial by an impartial jury of the State and district, wherein the crime shall have been committed; which district shall have been previously ascertained by law; and to be informed of the nature and cause of the accusation; to be confronted with the witnesses against him; to have compulsory process for obtaining witnesses in his favor; and to have the assistance of counsel for his defence."

§388. Upon the main provisions of these articles, a few remarks only will be made, since they are almost self-evident, and can require few illustrations to establish their utility and importance.

§389. The first clause requires the interposition of a grand jury, by way of presentment or indictment, before the party accused can be required to answer to any capital and infamous crime, charged against him. And this is regularly true at the common law, of all offences, above the grade of common misdemeanors. A grand jury, it is well known, is selected in the manner prescribed by law, and duly sworn to make inquiry, and present all offences committed against the authority of the State government, within the body of the county, for which they are impannelled. In the National courts, they are sworn to inquire, and present all offences committed against the authority of the National Government. The grand jury may consist of any number, not less than twelve, nor more than twenty-three; and twelve at least must concur in every accusation. They sit in secret, and examine the evidence laid before them by themselves. A presentment, properly speaking, is an accusation, made by a grand jury of its own mere motion, of an offence upon its own observation and knowledge, or upon evidence before it, and without any bill of indictment laid before it at the suit of the government. An indictment is a written accusation of an offence preferred to, and presented, upon oath, as true, by a grand jury, at the suit of the government. Upon a presentment, the proper officer of the court must frame an indictment, before the party accused can be put to answer it. But an indictment is usually, in the first instance, framed by the officers of the government, and laid before the grand jury. When the grand jury has heard the evidence, if they are of opinion, that the indictment is groundless, or not supported by evidence, they used formerly to endorse on the back of the bill, "ignoramus," or we know nothing of it, whence the bill was said to be *ignored*. But now, they assert, in plain English, "not a true bill," or, which is a better way, "not found;" and then the party is entitled to be discharged, if in custody, without further answer. But a fresh bill may be preferred against him by another grand jury. If the grand jury is satisfied of the truth of the accusation, then it writes on the back of the bill, "a true bill," (or anciently, *"billa vera."*) The bill is then said to be found, and is publicly returned into court; the party stands indicted, and may then be required to answer the matters charged against him.

§390. From this summary statement, it is obvious, that the grand jury performs most important public functions; and, is a great security to the citizens against vindictive prosecutions, either by the government, or by political partisans, or by private enemies. Nor is this all: the indictment must charge the time, and place, and nature, and circumstances, of the offence, with clearness and certainty; so that the party may have full notice of the charge, and be able to make his defence with all reasonable knowledge and ability.

§391. Another clause declares, that no person shall be subject, "for the same offence, to be twice put in jeopardy of life and limb." This, again, is another great privilege secured by the common law. The meaning of it is, that a party shall not be tried a second time, for the same offence, after he has once been convicted, or acquitted of the offence charged, by the verdict of a jury, and judgement has passed thereon for or against him. But it does not mean, that he shall not be tried for the offence a second time, if the jury has been discharged without giving any verdict; or, if, having given a verdict, judgement has been arrested upon it, or a new trial has been granted in his favor; for, in such a case, his life or limb cannot judicially be said to have been put in jeopardy.

§392. The next clause prohibits any person from being

compelled, in any criminal case, to be a witness against himself, or from being deprived of life, liberty, or property, without due process of law. This also is but an affirmance of a common-law privilege. But it is of inestimable value. It is well known, that in some countries, not only are criminals compelled to give evidence against themselves; but they are subjected to the rack or torture, in order to procure a confession of guilt. And what is worse, it has been (as if in mockery or scorn) attempted to excuse or justify it, upon the score of mercy and humanity to the accused. It has been contrived, (it is pretended,) that innocence should manifest itself by a stout resistance, or guilt by plain confession; as if a man's innocence were to be tried by the hardness of his constitution, and his guilt by the sensibility of his nerves! Cicero, many ages ago, although he lived in a state, wherein it was usual to put slaves to the torture, in order to furnish evidence, has denounced the absurdity and wickedness of the measure in terms of glowing eloquence, as striking, as they are brief. They are conceived in the spirit of Tacitus, and breathe all his pregnant and indignant sarcasm. Ulpian, also, at a still later period in Roman jurisprudence, stamped the practice with severe reproof.

§393. The other part of the clause is but an enlargement of the language of Magna Charta; "Neither will we pass upon him, or condemn him, but by the lawful judgement of his peers, or by the law of the land." Lord Coke says, that these latter words, "by the law of the land," mean, by due process of law; that is, without due presentment or indictment, and being brought in to answer thereto by due process of the common law. So that this clause, in effect, affirms the right of trial, according to the process and proceedings of the common law.

§394. The concluding clause is, that private property shall not be taken for public use without just compensation. This is an affirmance of a great doctrine established by the common law, for the protection of private property. It is founded in natural equity, and is laid down by jurists as a principle of universal law. Indeed, in a free government, almost all other rights would become utterly worthless, if the government possessed an uncontrollable power over the private fortune of every citizen. One of the fundamental objects of every good government must be, the due administration of justice; and how vain it would be, to speak of such an administration, where all property is subject to the will or caprice of the legislature and the rulers!

§395. The other article, in declaring, that the accused shall enjoy the right to a speedy and public trial, by an impartial jury of the State or district, wherein the crime shall have been committed, (which district shall be previously ascertained by law,) and to be informed of the nature and cause of the accusation, and to be confronted with the witnesses against him, does but follow out the established course of the common law in all trials for crimes. The trial is always public; the witnesses are sworn, and give in their testimony, (at least in capital cases,) in the presence of the accused; the nature and cause of the accusation is accurately laid down in the indictment; and the trial is at once speedy, impartial, and in the district where the offence is charged to be committed. Without in any measure impugning the propriety of these provisions, it may be suggested, that there seems to have been an undue solicitude to introduce into the Constitution some of the general guards and proceedings of the common law in criminal trials, (truly admirable in themselves,) without sufficiently adverting to the consideration, that, unless the whole system is incorporated, and especially the law of evidence, a corrupt legislature, or a debased and servile people, may render the whole little more than a solemn pageantry. If, on the other hand, the people are enlightened, and honest, and zealous in defence of their rights and liberties, it will be impossible to surprise them into a surrender of a single valuable appendage of the trial by jury.

§396. The remaining clauses are of more direct significance, and necessity. The accused is entitled to have compulsory process for obtaining witnesses in his favor, and to hav[e]
tance of counsel. A very short review of the s[tate of the]
common law, on these points, will put their prop[riety beyond]
question. In the first place, it was an anciently an[d]

received practice, derived from the civil law, and which Mr. Justice Blackstone says, in his day, still obtained in France, although, since the Revolution, it has been swept away, not to suffer the party accused in capital cases to exculpate himself by the testimony of any witnesses. Of this practice, the courts grew so heartily ashamed from its unreasonable and oppressive character, that another practice was gradually introduced, of examining witnesses for the accused, but not upon oath; the consequence of which was, that the jury gave less credit to this latter evidence, than to that produced by the government. Sir Edward Coke denounced the practice as tyrannical and unjust; and contended that, in criminal cases, the party accused was entitled to have witnesses sworn for him. The House of Commons, soon after the accession of the house Stuart to the throne of England, insisted, in a particular bill then pending, and, against the efforts both of the Crown and the House of Lords, carried a clause affirming the right, in cases tried under that act, of witnesses being sworn for, as well as against, the accused. By the statute of 7 Will. 3, ch. 3, the same measure of justice was established throughout the realm in cases of treason; and afterwards, in the reign of Queen Anne, the like rule was extended to all cases of treason and felony. The right seems never to have been doubted, or denied, in cases of mere misdemeanors. For what causes, and upon what grounds, this distinction was maintained, or even excused, it is impossible to assign any satisfactory, or even plausible reasoning. Surely, a man's life must be of infinitely more value than any subordinate punishment; and if he might protect himself against the latter, by proofs of his innocence, there would seem to be irresistible reasons for permitting him to do the same in capital offences. The common suggestion has been, that, in capital cases, no man could, or rather ought, to be convicted, unless upon evidence so conclusive and satisfactory, as to be above contradiction or doubt. But who can say, whether it be in any case so high, until all the proofs in favor, as well as against, the party have been heard? Witnesses for the government may swear falsely, and directly to the matter in charge; and, until opposing testimony is heard, there may not be the slightest ground to doubt its truth; and yet, when such is heard, it may be incontestable, that it is wholly unworthy of belief. The real fact seems to be, that the practice was early adopted into the criminal law in capital cases, in which the crown was supposed to take a peculiar interest, in base subserviency to the wishes of the latter. It is a reproach to the criminal jurisprudence of England, which the State trials, antecedently to the revolution of 1688, but too strongly sustain. These are crimsoned with the blood of persons, who were condemned to death, not only against law, but against the clearest rules of evidence.

§397. Another anomaly in the common law, is, that in capital cases, the prisoner is not, upon his trial upon the general issue, entitled to have counsel, unless some matter of law shall arise, proper to be debated. That is, in other words, that he shall not have the benefit of the talents and assistance of counsel in examining the witnesses or making his defence before the jury. Mr. Justice Blackstone, with all his habitual reverence for the institutions of English jurisprudence, as they actually exist, speaks out upon this subject with the free spirit of a patriot and a jurist. This (he says) is "a rule, which, however it may be palliated under cover of that noble declaration of the law, when rightly understood, that the judge shall be counsel for the prisoner, that is, shall see, that the proceedings against him are legal, and strictly regular, seems to be not of all a piece with the rest of the humane treatment of prisoners by the English law. For, upon what face of reason, can that assistance be denied to save the life of a man, which is yet allowed him in prosecutions for every petty trespass." The defect has indeed been cured in England in cases of treason; but it remained unprovided for in all other cases, to, what one can hardly help deeming, the discredit of the free genius of the English Constitution, until a very recent period.

§398. The wisdom of both of these provisions is, therefore, manifest, since they make matter of constitutional right, what the common law had left in a most imperfect and questionable state. The right to have witnesses sworn, and counsel employed for the prisoner, are scarcely less important privileges, than the right of a trial by jury. The omission of them in the Constitution is a matter of surprise; and their present incorporation into it is matter of honest congratulation among all the friends of rational liberty.

§399. We may bring also into view, in this place, two other amendments of the Constitution, connected with the subject of crimes. One is designed to guard the citizens from unreasonable and illegal searches of their persons, houses, papers, and effects, without probable cause of the commission of any offence; the other is, to prevent Congress, as well as the courts, from inflicting excessive and cruel punishments. The first is; "The right of the people to be secure in their persons, houses, papers, and effects, against unreasonable searches and seizures, shall not be violated. And no warrants shall issue, but upon probable cause, supported by oath or affirmation, and particularly describing the place to be searched, and the person or things to be seized." A warrant is a writ, or process under seal, issued by some court or magistrate, for the arrest of a person, who is accused on oath of some public offence or misdemeanor, requiring the officer, to whom it is directed, to arrest the offender, and to bring him before the court or magistrate, to answer for the offence, and otherwise to be dealt with according to law. Sometimes such warrants include, not only an authority to arrest the person, but also, in cases where the accusation is for stealing goods, authority to search the dwelling house, or other place of abode, of the party, for the stolen goods, and hence the latter are commonly called search-warrants. Formerly, search-warrants, in a general form, were issued form the State Department in England, authorizing officers to search houses and persons, without naming any persons or places in particular, so that, under color of such warrants, every man's house in the kingdom might, at the mere discretion of such officers, be searched, without any ground of accusation. Such warrants were, however, held illegal by the courts of justice in England. And this amendment not only pronounces them illegal; but prohibits Congress from passing any laws to give them effect.

§400. The second amendment is; "Excessive bail shall not be required; nor excessive fines imposed; nor cruel and unusual punishments inflicted." This amendment may, at first sight, be thought superfluous. It is, however, an exact transcript of a clause in the Bill of Rights, passed and ratified in the great Revolution of 1688, in England. It was thought, at that time, to be a most important constitutional provision for the security of the people against the wilful oppression of their rulers. The history of former ages had, indeed, taught the people the necessity of some such guards against the vindictiveness and the cruelty of the supple dependents of the Crown. In the arbitrary reigns of some of the princes of the house of Stuart, demands had often been made of excessive bail against persons, who were odious to the Court or its favorites; and on failing to procure such bail, (as often occurred,) they were committed to prison, and remained there for long periods, and always during the pleasure of the Crown. Enormous fines and assessments were also sometimes imposed by judges and magistrates, and cruel and vindictive punishments were inflicted, with a view to gratify the resentments of the prosecutors, or to subdue the unhappy victims to the will of their oppressors. The provision may now seem to be unnecessary, under our free Constitution, since it may be thought scarcely possible, that any department of our Government should authorize or justify such atrocious conduct. But the clause holds out a wise admonition to all departments of the National Government, to warn them against such violent proceedings, and to instruct them in the duties of clemency and moderation. A barrier is thus interposed against the use of those vindictive and atrocious punishments, which in former ages have disgraced the annals of many nations.

§401. The third section of the third article, contains the definition of treason, a crime, which is very apt to rouse public resentment, and, in times of party and political excitement, to be extended by construction to embrace acts of very slight misconduct, and even of an innocent character. Free governments, as well as despotic governments, have too often been guilty of the most outrageous injustice to their own citizens and subjects, upon accusations of this sort. They have been ready to accuse, upon the most unsatisfactory evidence, and to convict, upon the most slender proofs, some of their most distinguished and virtuous statesmen, as well as persons of inferior character. They have inflamed into the criminality of treason acts of just resistance to tyranny; and tortured a manly freedom of opinion into designs subversive of the government. To guard against the recurrence of these evils, the Constitution has declared, "Treason against the United States shall consist only in levying war against them, or in adhering to their enemies, giving them aid and comfort. No person shall be convicted of treason, unless on the testimony of two witnesses to the same overt act, or on confession in open court." "The Congress shall have power to declare the punishment of treason. But no attainder of treason shall work corruption of blood, or forfeiture, except during the life of the person attainted."

§402. Treason is generally deemed the highest crime, which can be committed in civil society, since its aim is an overthrow of the government, and a public resistance of its powers by force. Its tendency is to create universal danger and alarm; and on this account, it is peculiarly odious, and often visited with the deepest public resentment. Even a charge of this nature, made against an individual, is deemed so opprobrious, that, whether just or unjust, it subjects him to suspicion and hatred; and, in times of high political excitement, acts of a very subordinate nature are often, by popular prejudices, as well as by royal resentment, magnified into this fatal enormity. It is, therefore, of very great importance, that its true nature and limits should be exactly ascertained; and Montesquieu was so sensible of it, that he has not scrupled to declare, that if the crime of treason be indeterminate, that alone is sufficient to make any government degenerate into arbitrary power. The history of England itself is full of melancholy instruction on this subject. By the ancient common law, it was left very much to discretion to determine, what acts were, and what were not, treason, and the judges of those times, holding office at the pleasure of the Crown, became but too often the instruments, in its hands, of foul injustice. At the instance of tyrannical princes, they had abundant opportunities to create *constructive* treasons; that is, by forced and arbitrary constructions, to raise offences into the guilt and punishment of treason, which were not suspected to be such. The grievance of these constructive treasons was so enormous, and so often weighed down the innocent, and the patriotic, that it was found necessary, as early as the reign of Edward the Third, for Parliament to interfere, and arrest it, by declaring and defining all the different branches of treason. This statute has ever since remained the pole star of English jurisprudence upon this subject. And, although, upon temporary emergencies, and in arbitrary reigns, since that period, other treasons have been created, the sober sense of the nation has generally abrogated them, or reduced their power within narrow limits.

§403. Nor have republics been exempt from violence and tyranny of a similar character. It has been justly remarked, that new-fangled and artificial treasons have been the great engines, by which violent factions, the natural offspring of free governments, have usually wreaked their alternate malignity on each other.

§404. It was under the influence of these admonitions, furnished by history and human experience, that the Convention deemed it necessary to interpose an impassable barrier against arbitrary constructions, either by the courts, or by Congress, upon the crime of treason. It confines it to two species; first, the levying of war against the United States; and, secondly, adhering to their enemies, giving them aid and comfort. In so doing, they have adopted the very words of the Statute of Treason, of Edward the Third; and thus, by implication, in order to cut off, at once, all chances of arbitrary constructions, they have recognized the well-settled interpretation of these phrases in the administration of criminal law, which has prevailed for ages.

§405. The other part of the clause, requiring the testimony

of two witnesses to the same overt act, or a confession *in open court,* to justify a conviction, is founded upon the same reasoning. A like provision exists in British jurisprudence, founded upon the same great policy of protecting men against false testimony and unguarded confessions, to their utter ruin. It has been well remarked, that confessions are the weakest and most suspicious of all testimony; ever liable to be obtained by artifice, false hopes, promises of favor, or menaces; seldom remembered accurately, or reported with due precision; and incapable, in their nature, of being disproved by other negative evidence. To which it may be added, that they are easy to be forged, and the most difficult to guard against. An unprincipled demagogue, or a corrupt courtier, might otherwise hold the lives of the purest patriots in his hands, without the means of proving the falsity of the charge, if a secret confession, uncorroborated by other evidence, would furnish a sufficient foundation and proof of guilt. And wisely, also, has the Constitution declined to suffer the testimony of a single witness, however high, to be sufficient to establish such a crime, which rouses at once against the victim private honor and public hostility. There must, as there should, be a concurrence of two witnesses to the same overt act, that is, to the same open act of treason, who are above all reasonable exception.

§406. The subject of the power of Congress to declare the punishment of treason, and the consequent disabilities, have been already commented on in another place.

§407. We have thus passed in review all those provisions of the Constitution, which concern the establishment, jurisdiction, and duties, of the judicial department; and the rights and privileges of the citizens, connected with the administration of public justice.

CHAPTER XXXIII.

Privileges of Citizens.—Fugitive Criminals and Slaves.

§408. THE fourth article of the Constitution contains several important subjects, some of which have been already considered. Among those, which have been so considered, are, the clauses which respect the faith and credit to be given to the acts, records, judgements, and proceedings, of the different States, and the mode of proving them, and the effect thereof; the admission of new States into the Union; and the regulation and disposal of the territory, and other property, of the United States.

§409. Among those, which remain for consideration, the first is, "The citizens of each State shall be entitled to all privileges and immunities of citizens in the several States." It is obvious, that if the citizens of the different States were to be deemed aliens to each other, they could not inherit, or hold, or purchase real estate, or possess any political or municipal privileges in any other State, than that, in which they were born. And the States would be at liberty to make laws, giving preferences of rights and offices, and even privileges in trade and business, to those, who were Natives, over all other persons, who belonged to other States; or they might make invidious discriminations between the citizens of different States.

Such a power would have a tendency to generate jealousies and discontents, injurious to the harmony of all the States. And, therefore, the Constitution has wisely created, as it were, a general citizenship, communicating to the citizens of each State, who have their domicil in another, all the privileges and immunities enjoyed by the citizens of the latter.

§410. The next clause is, "A person, charged in any State with treason, felony, or other crime, who shall flee from justice, and be found in another State, shall, on demand of the Executive authority of the State, from which he fled, be delivered up, to be removed to the State, having jurisdiction of the crime." As doubts have existed, whether, by the law of nations, a surrender of fugitives from justice can lawfully be demanded from the government of the country, where they seek an asylum, there is great propriety in making this a positive right, in regard to the several States composing the United States. It is for their mutual benefit, convenience, and safety. It will promote harmony and good feeling between them. It will also add strength to a great moral duty, and operate indirectly to the suppression of crimes; and finally, it will thus increase the public sense of the blessings of the National Government.

§411. The next clause is, "No person held to service or labor in one State, under the laws thereof, escaping into another, shall, in consequence of any law or regulation therein, be discharged from such service or labor but shall be delivered up, on the claim of the party to whom such service or labor may be due." This clause was introduced into the Constitution solely for the benefit of the slave-holding States, to enable them to reclaim their fugitive slaves, who should escape into other States, where slavery is not tolerated. It is well known, that, at the common law, a slave escaping into a State, where slavery is not allowed, would immediately become free, and could not be reclaimed. Before the Constitution was adopted, the Southern States felt the want of some protecting provision against such an occurrence to be a grievous injury to them. And we here see, that the Eastern and Middle States have sacrificed their own opinions and feelings, in order to take away every source of jealousy, on a subject so delicate to Southern interests; a circumstance, sufficient of itself, to repel the delusive notion, that the South has not, at all times, had its full share in the blessings resulting from the Union.

CHAPTER XXXIV.

Guarantee of Republican Government.—
Mode of making Amendments.

§412. THE fourth section of the fourth article declares, "The United States shall guaranty to every State in this Union a republican form of Government; and shall protect each of them against invasion; and, on application of the Legislature, or of the Executive, when the Legislature cannot be convened, against domestic violence." The propriety of this provision will scarcely be doubted. If any of the States were to be at liberty to adopt any other form of Government, than a republican form, it would necessarily endanger, and might destroy, the safety of the Union. Suppose, for instance, a great State, like New York, should adopt a monarchical form of government, it might, under an enterprising and ambitious king, become formidable to, if not destructive of, the Constitution. And the PEOPLE of each State have a right to protection against the tyranny of a domestic faction, and to have a firm guarantee, that their political liberties shall not be overturned by a successful demagogue, who shall arrive at power by corrupt arts, and then plan a scheme for permanent possession of it. On the other hand, domestic violence by popular insurrection is equally repugnant to the good order and safety of the Union;

and one of the blessings arising from a National Government is the security which it affords, against a recurrence of evils of this sort. Accordingly, it is made an imperative duty of the General Government, on the application of the Legislature or Executive of a State, to aid in the suppression of such domestic insurrections; as well as to protect the State from foreign invasion.

§413. It may possibly be asked, what need there could be of such a precaution, and whether it may not become a pretext for alterations in the State governments, without the concurrence of the States themselves. These questions admit of ready answers. If the interposition of the General Government should not be needed, the provision for such an event will be a harmless superfluity only in the Constitution. But, who can say, what experiments may be produced by the caprice of particular States, by the ambition of enterprising leaders, or by the intrigues and influence of foreign powers? To the second question, it may be answered, that if the General Government should interpose, by virtue of this constitutional authority, it will, of course, be bound to pursue the authority. But the authority extends no further than to a *guarantee* of a republican form of Government, which supposes a pre-existing Government of the form, which is to be guaranteed. As long, therefore, as the existing republican forms are continued by the States, they are guaranteed by the Federal Constitution. Whenever the States may choose to substitute other republican forms, they have a right to do so, and to claim the federal guarantee for the latter. The only restriction imposed on them is, that they shall not exchange republican for anti-republican Constitutions: a restriction, which, it is presumed, will hardly be considered as a grievance.

§414. At first view, it might seem not to square with the republican theory, to suppose, either that a majority have not the right, or that a minority will have the force, to subvert a government; and, consequently, that the National interposition can never be required, but when it would be improper. But theoretic reasoning in this case, as in most other cases, must be qualified by the lessons of practice. Why may not illicit combinations, for purposes of violence, be formed, as well by a majority of a State, as by a majority of a county, or of a district of the same State; and if the authority of the State ought, in the latter case, to protect the local magistracy, ought not the National authority, in the former, to support the State authority? Besides; there are certain parts of the State Constitutions, which are so interwoven with the National Constitution, that a violent blow cannot be given to the one, without communicating the wound to the other. Insurrections in a State will rarely induce a National interposition, unless the number concerned in them bear some proportion to the friends of Government. It will be much better, that the violence in such cases, should be repressed by the superintending power, than that the majority should be left to maintain their cause by a bloody and obstinate contest. The existence of a right to interpose will generally prevent the necessity of exerting it.

§415. The next (the fifth) article, provides for the mode of making amendments to the Constitution. "The Congress, whenever two thirds of both Houses shall deem it necessary, shall propose amendments to this Constitution; or, on application of the Legislatures of two thirds of the several States, shall call a Convention for proposing amendments; which, in either case, shall be valid, to all intents and purposes, as part of this Constitution, when ratified by the Legislatures of three fourths of the several States, or by conventions in three fourths thereof, as the one, or the other mode of ratification may be proposed by the Congress; provided that no amendment, which may be made prior to the year one thousand eight hundred and eight, shall in any manner affect the first and fourth clauses in the ninth section of the first article; and that no State, without its consent, shall be deprived of its equal suffrage in the Senate."

§416. The importance of this power can scarcely be over estimated. It is obvious, that no human government can ever be perfect; and it is impossible to foresee, or guard against all the exigencies, which may, in different ages, require changes in the powers and modes of operation of a government, to suit the necessities and interests of the people. A government, which has no mode prescribed for any changes, will, in the lapse of time, become utterly unfit for the nation. It will either degenerate into a despotism, or lead to a revolution, by its oppressive inequalities. It is wise, therefore, in every government, and especially in a republic, to provide peaceable means for altering and improving the structure, as time and experience shall show it necessary, for the public safety and happiness. But, at the same time, it is equally important to guard against too easy and frequent changes; to secure due deliberation and caution in making them; and to follow experience, rather than speculation and theory. A government, which is always changing and changeable, is in a perpetual state of internal agitation, and incapable of any steady and permanent operations. It has a constant tendency to confusion and anarchy.

§417. In regard to the Constitution of the United States, it is confessedly a new experiment in the history of nations. Its framers were not bold or rash enough to believe, or to pronounce, it to be perfect. They made use of the best lights, which they possessed, to form and adjust its parts, and mould its materials. But they knew, that time might develop many defects in its arrangements, and many deficiencies in its powers. They desired, that it might be open to improvement; and, under the guidance of the sober judgement and enlightened skill of the country, to be perpetually approaching nearer and nearer to perfection. It was obvious, too, that the means of amendment might avert, or at least have a tendency to avert, the most serious perils, to which confederated republics are liable, and by which all have hitherto been shipwrecked. They knew, that the besetting sin of republics is a restlessness of temperament, and a spirit of discontent at slight evils. They knew the pride and jealousy of state power in confederacies; and they wished to disarm them of their potency, by providing a safe means to break the force, if not wholly to ward off the blows, which would, from time to time, under the garb of patriotism, or a love of the people, be aimed at the Constitution.

They believed, that the power of amendment was, if one may so say, the safety-valve to let off all temporary effervescences and excitements; and the real effective instrument to control and adjust the movements of the machinery, when out of order, or in danger of self-destruction.

§418. Upon the propriety of the power, in some form, there will probably be little controversy. The only question is, whether it is so arranged, as to accomplish its objects in the safest mode; safest for the stability of the Government; and safest for the rights and liberties of the people.

§419. The Constitution has adopted a middle course. It has provided for amendments being made; the mode is easy; and at the same time, it secures due deliberation, and caution. Congress may propose amendments, or a convention of the States. But, in any amendment proposed by Congress, two thirds of both Houses must concur; and no convention can be called, except upon the application of two thirds of the States. When amendments are proposed in either way, the assent of three fourths of all the States is necessary to their ratification. And, certainly, it may be said with confidence, that if three fourths of the States are not satisfied with the necessity of any particular amendment, the evils, which it proposes to remedy, cannot be of any general or pressing nature. That the power of amendment is not, in its present form, impracticable, is proved by the fact, that twelve amendments have been already proposed and ratified.

§420. The proviso excludes the power of amendment, until the year 1808, of the clauses in the Constitution, which respects the importation and migration of slaves, and the apportionment of direct taxes. And as the equality of the Representation of the States in the Senate might be destroyed by an amendment, it is expressly declared, that no amendment shall deprive any State, without its consent, of its equal suffrage in that body.

CHAPTER XXXV.

Public Debt—Supremacy of the Constitution, and Laws.

§421. THE first clause of the sixth article is, "All debts contracted, and engagements entered into, before the adoption of this Constitution, shall be as valid against the United States, under this Constitution, as under the Confederation." This can scarcely be deemed more than a solemn declaration of what the public law of nations recognizes as a moral obligation, binding on all nations, notwithstanding any changes in their forms of Government. It was important, however, to clear away all possible doubts, and to satisfy and quiet the public creditors, who might fear, that their just claims upon the Confederation might be disregarded or denied.

§422. The next clause is, "This Constitution, and the Laws of the United States, which shall be made in pursuance thereof, and all treaties made, or which shall be made, under the authority of the United States, shall be the supreme law of the land. And the judges in every State shall be bound thereby, any thing in the Constitution or laws of any State, to the contrary notwithstanding." The propriety of this power results from the very nature of the Constitution. To establish a National Government, and to affirm, that it shall have certain powers;

and yet, that in the exercise of those powers it shall not be supreme, but controllable by any State in the Union, would be a solecism, so mischievous, and so indefensible, that the scheme could never be attributed to the framers of the Constitution, without manifestly impeaching their wisdom, as well as their good faith. The want of such an effective practical supremacy was a vital defect in the Confederation; and furnished the most solid reason for abolishing it. It would be an idle mockery, to give powers to Congress, and yet at the same time to declare, that those powers might be suspended or annihilated, at the will of a single State; that the will of twenty-five States should be surrendered to the will of one. A government of such a nature would be as unworthy of public confidence, as it would be incapable of affording public protection, or private happiness.

§423. In regard to treaties, there is equal reason, why they should be held, when made, to be the supreme law of the land. It is to be considered, that treaties constitute solemn compacts of binding obligation among nations; and unless they are scrupulously obeyed, and enforced, no foreign nation would consent to negotiate with us; or if it did, any want of strict fidelity, on our part, in the discharge of the treaty stipulations, would be visited by reprisals, or by war. It is, therefore, indispensable, that they should have the obligation and force of a law, that they may be executed by the judicial power, and be obeyed like other laws. This will not prevent them from being cancelled, or abrogated, by the nation, upon grave and suitable occasions; for it will not be disputed, that they are subject to the legislative power, and may be repealed, like other laws, at its pleasure; or they may be varied by new treaties. Still, while they do subsist, they ought to have a positive binding efficacy, as laws, upon all the States, and all the citizens of the States. The peace of the nation, and its good faith, and moral dignity, indispensably require, that all State laws should be subjected to their supremacy. The difference between considering them as laws, and considering them as executory, or executed contracts, is exceedingly important in the actual administration of public justice. If they are supreme laws, courts of justice will enforce them directly in all cases, to which they can be judicially applied, in opposition to all State laws, as we all know was done in the case of the British debts, secured by the treaty of 1783, after the Constitution was adopted. If they are deemed but solemn compacts, promissory in their nature and obligation, courts of justice may be embarrassed in enforcing them, and may be compelled to leave the redress to be administered through other departments of the Government. It is notorious, that treaty stipulations (especially those of the treaty of peace of 1783) were grossly disregarded by the States under the Confederation. They were deemed by the States, not as laws, but like requisitions, of a mere moral obligation, and dependent upon the good will of the States for their execution. Congress, indeed, remonstrated against this construction, as unfounded in principle and justice. But their voice was not heard. Power and right were separated; the argument was all on one side; but the power was on the other. It was probably to obviate this very difficulty, that this clause was inserted in the Constitution; and it would redound to the immortal honor of its authors, if it had done no more, than thus to bring treaties within the sanctuary of justice, as laws of supreme obligation. There are, indeed, still cases, in which courts of justice can administer no effectual redress; for, when the terms of a stipulation import a contract, or when either of the parties engages to perform a particular act, the treaty addresses itself to the political, and not to the judicial, department; and the legislature must execute the contract, before it can become a rule for the courts.

§424. From this supremacy of the Constitution, and laws, and treaties, of the United States, within their constitutional scope, arises the duty of courts of justice to declare any unconstitutional law passed by Congress, or by a State legislature, void. So, in like manner, the same duty arises, whenever any other department of the National or State governments exceeds its constitutional functions. But the Judiciary of the United States has no general jurisdiction to declare acts of the several States void, unless they are repugnant to the Constitution of the United States, notwithstanding they are repugnant to the State Constitution. Such a power belongs to it only, where it sits to administer the local law of a State, and acts exactly, as a State tribunal is bound to act. But upon this subject it seems unnecessary to dwell, since the right of all courts, State as well as National, to declare unconstitutional laws void, seems settled beyond the reach of judicial controversy.

CHAPTER XXXVI.

Oath of Office.—Religious Test.—Ratification of the Constitution.

§425. THE next clause is, "The Senators and Representatives before mentioned, (that is, in Congress,) and the members of the several State Legislatures, and all executive and judicial officers, both of the United States and of the several States, shall be bound by oath of affirmation to support this Constitution. But no religious test shall ever be required, as a qualification to any office or public trust under the United States."

§426. That all those, who are intrusted with the execution of the powers of the National Government, should be bound, by some solemn obligation, to the due execution of the trusts reposed in them, and to support the Constitution, would seem to be a proposition too clear, to render any reasoning necessary in support of it. It results from the plain right of society, to require some guarantee from every officer, that he will be conscientious in the discharge of his duty. Oaths have a solemn obligation upon the minds of all reflecting men, and especially upon those, who feel a deep sense of accountability to a Supreme being. If , in the ordinary administration of justice, in cases of private rights, or personal claims, oaths are required of those, who try the cause, as well as of those, who give testimony, to guard against malice, falsehood, and evasion, surely like guards ought to be interposed in the administration of high public trusts, and especially in such, as may concern the welfare and safety of the whole community. But there are known denominations of men, who are conscientiously scrupulous of taking oaths, (among which is that pure and distinguished sect of Christians, commonly called Friends, or Quakers,) and, therefore, to prevent any unjustifiable exclusion from office, the Constitution has permitted a solemn affirmation to be made, instead of an oath, and as its equivalent.

§427. But it may not appear to all persons quite so clear, why the officers of the State governments should be equally bound to take a like oath or affirmation; and it has been even suggested, that there is no more reason to require that, than to require, that all of the United States officers should take an oath or affirmation to support the State Constitutions. A moment's reflection will show sufficient reasons for the requisition of it in the one case, and the omission of it in the other. The members and officers of the National Government have no agency in carrying into effect the State Constitutions. The members and officers of the State governments have an essential agency in giving effect to the National Constitution. The election of the President and the Senate will depend, in all cases, upon the Legislatures of the several States; and, in many cases, the election of the House of Representatives may be affected by their agency. The judges of the State courts will frequently be called upon to decide upon the Constitution, and laws, and treaties, of the United States; and upon rights and claims growing out of them. Decisions ought to be, as far as possible, uniform; and uniformity of obligation will greatly tend to such a result. The executive authority of the several States may be often called upon to exert powers, or to allow rights, given by the Constitution, as in filling vacancies in the Senate, during the recess of the Legislature; in issuing writs of election, to fill vacancies in the House of Representatives; in officering the militia, and giving effect to laws for calling them out; and in the surrender of fugitives from justice. These, and many other functions, devolving on the State authorities, render it highly important, that they should be under a solemn obligation to obey the Constitution. In common sense, there can be no well-founded objection to it. There may be serious evils growing out of an opposite course.

§428. The remaining part of the clause declares, that "no religious test shall ever be required, as a qualification to any office or public trust under the United States." This clause is recommended by its tendency to satisfy the minds of many delicate and scrupulous persons, who entertain great repugnance to religious tests, as a qualification for civil power or honor. But it has a higher aim in the Constitution. It is designed to cut off every pretence of an alliance between the Church and the State, in the administration of the National Government. The American people were too well read in the history of other countries, and had suffered too much in their colonial state, not to dread the abuses of authority resulting from religious bigotry, intolerance, and persecution. They knew but too well, that no sect could be safely trusted with power on such a subject; for all had in turns wielded it to the injury, and sometimes to the destruction, of their inoffensive, but, in their judgement, erring neighbors . And we shall presently see, that, by an amendment to the Constitution, evils of this sort in the National Government are still more effectually guarded against.

§429. The seventh and last article of the Constitution is, "The ratification of the Conventions of nine States, shall be sufficient for the establishment of this Constitution between the States so ratifying the same." It is unnecessary now to comment upon this article, as all the States have ratified the Constitution. But we know, that if unanimous ratification of it, by all the States, had been required, it would have been rejected; for North Carolina, and Rhode Island, did not, at first, accede to it.

§430. And here closes our review of the Constitution in the original form, in which it was adopted by the people of the United States. The concluding passage of it is valuable, as an historical reminiscence. "Done in Convention, by the unanimous consent of the States present, the seventeenth day of September, in the year of our Lord one thousand seven hundred and eighty seven, and of the Independence of the United States the twelfth. In witness whereof, we have hereunto subscribed our names." At the head of the illustrious men, who framed and signed it, stands the name of "George Washington, President, and Deputy from Virginia;" a name, at the utterance of which it is impossible not to feel the liveliest sense of gratitude to a gracious Providence, for a life of so much glory, such spotless integrity, and such exalted patriotism.

CHAPTER XXXVII.

Amendments to the Constitution.

§431. When the Constitution was before the people for adoption, several of the State conventions suggested certain amendments for the consideration of Congress, some of the most important of which were afterwards proposed to the people for adoption, by that body, at its first organization; and, having been since ratified, they are now incorporated into the Constitution. They are mainly clauses, in the nature of a Bill of Rights, which more effectually guard certain rights, already provided for in the Constitution, or prohibit certain exercises of authority, supposed to be dangerous to the public interests. We have already had occasion to consider several of them in the preceding pages; and the remainder will now be presented.

§432. Before, however, proceeding to the consideration of them, it may be proper to say a few words, as to the origin and objects of the first ten amendments, which may be considered as a Bill of Rights, and were proposed by the first Congress, and were immediately adopted by the people of the United States. The first amendment is, "Congress shall make no law respecting an establishment of religion, or prohibiting the free exercise thereof; or abridging the freedom of speech, or of the press; or the right of the people peaceably to assemble, and to petition the government for a redress of grievances."

§433. It has been already stated, that many objections were taken to the Constitution, not only on account of its actual provisions, but also on account of its deficiencies and omissions. Among the latter, none were proclaimed with more zeal, and pressed with more effect, than the want of a *Bill of Rights*. This, it was said, was a fatal defect; and sufficient of itself to bring on the ruin of the republic. To this objection, several answers were given; first, that the Constitution did, in fact, contain many provisions in the nature of a Bill of Rights, if the whole Constitution was not, in fact, a Bill of Rights; secondly, that a Bill of Rights was in its nature more adapted to a monarchy, than to a government, professedly founded upon the will of the people, and executed by their immediate representatives and agents; and, thirdly, that a formal Bill of Rights, beyond what was contained in it, was wholly unnecessary, and might even be dangerous.

§434. It was further added, that, in truth, the Constitution itself, was, in every rational sense, and to every useful purpose, a Bill of Rights for the Union. It specifies, and declares the political privileges of the citizens in the structure and administration of the Government. It defines certain immunities and modes of proceeding, which relate to their personal, private, and public rights and concerns. It confers on them the unalienable right of electing their rulers; and prohibits any tyrannical measures, and vindictive prosecutions. So that, at best, much of the force of the objection rests on mere nominal distinctions, or upon a desire to make a frame of government a code to regulate rights and remedies.

§435. Although it must be conceded, that there is much intrinsic force in this reasoning, it cannot in candor be admitted to be wholly satisfactory, or conclusive on the subject. It is rather the argument of an able advocate, than the reasoning of a constitutional salesman. In the first place, a Bill of Rights (in the very sense of this reasoning) is admitted in some cases to be important; and the Constitution itself adopts, and establishes its propriety to the extent of its actual provisions. Every reason, which establishes the propriety of any provision of this sort in the Constitution, such as a right of trial by jury in criminal cases, is, to that extent, proof, that it is neither unnecessary nor dangerous. It reduces the question to the consideration, not whether any Bill of Rights is necessary, but what such a Bill of Rights should properly contain. This is a point for argument, upon which different minds may arrive at different conclusions. That a Bill of Rights may contain too many enumerations, and especially such, as more correctly belong to the ordinary legislation of a government, cannot be doubted. Some of our State Bills of Rights contain clauses of this description, being either in their character and phraseology quite too loose, and general, and ambiguous; or covering doctrines quite debatable, both in theory and practice; or even leading to mischievous consequences, by restricting the Legislative power under circumstances, which were not foreseen, and if foreseen, the restraint would have been pronounced by all persons inexpedient, and perhaps unjust. Indeed, the rage of theorists to make constitutions a vehicle for the conveyance of their own crude and visionary aphorisms of government, requires to be guarded against with the most unceasing vigilance.

§436. In the next place, a Bill of Rights is important, and may often be indispensable, whenever it operates as a qualification upon powers, actually granted by the people to the government. This is the real ground of all the Bills of Rights in the parent country, in the Colonial constitutions and laws, and in the State constitutions. In England, the Bills of Rights were not demanded merely of the Crown, as withdrawing a power from the Royal prerogative; they were equally important, as withdrawing power from Parliament. A large proportion of the most valuable of the provisions in Magna Charta, and the Bill of Rights in 1688, consists of a solemn recognition of the limitations upon the powers of Parliament; that is, a declaration, that Parliament *ought* not to abolish, or restrict those rights. Such are the right of trial by jury; the right to personal liberty

311

and private property, according the the law of the land; that the subjects ought to have a right to bear arms; that elections of members of Parliament ought to be free; that freedom of speech and debate in Parliament ought not to be impeached, or questioned elsewhere; and that excessive bail ought not be required, nor excessive fines imposed, nor cruel or unusual punishments inflicted. Whenever, then, a general power exists, or is granted to a government, which may, in its actual exercise or abuse, be dangerous to the people, there seems a peculiar propriety in restricting its operations, and in excepting from it some at least of the most mischievous forms, in which it may be likely to be abused. And the very exception in such cases, will operate with a silent, but irresistible influence, to control the actual abuse of it in other analogous cases.

§437. In the next place, a Bill of Rights may be important, even when it goes beyond the powers supposed to be granted. It is not always possible to foresee the extent of the actual reach of certain powers, which are given in general terms. They may be construed to extend (and perhaps fairly) to certain classes of cases, which did not first appear to be within them. A Bill of Rights, then, operates, as a guard upon any extravagant or undue extension of such powers. Besides; (as has been justly remarked,) a Bill of Rights is of real efficiency in controlling the excesses of party spirit. It serves to guide and enlighten public opinion, and to render it more quickly to detect, and more resolute to resist, attempts to disturb private rights. It requires more than ordinary hardihood and audacity of character, to trample down principles, which our ancestors have consecrated with reverence; which we imbibed in our early education; which recommend themselves to the judgement of the world by their truth and simplicity; and which are constantly placed before the eyes of the people, accompanied with the imposing force and solemnity of a constitutional sanction. Bills of Rights are a part of the muniments of freemen, showing their title to protection; and they become of increased value, when placed under the protection of an independent judiciary, instituted as the appropriate guardian of the people and private rights of the citizens.

§438. In the next place, a Bill of Rights is an important protection against unjust and oppressive conduct on the part of the people themselves. In a government modified like that of the United States, (it has been said by a great statesman,) the great danger lies rather in the abuse of the community, than of the legislative body. The prescriptions in favor of liberty ought to be levelled against that quarter, where the greatest danger lies, namely, that which possesses the highest prerogative of power. But this is not found in the executive or legislative departments of government; but in the body of the people, operating by the majority against the minority. It may be thought, that all paper barriers against the power of the community are too weak to be worthy of attention. They are not so strong, as to satisfy all, who have seen and examined thoroughly the texture of such a defence. Yet, as they have a tendency to impress some degree of respect for them, to establish the public opinion in their favor, and to rouse the attention of the whole community, it may be one means to control the majority from those acts, to which they might otherwise be inclined.

§439. The want of a Bill of Rights, then, is not either an unfounded or illusory objection. The real question is not, whether every sort of right or privilege or claim ought to be affirmed in a constitution; but whether such, as in their own nature are of vital importance, and peculiarly susceptible of abuse, ought not to receive this solemn sanction. Doubtless, the want of a formal Bill of Rights in the Constitution was a matter of very exaggerated declamation and party zeal, for the mere purpose of defeating the Constitution. But, so far as the objection was well founded in fact, it was right to remove it by subsequent amendments; and Congress has (as we shall see) accordingly performed the duty with most prompt and laudable diligence.

§440. The first amendment is, "Congress shall make no law respecting an establishment of religion, or prohibiting the free exercise thereof; or abridging the freedom of speech, or of the press; or the right of the people peaceably to assemble, and to petition the government for a redress of grievances."

§441. The same policy, which introduced into the Constitution the prohibition of any religious test, led to the more extended prohibition of the interference of Congress in religious concerns. We are not to attribute this prohibition of a national religious establishment to an indifference to religion in general, and especially to Christianity, (which none could hold in more reverence, than the framers of the Constitution,) but to a dread by the people of the influence of ecclesiastical power in matters of government; a dread, which their ancestors brought with them from the parent country, and which, unhappily for human infirmity, their own conduct, after their emigration, had not, in any just degree, tended to diminish. It was also obvious, from the numerous and powerful sects existing in the United States, that there would be perpetual temptations to struggles for ascendency in the National councils, if any one might thereby hope to found a permanent and exclusive national establishment of its own, and religious persecutions might thus be introduced, to an extent utterly subversive of the true interests and good order of the Republic. The most effectual mode of suppressing evil, in the view of the people, was, to strike down the temptations of its introduction.

§442. How far any government has a right to interfere in matters touching religion, has been a subject much discussed by writers upon public and political law. The right and the duty of the interference of government in matters of religion have been maintained by many distinguished authors, as well by those, who were the warmest advocates of free governments, as by those, who were attached to governments of a more arbitrary character. Indeed, the right of a society or government to interfere in matters of religion, will hardly be contested by any persons, who believe that piety, religion, and morality are intimately connected with the well being of the state, and indispensable to the administration of civil justice. The promulgation of the great doctrines of religion, the being, and attributes, and providence of one Almighty God; the responsibility to Him for all our actions, founded upon moral accountability; a future state of rewards and punishments; the cultivation of all the personal, social, and benevolent virtues;—these never can be a matter of indifference in any well-ordered community. It is, indeed, difficult to conceive, how any civilized society can well exist without them. And, at all events, it is impossible for those, who believe in the truth of Christianity, as a Divine revelation, to doubt, that it is the especial duty of government to foster, and encourage it among all the citizens and subjects. This is a point wholly distinct from that of the right of private judgement in matters of religion, and of the freedom of public worship, according to the dictates of one's conscience.

§443. The real difficulty lies in ascertaining the limits, to which government may rightfully go, in fostering and encouraging religion. Three cases may easily be supposed. One, where a government affords aid to a particular religion, leaving all persons free to adopt any other; another, where it creates an ecclesiastical establishment for the propagation of the doctrines of a particular sect of that religion, leaving a like freedom of others; and a third, where it creates such an establishment, and excludes all persons, not belonging to it, either wholly, or in part, from any participation in the public honors, trusts, emoluments, privileges, and immunities of the state. For instance, a government may simply declare, that the Christian religion shall be the religion of the state, and shall be aided, and encouraged in all the varieties of sects belonging to it; or it may declare, that the Roman Catholic or Protestant religion shall be the religion of the state, leaving every man to the free enjoyment of his own religious opinions; or it may establish the doctrines of a particular sect, as of Episcopalians, as the religion of the state, with a like freedom; or it may establish the doctrines of a particular sect, as exclusively the religion of the state, tolerating others to a limited extent, or excluding all, not belonging to it, from all public honors, emoluments, privileges, and immunities.

§444. Probably, at the time of the adoption of the Constitution, and of the amendment to it, now under consideration, the general, if not the universal, sentiment in America was, that Christianity ought to receive encouragement from the State, so far as such encouragement was not incompatible with the private rights of conscience, and the freedom of religious worship. An attempt to level all religions, and to make it a matter of state policy to hold all in utter indifference, would have created universal disapprobation, if not universal indignation.

§445. The next clause respects the liberty of speech, and of the press. That this amendment was intended to secure to every citizen an absolute right to speak, or write, or print, whatever he might please, without any responsibility, public or private, therefor, is a supposition too wild to be indulged by any reasonable man. That would be to allow every citizen a right to destroy, at his pleasure, the reputation, the peace, the property, and even the personal safety of every other citizen. A man might then, out of mere malice or revenge, accuse another of infamous crimes; might excite against him the indignation of all his fellow citizens by the most atrocious calumnies; might disturb, nay, overturn his domestic peace, and embitter his domestic affections; might inflict the most distressing punishments upon the weak, the timid, and the innocent; might prejudice all the civil, political, and private rights to another; and might stir up sedition, rebellion, and even treason, against the government itself, in the wantonness of his passions, or the corruptions of his heart. Civil society could not go on under such circumstances. Men would be obliged to resort to private vengeance to make up for the deficiencies of the law. It is plain, then, that this amendment imports no more, than that every man shall have a right to speak, write, and print his opinions upon any subject whatsoever, without any prior restraint, so always that he does not injure any other person in his rights, property, or personal reputation; and so always that he does not thereby disturb the public peace, or attempt to subvert the government. *It is in fact designed to guard against those abuses of power, by which, in*

some foreign governments, men are not permitted to speak
upon political subjects, or to write or publish anything with-
out the express license of the government for that purpose.

§446. A little attention to the history of other countries, in other ages, will teach us the vast importance of this right. It is notorious, that, even to this day, in some foreign countries, it is a crime to speak on any subject, religious, philosophical, or political, what is contrary to the received opinions of the government, or the institutions of the country, however laudable may be the design, and however virtuous may be the motive. Even to animadvert upon the conduct of public men, of rulers, or of representatives, in terms of the strictest truth and courtesy, has been, and is, deemed a scandal upon the supposed sanctity of their stations and characters, subjecting the party to grievous punishment. In some countries, no works can be printed at all, whether of science, or literature, or philosophy, without the previous approbation of the government; and the press has been shackled, and compelled to speak only in the timid language, which the cringing courtier, or the capricious inquisitor, has been willing to license for publication. The Bible itself, the common inheritance, not merely of Christendom, but of the world, has been put exclusively under the control of the government; and has not been allowed to be seen, or heard, or read, except in a language unknown to the common inhabitants of the country. To publish a translation in the vernacular tongue, has been in former times a flagrant offence.

§447. There is a good deal of loose reasoning on the subject of the liberty of the press, as if its inviolability were constitutionally such, that, like the King of England, it could do no wrong, and was free from every inquiry, and afforded a perfect sanctuary for every abuse; that, in short, it implied a despotic sovereignty to do every sort of wrong, without the slightest accountability to private or public justice. Such a notion is too extravagant to be held by any sound constitutional lawyer, with regard to the rights and duties belonging to governments generally, or to the state governments in particular. If it were admitted to be correct, it might be justly affirmed, that the liberty of the press was incomparable with the permanent existence of any free government. Mr. Justice Blackstone has remarked, that the liberty of the press, properly understood, is essential to the nature of a free state; but that this consists in laying no *previous* restraints upon publications, and not in freedom from censure for criminal matter, when published. Every freeman has an undoubted right to lay what sentiments he pleases before the public. To forbid this is to destroy the freedom of the press. But, if he publishes what is improper, mischievous, or illegal, he must take the consequences of his own temerity. To subject the press to the restrictive power of licenser, as was formerly done before, and since the Revolution, (of 1688,) is to subject all freedom of sentiment to the prejudices of one man, and make him the arbitrary and infallible judge of all controverted points in learning, religion, and government. But to punish any dangerous or offensive writings, when published, shall, on a fair and impartial trial, be adjudged of a pernicious tendency, is necessary for the preservation of peace and good order, of government and religion, the only solid foundations of civil liberty. Thus, the will of individuals is still left free; the abuse only of that free will is the object of legal punishment. Neither is any restraint hereby laid upon freedom of thought or inquiry; liberty of private sentiment is still left; the disseminating, or making public of bad sentiments, destructive of the ends of society is the crime, which society corrects. A man may be allowed to keep poisons in his closet; but not publicly to vend them as cordials. And, after some additional reflections, he concludes with this memorable sentence: "So true will it be found, that to censure the licentiousness, is to maintain the liberty of the press."

§448. The remaining clause, secures "The right of the people peaceably to assemble and to petition for a redress of grievances," a right of inestimable in itself, but often prohibited in foreign governments, under the pretence of preventing insurrections, and dangerous conspiracies against the government.

§449. This would seem unnecessary to be expressly provided for in a republican government, since it results from the very nature of its structure and institutions. It is impossible, that it could be practically denied, until the spirit of liberty had wholly disappeared, and the people had become so servile and debased, as to be unfit to exercise any of the privileges of freemen.

§450. The next amendment is, "A well-regulated militia being necessary to the security of a free state, the right of the people to keep and bear arms shall not be infringed." One of the ordinary modes, by which tyrants accomplish their purposes without resistance, is, by disarming the people, and making it an offence to keep arms, and by substituting a regular army in the stead of a resort to the militia. The friends of a free government cannot be too watchful, to overcome the dangerous tendency of the public mind to sacrifice, for the sake of mere private convenience, this powerful check upon the designs of ambitious men.

§451. The importance of this article will scarcely be doubted by any persons, who have duly reflected upon the subject. The militia is the natural defence of a free country against sudden foreign invasions, domestic insurrections, and domestic usurpations of power by rulers. It is against sound policy for a free people to keep up large military establishments and standing armies in time of peace, both from the enormous expenses, with which they are attended, and the facile means, which they afford to ambitious and unprincipled rulers, to subvert the government, or trample upon the right of the people. The right of the citizens to keep and bear arms had justly been considered, as the palladium of the liberties of a republic; since it offers a strong moral check against the usurpations and arbitrary power of rulers; and it will generally, even if these are successful in the first instance, enable the people to resist and triumph over them. And yet, though this truth would seem so clear, and the importance of a well-regulated militia would seem so undeniable, it cannot be disguised, that among the American people there is a growing indifference to any system of militia discipline, and a strong disposition, from a sense of its burdens, to be rid of all regulations. How it is practicable to keep the people duly armed without some organization, it is difficult to see. There is certainly no small danger, that indifference may lead to disgust, and disgust to contempt; and thus gradually undermine all the protection intended by this clause of our National Bill of Rights.

§452. The next amendment is, "No soldier shall in time of peace be quartered in any house without the consent of the owner; nor in time of war, but in a manner to be prescribed by law." This provision speaks for itself. In arbitrary times it has not been unusual for military officers, with the connivance, or under the sanction of the government, to billet soldiers upon private citizens, without the slightest regard to their rights, or comfort.

§453. The next amendment is, "The enumeration in the Constitution of certain rights shall not be construed to deny, or disparage others retained by the People." The object of this clause is to get rid of a very common but perverse misapplication of a known maxim, that an affirmation of a power in particular cases, implies a negation of it in all other cases; and so, on the other hand, that a negation of a power in some cases, implies an affirmation of it in all others not denied. The maxim, when rightly understood, is perfectly sound and safe; but it has often been abused to purposes injurious to the rights of the people; and therefore the present clause was wisely inserted to prevent any such false interpretations and glosses of the Constitution.

§454. The next and last amendment, which has not been already considered, is, "The powers not delegated to the United States by the Constitution, nor prohibited by it to the States, are reserved to the States respectively, or to the People." This amendment follows out the object of the preceding; and is merely an affirmation of a rule of construction of the Constitution, which, upon any just reasoning, must have existed without it. Still, it is important as a security against two opposite tendencies of opinion, each of which is equally subversive of the true import of the Constitution. The one is to *imply* all powers, which may be useful to the National Government, which are not *expressly prohibited;* and the other is, to deny all powers to the National Government, which are not *expressly granted.* We have already seen, that there are many implied powers necessarily resulting from the nature of the express powers; and it is as clear, that no power can properly arise by implication from a mere prohibition. *The Government of the United States is one of limited powers; and no authority exists beyond the prescribed limits, marked out in the instrument itself. Whatever powers are not granted, necessarily belong to the respective States, or to the people of the respective States, if they have not been confided by them to the State Governments.*

CHAPTER XXXVIII.

Concluding Remarks

§455. WE have now reviewed all the provisions of the original Constitution of the United States, and all the Amendments, which have been incorporated into it. And here, the task, originally proposed in these Commentaries, is brought to a close. Many reflections naturally crowd upon the mind at such a moment; many grateful recollections of the past; and many anxious thoughts of the future. The past is secure. It is unalterable. The seal of eternity is upon it. The wisdom, which it has displayed, and the blessings, which it has bestowed, cannot be obscured; neither can they be debased by human folly, or by human infirmity. The future, is that, which may well awaken the most earnest solicitude, both for the virtue and the permanence of our Republic. The fate of other republics, their rise, their progress, their decline, and their fall, are written but too legibly on the pages of history, if, indeed, they were not continually before us in the startling fragments of their ruins. Those republics have perished; and have perished by their own hands. Prosperity has enervated them; corruption has debased them; and a venal populace has consummated their destruction. The people, alternately the prey of military chieftains at home, and of ambitious invaders from abroad, have been sometimes cheated out of their liberties by servile demagogues; sometimes betrayed into a surrender of them by false patriots; and sometimes they have willingly sold them for a price to the despot, who has bidden highest for his victims. They have disregarded the warning voice of their best statesmen; and have persecuted and driven from office their truest friends. They have listened to the councils of fawning sycophants, or base calumniators of the wise and the good. They have reverenced power more in its high abuses and summary movements, than in its calm and constitutional energy, when it dispensed blessings with an unseen, but a liberal hand. They have surrendered to faction, what belongs to the common interests and common rights of the country. Patronage and party, the triumph of an artful popular leader, and the discontents of a day, have outweighed, in their view, all solid principles and institutions of government. Such are the melancholy lessons of the past history of republics down to our own.

§456. It is not my design to detain the reader by any elaborate reflections addressed to his judgement, either by way of admonition or of encouragement. But it may not be wholly without use to glance at one or two considerations, upon which our meditations cannot be too frequently indulged.

§457. In the first place, it cannot escape our notice, how exceedingly difficult it is to settle the foundations of any government upon principles, which do not admit of some controversy or question. The very elements, out of which it is to be built, are susceptible of infinite modifications; and theory too often deludes us by the attractive simplicity of its plans, and imagination by the visionary perfection of its speculations. In theory, a government may promise the most perfect harmony of operations in all its various combinations. In practice, the whole machinery may be perpetually retarded, or thrown out of order by accidental maladjustments. In theory, a government may seem deficient in unity of design and symmetry of parts; and yet, in practice, it may work with astonishing accuracy and force for the general welfare. Whatever, then, has been found to work well by experience, should rarely be hazarded upon conjectural improvements. Time, and long and steady operations are indispensable to the perfection of all social institutions. To be of any value, these institutions must become cemented with the habits, the feelings, and the pursuits of the people. Every change discomposes for a while the whole arrangements of the system. What is safe, is not always expedient; what is new, is often pregnant with unforeseen evils, or attracts only by imaginary good.

§458. In the next place, the slighest attention to the history of the National Constitution must satisfy every reflecting mind, how many difficulties attended its formation and adoption, from real or imaginary difference of State interests, sectional feelings, and local institutions. It is an attempt to create a National sovereignty, and yet to preserve the State sovereignties; although it is impossible to assign definite boundaries in all cases to the power of each. The influence of the disturbing causes, which, more than once in the Convention, were on the point of breaking up the Union, have since immeasurably increased in concentration and vigor. The very inequalities of a government, confessedly founded in a compromise, were then felt with a strong sensibility; and every new source of discontent, whether accidental or permanent, has since added increased activity to the painful sense of these inequalities. The North cannot but perceive, that it has yielded to the South a superiority of Representative already amounting to twenty-five, beyond its due proportion; and the South imagines, that, with all this preponderance in representation, the other parts of the Union enjoy a more prefect protection of their interests, than its own. The West feels its growing power and weight in the Union; and the Atlantic States begin to learn, that the sceptre must soon, and perhaps forever, depart from them. If, under these circumstances, the Union should once be broken up, it is impossible, that a new Constitution should ever be formed, embracing the whole Territory. We shall be divided into several nations or confederacies, rivals in power, pursuits, and interests; too proud to brook injury, and too near to make retaliation distant or ineffectual. Our very animosities will, like those of all other kindred nations, become more deadly, because our lineage, our laws, and our language are the same. Let the history of the Grecian and Italian republics warn us of our dangers. The National Constitution is our last, and our only security. United we stand, divided we fall.

§459. If this Work shall but inspire the rising generation with a more ardent love of their country, and unquenchable thirst for liberty, and a profound reverence for the Constitution and the Union, then it will have accomplished all that its author ought to desire. Let the American youth never forget that they possess a noble inheritance, bought by the toils, and sufferings, and blood of their ancestors; and capable, if wisely improved, and faithfully guarded, of transmitting to their latest posterity all the substantial blessings of life, the peaceful enjoyment of liberty, of property, of religion, and of independence. The structure has been erected by architects of consummate skill and fidelity; its foundations are solid; its compartments are beautiful, as well as useful; its arrangements are full of wisdom and order; and its defences are impregnable from without. It has been reared for immortality, if the work of man may justly aspire to such a title. It may, nevertheless, perish in an hour, by the folly, or corruption, or negligence of its only keepers, THE PEOPLE. Republics are created by the virtue, public spirit, and intelligence of the citizens. They fall, when the wise are banished from the public councils, because they dare to be honest, and the profligate are rewarded, because they flatter the people, in order to betray them.

APPENDIX.

DECLARATION OF RIGHTS

OF THE CONTINENTAL CONGRESS, OCTOBER 14, 1774

WHEREAS, since the close of the last war, the British Parliament, claiming a power of right, to bind the people of America by Statutes in all cases whatsoever, hath in some Acts expressly imposed taxes on them, and in others, under various pretences, but in fact for the purpose of raising a revenue, hath imposed rates and duties payable in these Colonies, established a Board of Commissioners, with unconstitutional powers, and extended the jurisdiction of Courts of Admiralty, not only for collecting the said duties, but for the trial of causes merely arising within the body of a county:

And whereas, in consequences of other Statutes, judges, who before held only estates at will in their offices, have been made dependent on the Crown alone, for their salaries, and standing armies kept in times of peace; and whereas, it has lately been resolved in Parliament, that by force of a Statute, made in the thirty-fifth year of the reign of King Henry the VII., Colonists may be transported to England, and tried there, upon accusations for treasons and misprisions, or concealments, of treasons committed in the Colonies, and by a late

Statute, such trials have been directed in cases therein mentioned:

And whereas, in the last session of Parliament, three Statutes were made; one entitled, 'An Act to discontinue, in such manner, and for such time, as are therein mentioned, the landing and discharging, lading, or shipping of goods, wares, and merchandize, at the town, and within the harbor, of Boston, in the Province of Massachusetts Bay in North America;' another entitled, 'An Act for the better regulating the government of the Province of Massachusetts Bay in New England,' and another entitled, 'An Act for the impartial administration of justice, in the cases of persons questioned for any act done by them in the execution of the law, or for the suppression of riots and tumults, in the Province of the Massachusetts Bay in New England:' And another Statute was then made, "for making more effectual provision for the government of the Province of Quebec," &c. All which Statutes are impolitic, unjust, and cruel, as well as unconstitutional, and most dangerous and destructive of American rights:

And whereas, Assemblies have been frequently dissolved, contrary to the rights of the People, when they attempted to deliberate on grievances; and their dutiful, humble, loyal, and reasonable, petitions to the Crown for redress, have been repeatedly treated with contempt, by his Majesty's ministers of state:

The good People of the several Colonies of New Hampshire, Massachusetts Bay, Rhode Island and Providence Plantations, Connecticut, New York, New Jersey, Pennsylvania, Newcastle, Kent, and Sussex, on Delaware, Maryland, Virginia, North Carolina, and South Carolina, justly alarmed at these arbitrary proceedings of Parliament and Administration, have severally elected, constituted, and appointed Deputies to meet and sit in General Congress, in the city of Philadelphia, in order to obtain such establishment, as that their religion, laws and liberties, may not be subverted; whereupon the Deputies so appointed being now assembled, in a full and free representation of these Colonies, taking into their most serious consideration, the best means of attaining the ends aforesaid, do, in the first place, as Englishmen their ancestors in like cases have usually done, for asserting and vindicating their rights and liberties, DECLARE,

That the inhabitants of the English Colonies in North America, by the immutable laws of Nature, the principles of the English Constitution, and the several Charters or Compacts, have the following RIGHTS.

Resolved, N.C.D.* 1. That they are entitled to life, liberty, and property; and they have never ceded to any Sovereign power whatever, a right to dispose of either, without their consent.

Resolved, N.C.D. 2. That our ancestors, who first settled these Colonies, were, at the time of their emigration from the mother Country, entitled to all the rights, liberties, and immunities, of free and natural-born subjects, within the realm of England.

Resolved, N.C.D. 3. That, by such emigration, they by no means forfeited, surrendered, or lost, any of those rights, but that they were, and their descendants now are, entitled to the exercise and enjoyment of all such of them, as their local and other circumstances enable them to exercise and enjoy.

Resolved, 4. That the foundation of English liberty, and of all free government, is, a right in the People to participate in their legislative council; and as the English Colonists are not represented, and, from their local and other circumstances, cannot properly be represented, in the British Parliament, they are entitled to a free and exclusive power of legislation in their several provincial legislatures, where their right of representation can alone be preserved, in all cases of taxation and internal polity, subject only to the negative of their Sovereign, in such manner as has been heretofore used and accustomed; but, from the necessity of the case, and a regard to the mutual interests of both Countries, we cheerfully consent to the operation of such Acts of the British Parliament, as are, *bonâ fide,*

---

* *Nemine contradicente,* no person opposing, or disagreeing.

restrained to the regulation of our external commerce, for the purpose of securing the commercial advantages of the whole empire to the mother Country, and the commercial benefits of its respective members; excluding every idea of taxation, internal or external, for raising a revenue on the subjects in America, without their consent.

Resolved, N.C.D. 5. That the respective Colonies are entitled to the common law of England, and more especially to the great and inestimable privilege of being tried by their peers of the vicinage, according to the course of that law.

Resolved, 6. That they are entitled to the benefit of such of the English Statutes, as existed at the time of their colonization; and which they have, by experience, respectively found to be applicable to their several local and other circumstances.

Resolved, N.C.D. 7. That these, his Majesty's Colonies, are likewise entitled to all the immunities and privileges, granted and confirmed to them by royal Charters, or secured by their several codes of provincial laws.

Resolved, N.C.D. 8. That they have a right peaceably to assemble, consider of their grievances, and petition the King; and that all prosecutions, prohibitory proclamations, and commitments for the same, are illegal.

Resolved, N.C.D. 9. That the keeping a standing army in these Colonies, in times of peace, without the consent of the legislature of that Colony in which such army is kept, is against law.

Resolved, N.C.D. 10. It is indispensably necessary to good government, and rendered essential by the English Constitution, that the constituent branches of the legislature be independent of each other; that, therefore, the exercise of legislative power, in several Colonies, by a Council appointed, during pleasure, by the Crown, is unconstitutional, dangerous, and destructive to the freedom of American legislation.

All and each of which, the aforesaid Deputies, in behalf of themselves, and their Constituents, do claim, demand, and insist on, as their indubitable rights and liberties; which cannot be legally taken from them, altered, or abridged, by any power

whatever, without their own consent, by the ⟍
in their several provincial Legislatures.

DECLARATION OF INDEPENDENCE.

A DECLARATION by the Representatives of the United
of America, in Congress assembled.

When, in the course of human events, it becomes necess⟍y
for one people to dissolve the political bands which have connected them with another, and to assume, among the powers
of the earth, the separate and equal station to which the laws
of nature, and of nature's God, entitle them, a decent respect
to the opinions of mankind requires, that they should declare
the causes which impel them to the separation.

We hold these truths to be self-evident: that all men are created equal; that they are endowed, by their Creator, with certain unalienable rights; that among these, are life, liberty, and
the pursuit of happiness. That, to secure these rights, governments are instituted among men, deriving their just powers
from the consent of the governed; that, whenever any form of
government becomes destructive of these ends, it is the right
of the people to alter or to abolish it, and to institute new government, laying its foundation on such principles, and organizing its powers in such form, as to them shall seem most
likely to effect their safety and happiness. Prudence, indeed,
will dictate, that governments, long established, should not be
changed for light and transient causes; and, accordingly, all experience hath shown, that mankind are more disposed to suffer, while evils are sufferable, than to right themselves, by
abolishing the forms to which they are accustomed. But, when
a long train of abuses and usurpations, pursuing invariably the
same object, evinces a design to reduce them under absolute
despotism, it is their right, it is their duty, to throw off such
government, and to provide new guards for their future security. Such has been the patient sufferance of these Colonies;
and such is now the necessity which constrains them to alter
their former systems of government. The history of the
present King of Great Britain is a history of repeated injuries

and usurpations, all having, in direct object, the establishment of an absolute tyranny over these States. To prove this, let facts be submitted to a candid world.

He has refused his assent to laws the most wholesome and necessary for the public good.

He has forbidden his governors to pass laws of immediate and pressing importance, unless suspended in their operation till his assent should be obtained; and, when so suspended, he has utterly neglected to attend to them.

He has refused to pass other laws for the accommodation of large districts of people, unless those people would relinquish the right of representation in the legislature: a right inestimable to them, and formidable to tyrants only.

He has called together legislative bodies at places unusual, uncomfortable, and distant from the depository of their public records, for the sole purpose of fatiguing them into compliance with his measures.

He has dissolved representative houses, repeatedly, for opposing, with manly firmness, his invasions on the rights of the people.

He has refused, for a long time, after such dissolutions, to cause others to be elected; whereby the legislative powers, incapable of annihilation, have returned to the people at large for their exercise; the State remaining, in the mean time, exposed to all the dangers of invasion from without, and convulsions within.

He has endeavored to prevent the population of these States; for that purpose, obstructing the laws for naturalization of foreigners; refusing to pass others to encourage their migrations hither, and raising the conditions of new appropriations of lands.

He has obstructed the administration of justice, by refusing his assent to laws for establishing judiciary powers.

He has made judges dependent on his will alone, for the tenure of their offices, and the amount and payment of their salaries.

He has erected a multitude of new offices, and sent hither

swarms of officers to harass our people, and eat out their substance.

He has kept among us, in time of peace, standing armies, without the consent of our legislature.

He has affected to render the military independent of, and superior to, the civil power.

He has combined, with others, to subject us to a jurisdiction foreign to our constitution, and unacknowledged by our laws; giving his assent to their acts of pretended legislation:

For quartering large bodies of armed troops among us:

For protecting them, by a mock-trial, from punishment, for any murders which they should commit on the inhabitants of these States:

For cutting off our trade with all parts of the world:

For imposing taxes on us, without our consent:

For depriving us, in many cases, of the benefits of trial by jury:

For transporting us beyond seas, to be tried for pretended offences:

For abolishing the free system of English laws in a neighboring Province, establishing therein an arbitrary government, and enlarging its boundaries, so as to render it, at once, an example and fit instrument for introducing the same absolute rule into these Colonies:

For taking away our charters, abolishing our most valuable laws, and altering, fundamentally, the forms of our governments:

For suspending our own legislatures, and declaring themselves invested with power to legislate for us, in all cases whatsoever.

He has abdicated government here, by declaring us out of his protection, and waging war against us.

He has plundered our seas, ravaged our coasts, burnt our towns, and destroyed the lives of our people.

He is, at this time, transporting large armies of foreign mercenaries, to complete the works of death, desolation, and tyranny, already begun with circumstances of cruelty and perfidy, scarcely paralleled in the most barbarous ages, and totally unworthy the head of a civilized nation.

He has constrained our fellow-citizens, taken captive on the high seas, to bear arms against their country, to become the executioners of their friends and bretheren, or to fall themselves by their hands.

He has excited domestic insurrections amongst us, and has endeavored to bring on the inhabitants of our frontiers, the merciless Indian savages, whose known rule of warfare is an undistinguished destruction of all ages, sexes, and conditions.

In every state of these oppressions, we have petitioned for redress, in the most humble terms: Our repeated petitions have been answered only by repeated injury. A prince, whose character is thus marked by every act which may define a tyrant, is unfit to be the ruler of a free people.

Nor have we been wanting in attentions to our British bretheren. We have warned them, from time to time, of attempts, by their legislature, to extend an unwarrantable jurisdiction over us. We have reminded them of the circumstances of our emigration and settlement here. We have applied to their native justice and magnanimity, and we have conjured them, by the ties of our common kindred, to disavow these usurpations, which would inevitably interrupt our connexions and correspondence. They too, have been deaf to the voice of justice and of consanguinity. We must, therefore, acquiesce in the necessity, which denounces our separation, and hold them, as we hold the rest of mankind, enemies in war, in peace, friends.

We, therefore, the representatives of the UNITED STATES OF AMERICA, in GENERAL CONGRESS assembled, appealing to the Supreme Judge of the World, for the rectitude of our intentions, do, in the name, and by authority, of the good People of these Colonies, solemnly publish and declare, That these United Colonies are and of right ought to be, FREE AND INDEPENDENT STATES, they have full power to levy war, conclude peace, contract alliances, establish commerce, and to do all other acts and things, which INDEPENDENT STATES may of right do. And, for the support of this declaration, with a firm reliance on the protection of DIVINE PROVIDENCE, we mutually pledge to each other, our lives, our fortunes, and our sacred honor.

ARTICLES OF CONFEDERATION

And perpetual union, between the States of New Hampshire, Massachusetts Bay, Rhode Island and Providence Plantations, Connecticut, New York, New Jersey, Pennsylvania, Delaware, Maryland, Virginia, North Carolina, South Carolina, and Georgia.

ARTICLE I.

THE style of this confederacy shall be, "THE UNITED STATES OF AMERICA."

ARTICLE II.

Each State retains its sovereignty, freedom, and independence, and every power, jurisdiction, and right, which is not by this Confederation, expressly delegated to the United States in Congress assembled.

ARTICLE III.

The said States hereby severally enter into a firm league of friendship with each other, for their common defence, the security of their liberties, and their mutual and general welfare; binding themselves to assist each other against all force offered to, or attacks made upon, them, or any of them, on account of religion, sovereignty, trade, or any other pretence whatever.

ARTICLE IV.

The better to secure and perpetuate mutual friendship and intercourse among the people of the different States in this Union, the free inhabitants of each of these States, paupers, vagabonds, and fugitives from justice, excepted, shall be entitled to all privileges and immunities of free citizens, in the several States; and the people of each State shall have free ingress and regress to and from any other State; and shall enjoy therein all the privileges of trade and commerce, subject to the same duties, impositions, and restrictions, as the inhabitants thereof respectively; provided, that such restriction shall not extend so far as to prevent the removal of property imported into any State, to any other State of which the owner is an inhabitant; provided also, that no imposition, duties, or restriction, shall be laid by any State, on the property of the United States, or either of them.

If any person guilty of, or charged with, treason, felony, or other high misdemeanor, in any State, shall flee from justice, and be found in any of the United States, he shall, upon demand of the governor or executive power of the State from which he fled, be delivered up, and removed to the State having jurisdiction of his offence.

Full faith and credit shall be given in each of these States to the records, acts, and judicial proceedings, of the courts and magistrates of every other State.

ARTICLE V.

For the more convenient management of the general interests of the United States, delegates shall be annually appointed in such manner as the legislature of each State shall direct, to meet in Congress on the first Monday in November, in every year, with a power reserved to each State to recall its delegates, or any of them, at any time within the year, and send others in their stead, for the remainder of the year.

No State shall be represented in Congress by less than two, nor by more than seven, members; and no person shall be capable of being a delegate for more than three years in any term of six years; nor shall any person, being a delegate, be capable of holding any office under the United States, for which he, or another for his benefit, receives any salary, fees, or emolument of any kind.

Each State shall maintain its own delegates in a meeting of the States, and while they act as members of the committee of the States.

In determining questions in the United States in Congress assembled, each State shall have one vote.

Freedom of speech and debate in Congress shall not be impeached or questioned, in any court or place out of Congress;

and the members of Congress shall be protected in their persons from arrests and imprisonment, during the time of their going to, and from, and attendance on, Congress, except for treason, felony, or breach of the peace.

ARTICLE VI.

No State, without the consent of the United States in Congress assembled, shall send any embassy to, or receive any embassy from, or enter into any conference, agreement, alliance, or treaty, with any king, prince, or state; nor shall any person, holding any office of profit, or trust, under the United States, or any of them, accept of any present, emolument, office, or title, of any kind whatever, from being king, prince, or foreign state; nor shall the United States in Congress assembled, or any of them, grant any title of nobility.

No two or more States shall enter into any treaty, confederation, or alliance whatever, between them, without the consent of the United States in Congress assembled, specifying accurately the purposes for which the same is to be entered into, and how long it shall continue.

No State shall lay any imposts or duties, which may interfere with any stipulations in treaties entered into, by the United States in Congress assembled, with any king, prince, or state, in pursuance of any treaties, already proposed by Congress to the courts of France and Spain.

No vessels of war shall be kept up, in time of peace, by any State, except such number only, as shall be deemed necessary, by the United States in Congress assembled, for the defence of such State, or its trade; nor shall any body of forces be kept up by any State, in time of peace, except such number only, as in the judgement of the United States in Congress assembled, shall be deemed requisite to garrison the forts necessary for the defence of such State: but every State shall always keep up a well-regulated and disciplined militia, sufficiently armed and accoutred; and shall provide and constantly have ready for use, in public stores, a due number of field-pieces and tents, and a proper quantity of arms, ammunition, and camp equipage.

No State shall engage in any war, without the consent of the

United States in Congress assembled, unless such State be actually invaded by enemies, or shall have received certain advice of a resolution being formed by some nation of Indians to invade such State, and the danger is so imminent as not to admit of a delay, till the United States in Congress assembled can be consulted; nor shall any State grant commissions to any ship or vessels of war, nor letters of marque or reprisal, except it be after a declaration of war by the United States in Congress assembled; and then only against which war has been so declared, and under such regulations as shall be established by the United States in Congress assembled; unless such State be infested by pirates, in which vessels of war may be fitted out for that occasion, and kept so long as the danger shall continue, or until the United States in Congress assembled shall determine otherwise.

ARTICLE VII.

When land forces are raised by any State for the common defence, all officers of, or under, the rank of colonel, shall be appointed by the legislature of each State respectively, by whom such forces shall be raised, or in such manner as such State shall direct; and all vacancies shall be filled up by the State which first made the appointment.

ARTICLE VIII.

All charges of war, and all other expenses that shall be incurred for the common defence, or general welfare, and allowed by the United States in Congress assembled, shall be defrayed out of a common treasury, which shall be supplied by the several States in proportion to the value of all land within each State, granted to, or surveyed for, any person, as such land and the buildings and improvements thereon shall be estimated, according to such mode as the United States in Congress assembled shall, from time to time, direct and appoint. The taxes for paying that proportion, shall be laid and levied by the authority and direction of the legislatures of the several States, within the time agreed upon by the United States in Congress assembled.

ARTICLE IX.

The United States in Congress assembled, shall have the sole and exclusive right and power, of determining on peace and war, except in the cases, mentioned in the sixth article: Of sending and receiving ambassadors: Entering into treaties and alliances; provided that no treaty of commerce shall be made, whereby the legislative power of the respective States shall be restrained from imposing such imposts and duties on foreigners as their own people are subjected to, or from prohibiting the exportation or importation of any species of goods or commodities whatever: Of establishing rules for deciding, in all cases, what captures on land or water shall be legal; and in what manner prizes, taken by land or naval forces, in the service of the United States, shall be divided or appropriated: Of granting letters of marque and reprisal, in times of peace: Appointing courts, for the trial of piracies and felonies, committed on the high seas; and establishing courts, for receiving and determining, finally, appeals in all cases of captures; provided, that no member of Congress shall be appointed a judge of any of the said courts.

The United States in Congress assembled shall also be the last resort, on appeal, in all disputes and differences now subsisting, or that hereafter may arise, between two or more States, concerning boundary, jurisdiction, or any other cause whatever; which authority shall always be exercised in the manner following: Whenever the legislative or executive authority, or lawful agent, of any State, in controversy with another, shall present a petition to Congress, stating the matter in question, and praying for a hearing, notice thereof shall be given, by order of Congress, to the legislative or executive authority of the other State in controversy; and a day assigned, for the appearances of the parties by their lawful agents, who shall then be directed to appoint, by joint consent, commissioners or judges, to constitute a court for hearing and determining the matter in question: but if they cannot agree, Congress shall name three persons, out of each of the United States; and from the list of such persons, each party shall alternately strike out one, the petitioners beginning, until the number shall be reduced to thirteen; and from that number, not less than seven, nor more than nine, names, as Congress shall direct, shall, in the presence of Congress, be drawn out, by lot; and the persons whose names shall be so drawn, or any five of them, shall be commissioners or judges, to hear and finally determine the controversy so always as a major part of the judges, who shall hear the cause, shall agree in the determination. And if either party shall neglect to attend at the day appointed, without showing reasons which Congress shall judge sufficient, or being present shall refuse to strike, the Congress shall proceed to nominate three persons out of each State; and the Secretary of Congress shall strike in behalf of such party absent or refusing; and the judgement and sentence of the court, to be appointed in the manner before prescribed, shall be final and conclusive. And if any of the parties shall refuse to submit to the authority of such court, or to appear, or defend their claim or cause, the court shall, nevertheless, proceed to pronounce sentence or judgement, which shall in like manner be final and decisive; the judgement, or sentence, and other proceedings, being, in either case, transmitted to Congress, and lodged among the acts of Congress, for the security of the parties concerned: Provided, that every commissioner, before he sits in judgement, shall take an oath, to be administered by one of the judges of the supreme or superior court of the State, where the cause shall be tried. 'Well and truly to hear and determine the matter in question, according to the best of his judgement, without favor, affection, or hope of reward:' Provided, also, that no State shall be deprived of territory for the benefit of the United States.

All controversies concerning the private right of soil claimed under different grants of two or more States, whose jurisdictions, as they may respect such lands and the States which passed such grants, are adjusted, the said grants, or either of them, being at the same time claimed to have originated antecendent to such settlement of jurisdiction, shall, on the petition of either party to the Congress of the United States, be finally determined, as near as may be, in the same manner as is before prescribed for deciding disputes respecting territorial jurisdiction between different States.

The United States in Congress assembled shall also have the sole and exclusive right and power of regulating the alloy and value of coin struck by their own authority; or by that of the respective States: Fixing the standard of weights and measures throughout the United States: Regulating the trade and managing all affairs with the Indians, not members of any of the States; provided that the legislative right of any State within its own limits be not infringed or violated: Establishing and regulating post-offices from one State to another, throughout all the United States, and exacting such postage on the papers passing through the same as may be requisite to defray the expenses of the said officers: Appointing all the officers of the naval forces, and commissioning all officers whatever in the service of the United States: Making rules for the government and regulation of the land and naval forces, and directing their operations.

The United States in Congress assembled shall have the authority to appoint a committee, to sit in the recess of Congress, to be denominated A COMMITTEE OF THE STATES, and to consist of one delegate from each State; and to appoint such other committees and civil officers as may be necessary for managing the general affairs of the United States under their direction: To appoint one of their number to preside; provided, that no person be allowed to serve in the office of President more than one year in any term of three years. To ascertain the necessary sums of money to be raised for the service of the United States, and to appropriate and apply the same for defraying the public expenses: To borrow money, or emit bills on the credit of the United States, transmitting every half year to the respective States an account of the sums of money so borrowed or emitted: To build and equip a navy: To agree upon the number of land forces, and to make requisitions from each State for its quota, in proportion to the number of white inhabitants in such State, which requisition shall be binding; and thereupon the legislature of each State shall appoint the regimental officers, raise the men, and clothe, arm, and equip them, in a soldierlike manner, at the expense of the United States; and the

341

officers and men so clothed, armed, and equipped, shall march to the place appointed, and within the time agreed on, by the United States in Congress assembled: but if the United States in Congress assembled shall, on consideration of circumstances, judge proper that any State should not raise men, or should raise a smaller number than its quota, and that any other State should raise a greater number of men than its quota thereof, such extra number shall be raised, officered, clothed, armed, and equipped, in the same manner as the quota of such State; unless the legislature of such State shall judge that such extra number cannot be safely spared out of the same; in which case they shall raise, officer, clothe, arm, and equip, as many of such extra number as they judge can be safely spared: and the officers and men so clothed, armed, and equipped, shall march to the place appointed, and within the time agreed on, by the United States in Congress assembled.

The United States in Congress assembled shall never engage in a war; nor grant letters of marque and reprisal in time of peace; nor enter into any treaties or alliances; nor coin money; nor regulate the value thereof, nor ascertain the sums and expenses necessary for the defence and welfare of the United States, or any of them; nor emit bills; nor borrow money on the credit of the United States; nor appropriate money; nor agree upon the number of vessels of war to be built or purchased, or the number of land or sea forces to be raised; nor appoint a Commander-in-Chief of the army or navy; unless nine States assent to the same; nor shall a question on any other point, except for adjourning from day to day, be determined, unless by the votes of a majority of the United States in Congress assembled.

The Congress of the United States shall have power to adjourn to any time within the year, and to place within the United States, so that no period of adjournment be for a longer duration than the space of six months; and shall publish the journal of their proceedings monthly except such parts thereof relating to treaties, alliances, or military operations, as in their judgement require secrecy, and the yeas and nays of the delegates of each State, on any question, shall be entered on the journal, when it is desired by any delegate; and the delegates of a State, or any of them, at his or their request, shall be furnished with a transcript of the said journal, except such parts as are above expected, to lay before the legislatures of the several States.

ARTICLE X.

The Committee of the States, or any nine of them, shall be authorized to execute, in the recess of Congress, such of the powers of Congress as the United States in Congress assembled, by the consent of nine States, shall, from time to time, think expedient to vest them with; provided, that no power be delegated to the said Committee, for the exercise of which, by the articles of Confederation, the voice of nine States in the Congress of the United States assembled is requisite.

ARTICLE XI.

Canada, acceding to this Confederation, and joining in the measures of the United States, shall be admitted into, and entitled to all the advantages of, this Union. But no other Colony shall be admitted into the same, unless such admission be agreed to by nine States.

ARTICLE XII.

All bills of credit emitted, moneys borrowed, and debts contracted, by or under the authority of Congress, before the assembling of the United States, in pursuance of the present Confederation, shall be deemed and considered as a charge against the United States, for payment and satisfaction whereof, the said United States, and the public faith, are hereby solemnly pledged.

ARTICLE XIII.

Every State shall abide by the determinations of the United States in Congress assembled, on all questions which, by this Confederation, are submitted to them. And the Articles of this Confederation shall be inviolably observed by every State; and the Union shall be perpetual. Nor shall any alteration at any time hereafter be made in any of them, unless such alteration be agreed to, in a Congress of the United States, and be afterwards confirmed by the legislatures of every State.

And whereas, it hath pleased the great Governor of the World, to incline the hearts of the legislatures we respectively represent in Congress to approve of, and to authorize us to ratify, the said Articles of Confederation and Perpetual Union:

KNOW YE, That we, the undersigned delegates, by virtue of the power and authority to us given for that purpose, do, by these presents, in the name, and in behalf, of our respective constituents, fully and entirely ratify and confirm each and every of the said Articles of Confederation and Perpetual Union, and all and singular the matters and things therein contained. And we do further solemnly plight and engage the faith of our respective constituents, that they shall abide by the determinations of the United States in Congress assembled, on all questions, which by the said Confederation, are submitted to them; and that the articles thereof shall be inviolably observed by the States we respectively represent; and that the Union shall be perpetual.

In witness whereof, we have hereunto set our hands in Congress.

Done at Philadelphia, in the State of Pennsylvania, the ninth day of July, in the year of our Lord one thousand seven hundred and seventy-eight, and in the third year of the Independence of America.

CONSTITUTION

OF THE

UNITED STATES OF AMERICA

WE, the People of the United States, in order to form a more perfect union, establish justice, insure domestic tranquility, provide for the common defence, promote the general welfare, and secure the blessings of liberty to ourselves and our posterity, do ordain and establish this Constitution for the United States of America.

ARTICLE I.

SECTION 1.

1. All Legislative powers herein granted, shall be vested in a Congress of the United States, which shall consist of a Senate and House of Representatives.

SECTION 2.

1. The House of Representatives shall be composed of members chosen every second year by the people of the several States, and the electors in each State shall have the qualifications requisite for electors of the most numerous branch of the State Legislature.

2. No person shall be a Representative who shall not have attained to the age of twenty-five years, and been seven years a citizen of the United States, and who'll not, when elected, be an inhabitant of that State in which he shall be chosen.

3. Representatives and direct taxes shall be apportioned among the several States which may be included within this Union, according to their respective numbers, which shall be determined by adding to the whole number of free persons, including those bound to service for a term of years, and excluding Indians not taxed, three fifths of all other persons. The actual enumeration shall be made within three years after the first meeting of the Congress of the United States, and within every subsequent term of ten years, in such manner as they shall by law direct. The number of Representatives shall not exceed one for every thirty thousand, but each State shall have at least one Representative; and until such enumeration shall be made, the State of New Hampshire shall be entitled to choose three, Massachusetts eight, Rhode Island and Providence Plantations one, Connecticut five, New York six, New Jersey four, Pennsylvania eight, Delaware one, Maryland six, Virginia ten, North Carolina five, South Carolina five, and Georgia three.

4. When vacancies happen in the representation from any State, the executive authority thereof shall issue writs of election to fill such vacancies.

5. The House of Representatives shall choose their Speaker and other officers; and shall have the sole power of impeachment.

SECTION 3.

1. The Senate of the United States shall be composed of two Senators from each State, chosen by the legislature thereof, for six years; and each Senator shall have one vote.

2. Immediately after they shall be assembled in consequence of the first election, they shall be divided, as equally as may be, into three classes. The seats of the Senators of the first class shall be vacated at the expiration of the second year; of the second class, at the expiration of the fourth year; and of the third class, at the expiration of the sixth year; so that one third may be chosen every second year; and if vacancies happen by resignation, or otherwise, during the recess of the legislature of any State, the executive thereof may make temporary appointments until the next meeting of the legislature, which shall then fill such vacancies.

3. No person shall be a Senator who shall not have attained to the age of thirty years, and been nine years a citizen of the United States, and who shall not, when elected, be an inhabitant of that State for which he shall be chosen.

4. The Vice-President of the United States shall be President of the Senate, but shall have no vote, unless they be equally divided.

5. The Senate shall choose their other officers, and also a President *pro tempore,* in the absence of the Vice-President, or when he shall exercise the office of President of the United States.

6. The Senate shall have the sole power to try all impeachments. When sitting for that purpose, they shall be on oath or affirmation. When the President of the United States is tried, the Chief Justice shall preside and no person shall be convicted without the concurrence of two thirds of the members present.

7. Judgement in cases of impeachment shall not extend further than to removal from office, and disqualification to hold and enjoy any office of honor, trust, or profit, under the United States; but the party convicted shall, nevertheless, be liable and subject to indictment, trial, judgement, and punishment, according to law.

SECTION 4.

1. The times, places, and manner, of holding elections for Senators and Representatives, shall be prescribed in each State by the legislature thereof: but the Congress may at any time, by law, make or alter such regulations, except as to the place of choosing Senators.

2. The Congress shall assemble at least once in every year, and such meeting shall be on the first Monday in December, unless they shall by law appoint a different day.

SECTION 5.

1. Each House shall be the judge of the elections, returns, and qualifications, of its own members, and a majority of each shall constitute a quorum to do business; but a smaller number may adjourn from day to day, and may be authorized to compel the attendance of absent members, in such manner, and under such penalties, as each House may provide.

2. Each House may determine the rules of its proceedings, punish its members for disorderly behavior, and, with the concurrence of two thirds, expel a member.

3. Each House shall keep a journal of its proceedings, and, from time to time, publish the same, excepting such parts as may, in their judgement, require secrecy; and the yeas and nays of the members of either House, on any question, shall, at the desire of one fifth of those present, be entered on the journal.

4. Neither House, during the session of Congress, shall, without the consent of the other, adjourn for more than three days, nor to any other place than that in which the two Houses shall be sitting.

SECTION 6.

1. The Senators and Representatives shall receive a compen-

sation for their services, to be ascertained by law, and paid out of the treasury of the United States. They shall, in all cases, except treason, felony, and breach of the peace, be privileged from arrest during their attendance at the session of their respective Houses, and in going to, and returning from, the same; and for any speech or debate in either House, they shall not be questioned in any other place.

2. No Senator or Representative shall, during the time for which he was elected, be appointed to any civil office under the authority of the United States, which shall have been created, or the emoluments whereof shall have been increased, during such time; and no person, holding any office under the United States, shall be a member of either House during his continuance in office.

SECTION 7.

1. All bills for raising revenue shall originate in the House of Representatives; but the Senate may propose or concur with amendments, as on other bills.

2. Every bill, which shall have passed the House of Representatives and the Senate, shall, before it become a law, be presented to the President of the United States; if he approve, he shall sign it, but if not, he shall return it, with his objections, to that House in which it shall have originated, who shall enter the objections at large on their journal, and proceed to reconsider it. If, after such reconsideration, two thirds of that House shall agree to pass the bill, it shall be sent, together with the objections, to the other House, by which it shall likewise be reconsidered, and, if approved by two thirds of that House, it shall become a law. But in all such cases the votes of both Houses shall be determined by yeas and nays, and the names of the persons voting for and against the bill shall be entered on the journal of each House, respectively. If any bill not be returned by the President within ten days (Sundays excepted) after it shall have been presented to him, the same shall be a law, in like manner as if he had signed it, unless the Congress, by their adjournment, prevent its return, in which case it shall not be a law.

3. Every order, resolution, or vote, to which the concur-

rence of the Senate and House of Representatives may be necessary, (except on a question of adjournment,) shall be presented to the President of the United States; and before the same shall take effect, shall be approved by him, or, being disapproved by him, shall be re-passed by two thirds of the Senate and House of Representatives, according to the rules and limitations prescribed in the case of a bill.

SECTION 8.

The Congress shall have power,

1. To lay and collect taxes, duties, imposts, and excises, to pay the debts, and provide for the common defence and general welfare, of the United States; but all duties, imposts, and excises, shall be uniform throughout the United States:

2. To borrow money on the credit of the United States:

3. To regulate commerce with foreign nations, and among the several States, and with the Indian tribes:

4. To establish a uniform rule of naturalization, and uniform laws on the subject of bankruptcies, throughout the United States:

5. To coin money, regulate the value thereof, and of foreign coin, and fix the standard of weights and measures:

6. To provide for the punishment of counterfeiting the securities and current coin of the United States:

7. To establish post-offices and post-roads:

8. To promote the progress of science and useful arts, by securing, for limited times, to authors and inventors the exclusive rights to their respective writings and discoveries:

9. To constitute tribunals inferior to the Supreme Court.

10. To define and punish piracies and felonies, committed on the high seas, and offences against the law of nations:

11. To declare war, grant letters of marque and reprisal, and make rules concerning captures on land and water:

12. To raise and support armies; but no appropriation of money to that use shall be for a longer term than two years:

13. To provide and maintain a navy:

14. To make rules for the government and regulation of the land and naval forces:

15. To provide for calling forth the militia to execute the

laws of the Union, suppress insurrections, and repel invasions:

16. To provide for organizing, arming, and disciplining, the militia, and for governing such part of them as may be employed in the service of the United States, reserving to the States respectively, the appointment of the officers, and the authority of training the militia, according to the discipline prescribed by Congress:

17. To exercise exclusive legislation in all cases whatsoever, over such district, (not exceeding ten miles square,) as may, by cession of particular States, and the acceptance of Congress, become the seat of the government of the United States, and to exercise like authority over all places, purchased by the consent of the legislature of the State in which the same shall be, for the erection of forts, magazines, arsenals, dock-yards, and other needful buildings:—And

18. To make all laws which shall be necessary and proper for carrying into execution for foregoing powers, and all other powers vested by this Constitution in the government of the United States, or in any department or officer thereof.

SECTION 9.

1. The migration or importation of such persons, as any of the States, now existing, shall think proper to admit, shall not be prohibited by the Congress prior to the year one thousand eight hundred and eight; but a tax or duty may be imposed on such importation, not exceeding ten dollars for each person.

2. The privilege of the writ of *habeas corpus* shall not be suspended, unless when, in cases of rebellion or invasion, the public safety may require it.

3. No bill of attainder, or *ex post facto* law, shall be passed.

4. No capitation or other direct tax, shall be laid, unless in proportion to the *census* or enumeration, herein before directed to be taken.

5. No tax or duty shall be laid on articles exported from any State. No preference shall be given by any regulation of commerce or revenue, to the ports of one State over those of another; nor shall vessels bound to, or from, one State, be obliged to enter, clear, or pay duties, in another.

6. No money shall be drawn from the treasury, but in consequence of appropriations made by law, and a regular statement and account of the receipts and expenditures of all public money shall be published, from time to time.

7. No title of nobility shall be granted by the United States: And no person, holding any office of profit or trust under them, shall without the consent of the Congress, accept of any present, emolument, office, or title, of any kind whatever, from any king, prince, or foreign state.

SECTION 10.

1. No State shall enter into any treaty, alliance, or confederation; grant letters of marque and reprisal; coin money; emit bills of credit; make any thing but gold and silver coin a tender in payment of debts; pass any bill of attainder, *ex post facto* law, or law impairing the obligation of contracts, or grant any title of nobility.

2. No State shall, without the consent of the Congress, lay any imposts or duties on imports or exports, except what may be absolutely necessary for executing its inspection laws; and the net produce of all duties and imposts, laid by any State on imports or exports, shall be for the use of the treasury of the United States; and all such laws shall be subject to the revision and control of the Congress. No State shall, without the consent of Congress, lay any duty of tonnage, keep troops, or ships of war, in time of peace, enter into any agreement or compact with another State, or with a foreign power, or engage in wars, unless actually invaded, or in such imminent danger, as will not admit of delay.

ARTICLE II.

SECTION I.

1. The Executive power shall be vested in a President of the United States of America. He shall hold his office during the term of four years, and together with the Vice-President, chosen for the same term, be elected as follows:

2. Each State shall appoint, in such manner as the Legislature thereof may direct, a number of Electors, equal to the

whole number of Senators and Representatives, to which the State may be entitled in the Congress: but no Senator or Representative, or person holding an office of trust or profit, under the United States, shall be appointed an Elector.

3. The Electors shall meet in their respective States, and vote by ballot for two persons, of whom one, at least, shall not be inhabitant of the same State with themselves. And they shall make a list of all the persons voted for, and of the number of votes for each; which list they shall sign and certify, and transmit, sealed, to the seat of the government of the United States, directed to the President of the Senate. The President of the Senate shall, in the presence of the Senate and House of Representatives, open all the certificates, and the votes shall then be counted. The person having the greatest number of votes shall be the President, if such number be a majority of the whole number of Electors apppointed; and if there be more than one, who have such majority, and have an equal number of votes, then the House of Representatives shall immediately choose, by ballot, one of them for President; and if no person have a majority, then, from the five highest on the list, the said House shall, in like manner, choose the President. But in choosing the President, the votes shall be taken by States, the representation from each State having one vote; a quorum for this purpose, shall consist of a member or members from two thirds of the States, and a majority of all the States shall be necessary to a choice. In every case, after the choice of the President, the person having the greatest number of votes of the Electors shall be the Vice-President. But if there should remain two or more who have equal votes, the Senate shall choose from them, by ballot, the Vice-President.

4. The Congress may determine the time of choosing the Electors, and the day on which they shall give their votes; which day shall be the same throughout the United States.

5. No person, except a natural-born citizen, or a citizen of the United States at the time of the adoption of this Constitution, shall be eligible to the office of President; neither shall any person be eligible to that office, who shall not have at-

tained to the age of thirty-five years, and been fourteen years a resident within the United States.

6. In case of the removal of the President from office, or of his death, resignation, or inability to discharge the powers and duties of the said office, the same shall devolve on the Vice-President, and the Congress may by law provide for the case of removal, death, resignation, or inability, both of the President and Vice-President, declaring what officer shall then act as President, and such officer shall act accordingly, until the disability be removed, or a President shall be elected.

7. The President shall, at stated times, receive for his services, a compensation, which shall neither be increased nor diminished during the period for which he shall have been elected, and he shall not receive within that period, any other emolument from the United States, or any of them.

8. Before he enter on the execution of his office, he shall take the following oath or affirmation:

9. "I do solemnly swear, (or affirm,) that I will faithfully execute the office of President of the United States, and will, to the best of my ability, preserve, protect, and defend, the Constitution of the United States."

SECTION 2.

1. The President shall be commander-in-chief of the army and navy of the United States, and of the militia of the several States, when called into the actual service of the United States; he may require the opinion, in writing, of the principal officer in each of the executive departments, upon any subject relating to the duties of their respective offices, and he shall have power to grant reprieves and pardons for offences against the United States, except in cases of impeachment.

2. He shall have power, by and with the advice and consent of the Senate, to make treaties, provided two thirds of the Senators present concur; and he shall nominate, and by and with the advice and consent of the Senate, shall appoint ambassadors, other public ministers, and consuls, judges of the Supreme Court, and all other officers of the United States, whose

appointments are not herein otherwise provided for, and which shall be established by law: but the Congress may by law vest the appointment of such inferior officers, as they think proper, in the President alone, in the courts of law, or in the heads of Departments.

3. The President shall have power to fill up all vacancies that may happen, during the recess of the Senate, by granting commission, which shall expire at the end of their next session.

SECTION 3.

1. He shall, from time to time, give to the Congress information of the state of the Union, and recommend to their consideration such measures as he shall judge necessary and expedient; he may, on extraordinary occasions, convene both Houses, or either of them, and in case of disagreement between them, with respect to the time of adjournment, he may adjourn them to such time as he shall think proper; he shall receive ambassadors and other public ministers; he shall take care that the laws be faithfully executed, and shall commission all the officers of the United States.

SECTION 4.

1. The President, Vice-President, and all civil officers of the United States, shall be removed from office, on impeachment for, and conviction of, treason, bribery, or other high crimes and misdemeanors.

ARTICLE III.

SECTION 1.

1. The Judicial power of the United States shall be vested in one Supreme Court, and in such inferior courts as the Congress may, from time to time, ordain and establish. The judges, both of the Supreme and inferior courts, shall hold their offices during good behavior, and shall, at stated times, receive for their services a compensation, which shall not be diminished during their continuance in office.

SECTION 2.

1. The Judicial power shall extend to all cases, in law and

equity, arising under this Constitution, the laws of the United States, and treaties made, or which shall be made, under their authority; to all cases affecting ambassadors, other public ministers, and consuls; to all cases of admiralty and maritime jurisdiction; to controversies to which the United States shall be a party; to controversies between two or more States, between a State and citizens of another State, between citizens of different States, between citizens of the same State claiming lands under grants of different States, and between a State, or the citizens thereof, and foreign states, citizens, or subjects.

2. In all cases affecting ambassadors, other public ministers, and consuls, and those in which a State shall be a party, the Supreme Court shall have original jurisdiction. In all the other cases before mentioned, the Supreme Court shall have appellate jurisdiction, both as to law and fact, with such exceptions, and under such regulations, as the Congress shall make.

3. The trial of all crimes, except in cases of impeachment, shall be by jury; and such trial shall be held in the State where the said crimes shall have been committed; but when not committed within any State, the trial shall be at such place, or places, as the Congress may by laws have directed.

SECTION 3.

1. Treason against the United States shall consist only in levying war against them, or in adhering to their enemies, giving them aid and comfort. No person shall be convicted of treason, unless on the testimony of two witnesses to the same overt act, or on confession in open court.

2. The Congress shall have power to declare the punishment of treason, but no attainder of treason shall work corruption of blood, or forfeiture, except during the life of the person attainted.

ARTICLE IV

SECTION 1.

1. Full faith and credit shall be given in each State to the public acts, records, and judicial proceedings, of every other State. And the Congress may, by general laws, prescribe the

manner in which such acts, records, and proceedings, shall be proved, and the effect thereof.

SECTION 2.

1. The citizens of each State shall be entitled to all privileges and immunities of citizens in the several States.

2. A person charged in any State with treason, felony, or other crime, who shall flee from justice, and be found in another State, shall, on demand of the executive authority of the State from which he fled, be delivered up, to be removed to the State having jurisdiction of the crime.

3. No person held to service or labor in one State, under the laws thereof, escaping into another, shall, in consequence of any law or regulation therein, be discharged from such service or labor, but shall be delivered up on claim of the party to whom such service or labor may be due.

SECTION 3.

1. New States may be admitted by the Congress into this Union; but no new State shall be formed, or erected, within the jurisdiction of any other State; nor any State be formed, by the junction of two or more States, or parts of States, without the consent of the legislatures of the States concerned, as well as of the Congress.

2. The Congress shall have power to dispose of and make all needful rules and regulations respecting the territory, or other property, belonging to the United States; and nothing in this Constitution shall be so construed as to prejudice any claims of the United States, or of any particular State.

SECTION 4.

1. The United States shall guaranty to every State in this Union a republican form of government, and shall protect each of them against invasion; and, on application of the legislature, or of the executive, (when the legislature cannot be convened,) against domestic violence.

ARTICLE V.

1. The Congress, whenever two thirds of both Houses shall

deem it necessary, shall propose amendments to this Constitution, or, on the application of the legislatures of two thirds of the several States, shall call a convention for proposing amendments, which, in either case, shall be valid to all intents and purposes, as part of this Constitution, when ratified by the legislature of three fourths of the several States, or by conventions in three fourths thereof, as the one or the other mode of ratification may be proposed by the Congress: Provided, that no amendment, which may be made prior to the year one thousand eight hundred and eight, shall, in any manner, affect the first and fourth clauses in the ninth section of the first article; and that no State, without its consent, shall be deprived of its equal suffrage in the Senate.

ARTICLE VI.

1. All debts contracted, and engagements entered into, before the adoption of this Constitution, shall be as valid against the United States, under this Constitution, as under the Confederation.

2. This Constitution, and the laws of the United States which shall be made in pursuance thereof, and all treaties made, or which shall be made, under the authority of the United States, shall be the supreme law of the land; and the judges in every State shall be bound thereby, any thing in the Constitution or laws of any State to the contrary notwithstanding.

3. The Senators and Representatives before mentioned, and the members of the several State legislatures, and all executive and judicial officers, both of the United States, and of the several States, shall be bound, by oath or affirmation, to support this Constitution; but no religious test shall ever be required as a qualification to any office or public trust, under the United States.

ARTICLE VII.

1. The ratification of the Conventions of nine States shall be sufficient for the establishment of this Constitution between the States so ratifying the same.

AMENDMENTS TO THE CONSTITUTION.

ARTICLE I.

Congress shall make no law respecting an establishment of religion, or prohibiting the free exercise thereof; or abridging the freedom of speech, or of the press; or the right of the people peaceably to assemble, and to petition the government for a redress of grievances.

ARTICLE II.

A well regulated militia being necessary to the security of a free State, the right of the people to keep and bear arms shall not be infringed.

ARTICLE III.

No soldier shall, in time of peace, be quartered in any house, without the consent of the owner; nor, in time of war, but in a manner to be prescribed by law.

ARTICLE IV.

The right of the people to be secure in their persons, houses, papers, and effects, against unreasonable searches and seizures, shall not be violated; and no warrants shall issue, but upon probable cause, supported by oath or affirmation, and particularly describing the place to be searched, and the persons or things to be seized.

ARTICLE V.

No person shall be held to answer for a capital, or otherwise infamous, crime, unless on a presentment or indictment of a grand jury, except in cases arising in the land or naval forces, or in the militia, when in actual service, in time of war, or public danger; nor shall any person be subject, for the same offence, to be twice put in jeopardy of life or limb; nor shall be compelled, in any criminal case, to be a witness against himself, nor be deprived of life, liberty, or property, without due process of law; nor shall private property be taken for public use, without just compensation.

ARTICLE VI.

In all criminal prosecutions, the accused shall enjoy the right to a speedy and public trial, by an impartial jury of the State and district wherein the crime shall have been committed, which district shall have been previously ascertained by law; and to be informed of the nature and cause of the accusation; to be confronted with the witnesses against him; to have compulsory process for obtaining witnesses in his favor; and to have the assistance of counsel for his defence.

ARTICLE VII.

In suits at common law, where the value in controversy shall exceed twenty dollars, right of trial by jury shall be preserved; and no fact, tried by a jury, shall be otherwise re-examined in any court of the United States, than according to the rules of the common law.

ARTICLE VIII.

Excessive bail shall not be required, nor excessive fines imposed, nor cruel and unusual punishments inflicted.

ARTICLE IX.

The enumeration in the Constitution of certain rights shall not be construed to deny or disparage others retained by the people.

ARTICLE X.

The powers not delegated to the United States by the Constitution, nor prohibited by it to the States, are reserved to the States respectively, or to the people.

ARTICLE XI.

The judicial power of the United States shall not be construed to extend to any suit in law or equity, commenced or prosecuted against one of the United States by citizens of another State, or by citizens or subjects of any foreign State.

ARTICLE XII.

1. The Electors shall meet in their respective States, and vote

by ballot for President and Vice-President, one of whom, at least, shall not be an inhabitant of the same State with themselves; they shall name in their ballots the person voted for as President, and in distinct ballots the person voted for as Vice-President; and they shall make distinct lists of all persons voted for as President, and of all persons voted for as Vice-President, and of the number of votes for each, which lists they shall sign, and certify, and transmit, sealed, to the seat of the government of the United States, directed to the President of the Senate; the President of the Senate shall, in the presence of the Senate and House of Representatives, open all the certificates, and the votes shall then be counted; the person having the greatest number of votes for President shall be the President, if such number be a majority of the whole number of Electors appointed; and if no person have such majority, then, from the persons having the highest numbers, not exceeding three, on the list of those voted for as President, the House of Representatives shall choose immediately, by ballot, the President. But in choosing the President, the votes shall be taken by States, the representation from each State having one vote; a quorum for this purpose shall consist of a member or members from two thirds of the States, and a majority of all the States shall be necessary to a choice. And if the House of Representatives shall not choose a President, whenever the right of choice shall devolve upon them, before the fourth day of March next following, then the Vice-President shall act as President, as in case of death, or other constitutional disability, of the President.

2. The person having the greatest number of votes as Vice-President shall be the Vice-President, if such number be a majority of the whole number of electors appointed; and if no person have a majority, then, from the two highest numbers on the list, the Senate shall choose the Vice-President; a quorum for the purpose shall consist of two thirds of the whole number of Senators; a majority of the whole number shall be necessary to a choice.

3. But no person constitutionally ineligible to the office of

President, shall be eligible to that of Vice-President of the United States.

WASHINGTON'S FAREWELL ADDRESS
TO THE PEOPLE OF THE UNITED STATES.

SEPTEMBER 17, 1796.

FRIENDS AND FELLOW CITIZENS,

The period for a new election of a citizen to administer the executive government of the United States being not far distant, and the time actually arrived, when your thoughts must be employed in designating the person who is to be clothed with that important trust, it appears to me proper, especially as it may conduce to a more distinct expression of the public voice, that I should now apprise you of the resolution I have formed, to decline being considered among the number of those out of whom a choice is to be made.

I beg you, at the same time, to do me the justice to be assured, that this resolution has not been taken, without a strict regard to all the considerations appertaining to the relation which binds a dutiful citizen to his country; and that, in withdrawing the tender of service, which silence, in my situation, might imply, I am influenced by no diminution of zeal for your future interest; no deficiency of grateful respect for your past kindness; but am supported by a full conviction that the step is compatible with both.

The acceptance of, and continuance hitherto in, the office to which your suffrages have twice called me, have been a uniform sacrifice of inclination to the opinion of duty, and to a deference for what appeared to be your desire. I constantly hoped, that it would have been much earlier in my power, consistently with motives which I was not at liberty to disregard, to return to that retirement from which I had been reluctantly drawn. The strength of my inclination to do this, previous to the last election, had even led to the preparation of an address, to declare it to you; but mature reflection on the then perplexed and critical posture of our affairs with foreign nations, and the unanimous advice of persons entitled to my confidence, impelled me to abandon the idea.

I rejoice that the state of your concerns, external as well as internal, no longer renders the pursuit of inclination incompatible with the sentiment of duty or propriety; and am persuaded, whatever partiality may be retained for my services, that, in the present circumstances of our country, you will not disapprove my determination to retire.

The impressions, with which I first undertook the arduous trust, were explained on the proper occasion. In the discharge of this trust, I will only say, that I have, with good intentions, contributed towards the organization and administration of the government, the best exertions of which a very fallible judgement was capable. Not unconscious, in the outset, of the inferiority of my qualifications, experience in my own eyes, perhaps still more in the eyes of others, has strengthened the motives to diffidence of myself; and, every day, the increasing weight of years admonishes me, more and more, that the shade of retirement is as necessary to me, as it will be welcome. Satisfied that, if any circumstances have given peculiar value to my services, they were temporary, I have the consolation to believe, that, while choice and prudence invite me to quit the political scene, patriotism does not forbid it.

In looking forward to the moment which is intended to terminate the career of my public life, my feelings do not permit me to suspend the deep acknowledgment of that debt of gratitude which I owe to my beloved country, for the many honors it has conferred upon me; still more for the steadfast confidence with which it has supported me; and for the opportunities I have thence enjoyed, of manifesting my inviolable attachment, by services faithful and persevering, though in usefulness unequal to my zeal. If benefits have resulted to our country from these services, let it always be remembered to your praise, and as an instructive example in our annals, that, under circumstances in which the passions, agitated in every

direction, were liable to mislead, amidst appearances sometimes dubious, vicissitudes of fortune often discouraging, in
situations in which, not unfrequently, want of success has
countenanced the spirit of criticism, the constancy of your
support was the essential prop of the efforts, and a guarantee
of the plans, by which they were effected. Profoundly pene-
trated with this idea, I shall carry it with me to my grave, as a
strong incitement to unceasing vows, that Heaven may continue to you the choicest tokens of its beneficence; that your
union and brotherly affection may be perpetual; that the free
Constitution, which is the work of your hands, may be sacredly maintained; that its administration, in every department, may be stamped with wisdom and virtue; that, in fine,
the happiness of the people of these States, under the auspices
of liberty, may be made complete, by so careful a preservation
and so prudent a use of this blessing, as will acquire to them
the glory of recommending it to the applause, the affection,
and adoption, of every nation which is yet a stranger to it.

Here, perhaps, I ought to stop; but a solicitude for your welfare, which cannot end but with my life, and the apprehension
of danger natural to that solicitude, urge me, on an occasion
like the present, to offer to your solemn contemplation, and to
recommend to your frequent review, some sentiments, which
are the result of much reflection; of no inconsiderable observation; and which appear to me all important to the permanency
of your felicity, as a people. These will be offered to you with
the more freedom, as you can only see in them the disinterested warnings of a parting friend, who can possibly have no
personal motive to bias his counsel; nor can I forget, as an encouragement to it, your indulgent reception of my sentiments
on a former, and not dissimilar, occasion.

Interwoven as is the love of liberty with every ligament of
your hearts, no recommendation of mine is necessary to for-
tify, or confirm, the attachment.

The unity of government, which constitutes you one people, is also now dear to you. It is justly so; for it is a main pillar
in the edifice of your real independence; the support of your

tranquility at home, your peace abroad; of your safety; of your prosperity; of that very liberty which you so highly prize. But, as it is easy to foresee, that, from different causes, and from different quarters, much pains will be taken, many artifices employed, to weaken, in your minds, the conviction of this truth; as this is the point in your political fortress, against which the batteries of internal and external enemies will be most constantly and actively (though often covertly and insidiously) directed, it is of infinite moment that you should properly estimate the immense value of your National Union, to your collective and individual happiness; that you should cherish a cordial, habitual, and immovable, attachment to it; accustoming yourselves to think and speak of it as of the palladium of your political safety and prosperity; watching for its preservation with jealous anxiety; discountenancing whatever may suggest even a suspicion that it can, in any event, be abandoned; and indignantly frowning upon the first dawning of every attempt to alienate any portion of our country from the rest, or to enfeeble the sacred ties which now link together the various parts.

For this you have every inducement of sympathy and interest. Citizens, by birth or choice, of a common country, that country has a right to concentrate your affections. The name of AMERICAN, which belongs to you in your National capacity, must always exalt the just pride of patriotism, more than any appellation derived from local discriminations. With slight shades of difference, you have the same religion, manners, habits, and political principles. You have, in a common cause, fought and triumphed together: the independence and liberty you possess are the work of joint councils and joint efforts, of common dangers, sufferings, and successes.

But these considerations, however powerfully they address themselves to your sensibility, are greatly outweighed by those which apply more immediately to your interest. Here every portion of our country finds the most commanding motives for carefully guarding and preserving the union of the whole.

The *North,* in an unrestrained intercourse with the *South,* protected by the equal laws of a common government, finds, in the productions of the latter, great additional resources of maritime and commercial enterprise, and precious materials of manufacturing industry. The *South,* in the same intercourse, benefitting by the agency of the *North,* sees its agriculture grow, and its commerce expand. Turning partly into its own channels the seamen of the North, it finds its particular navigation invigorated and, while it contributes, in different ways, to nourish and increase the general mass of the National navigation, it looks forward to the protection of a maritime strength, to which itself is unequally adapted. The *East,* in like intercourse with the *West,* already finds, and in the progressive improvement of interior communications, by land and water, will more and more find, a valuable vent for the commodities which it brings from abroad, or manufactures at home. The *West* derives from the *East* supplies requisite to its growth and comfort; and, what is, perhaps, of still greater consequence, it must, of necessity, owe the secure enjoyment of indispensable *outlets* for its own productions, to the weight, influence, and the future maritime strength of the Atlantic side of the Union, directed by an indissoluble community of interest as *one* nation. Any other tenure by which the *West* can hold this essential advantage, whether derived from its own separate strength, or from an apostate and unnatural connexion with any foreign power, must be intrinsically precarious.

While, then, every part of our country thus feels an immediate and particular interest in union, all the parts combined cannot fail to find, in the united mass of means and efforts, greater strength, greater resource, proportionably greater security from external danger, a less frequent interruption of their peace by foreign nations; and, what is of inestimable value, they must derive from union an exemption from those broils and wars between themselves, which so frequently afflict neighboring countries, not tied together by the same governments; which their own rivalships alone would be sufficient to produce, but which opposite foreign alliances, attachments, and intrigues, would stimulate and embitter. Hence, likewise, they will avoid the necessity of those overgrown military establishments, which, under any form of government, are inauspicious to liberty, and which are to be regarded as . particularly hostile to republican liberty; in this sense it is that your union ought to be considered as a main prop of your liberty, and that the love of the one ought to endear to you the preservation of the other.

These considerations speak a persuasive language to every reflecting and virtuous mind, and exhibit the continuance of the Union as a primary object of patriotic desire. Is there a doubt, whether a common government can embrace so large a sphere? Let experience solve it. To listen to mere speculation in such a case, were criminal. We are authorized to hope, that a proper organization of the whole, with the auxiliary agency of governments for the respective subdivisions, will afford a happy issue to the experiment. It is well worth a fair and full experiment. With such powerful and obvious motives to union, affecting all parts of our country, while experience shall not have demonstrated its impracticability, there will always be reason to distrust the patriotism of those, who, in any quarter, may endeavor to weaken its bands.

In contemplating the causes, which may disturb our union, it occurs, as matter of serious concern, that any ground should have been furnished for characterizing parties by geographical discriminations, *Northern* and *Southern, Atlantic* and *Western;* whence designing men may endeavor to excite a belief, that there is a real difference of local interests and views. One of the expedients of party to acquire influence, within particular districts, is, to misrepresent the opinions and aims of other districts. You cannot shield yourselves too much against the jealousies and heart-burnings, which spring from these misrepresentations; they tend to render alien to each other those who ought to be bound together by fraternal affection. The inhabitants of our western country have lately had a useful lesson on this head; they have seen, in the negotiation by the Executive, and in the unanimous ratification by the Senate, of the treaty with Spain, and in the universal satisfaction at that event, throughout the United States, a decisive proof how unfounded were the suspicions propagated among them, of a policy in the General Government, and in the Atlantic States, unfriendly to their interests, in regard to the Mississippi; they have been witnesses to the formation of two treaties, that with Great Britain, and that with Spain, which secure to them everything they could desire, in respect to our foreign relations, towards confirming their prosperity. Will it not be their wisdom to rely, for the preservation of these advantages, on the UNION by which they were procured? Will they not henceforth be deaf to those advisers, if such there are, who would sever them from their brethren, and connect them with aliens?

To the efficacy and permanency of your Union, a government for the whole is indispensable. No alliances, however strict, between the parts, can be an adequate substitute; they must inevitably experience the infractions and interruptions which all alliances, in all times, have experienced. Sensible of this momentous truth, you have improved upon your first essay, by the adoption of a Constitution of Government better calculated than your former, for an intimate Union, and for the efficacious management of your common concerns. This Government, the offspring of our own choice, uninfluenced and unawed, adopted upon full investigation and mature deliberation, completely free in its principles, in the distribution of its powers uniting security with energy, and containing within itself a provision for its own amendment, has a just claim to your confidence and your support. Respect for its authority, compliance with its laws, acquiescence in its measures, are duties enjoined by the fundamental maxims of true liberty. The basis of our political systems is, the right of the people to make and to alter their Constitutions of Government. But the Constitution which at any time exists, till changed by an explicit and authentic act of the whole people, is sacredly obligatory upon all. The very idea of the power and the right of the people to establish Government, pre-supposes the duty of every individual to obey the established Government.

All obstructions to the execution of the Laws, all combinations and associations, under whatever plausible character, with the real design to direct, control, counteract, or awe, the regular deliberation and action of the constituted authorities, are destructive of this fundamental principle, and of fatal tendency. They serve to organize faction, to give it an artificial and extraordinary force; to put, in the place of the delegated will of the nation, the will of a party, often a small but artful and enterprising minority of the community; and, according to the alternate triumphs of different parties, to make the public administration the mirror of the ill-concerted and incongruous projects of faction, rather than the organ of consistent and wholesome plans, digested by common councils, and modified by mutual interests.

However combinations or associations of the above description may now and then answer popular ends, they are likely, in the course of time and things, to become potent engines, by which cunning, ambitious, and unprincipled, men will be enabled to subvert the power of the people, and to usurp for themselves the reins of government; destroying, afterwards, the very engines, which had lifted them to unjust dominion.

Towards the preservation of your government, and the permanency of your present happy state, it is requisite, not only that you steadily discountenance irregular oppositions to its acknowledged authority, but also that you resist with care the spirit of innovation upon its principles, however specious the pretexts. One method of assault may be to effect, in the forms of the Constitution, alterations which will impair the energy of the system, and thus to undermine what cannot be directly overthrown. In all the changes to which you may be invited, remember that time and habit are at least as necessary to fix the true character of governments, as of other human institutions; that experience is the surest standard, by which to test the real tendency of the existing Constitution of a country; that facility in changes, upon the credit of mere hypothesis and opinion, exposes to perpetual change, from the endless variety of hypothesis and opinion; and remember, especially, that, for the efficient management of your common interests, in a country so extensive as ours, a government of as much vigor as is consistent with the perfect security of liberty is indispensable. Liberty itself will find in such a government, with powers properly distributed and adjusted, its surest guardian. It is, indeed, little else than a name, where the government is too feeble to withstand the enterprises of faction, to confine each member of the society within the limits prescribed by the laws, and to maintain all in the secure and tranquil enjoyment of the rights of person and property.

I have already intimated to you the danger of parties in the state, with particular reference to the founding of them on geographical discriminations. Let me now take a more comprehensive view, and warn you in the most solemn manner against the baneful effects of the spirit of party, generally.

This, spirit, unfortunately, is inseparable from our nature, having its root in the strongest passions of the human mind. It exists, under different shapes, in all governments, more or less stifled, controlled, or repressed; but, in those of the popular form, it is seen in its greatest rankness, and is truly their worst enemy.

The alternate domination of one faction over another, sharpened by the spirit of revenge, natural to party dissension, which in different ages and countries has perpetrated the most horrid enormities, is itself a frightful despotism. But this leads at length to a more formal and permanent despotism. The disorders and miseries, which result, gradually incline the minds of men to seek security and repose in the absolute power of an individual; and sooner or later the chief of some prevailing faction, more able or more fortunate than his competitors, turns this disposition to the purposes of his own elevation, on the ruins of Public Liberty.

Without looking forward to an extremity of this kind, (which nevertheless ought not to be entirely out of sight,) the common and continual mischiefs of the spirit of party are sufficient to make it the interest and duty of a wise people to discourage and restrain it.

It serves always to distract the Public Councils, and enfeeble the Public Administration. It agitates the Community with ill-founded jealousies and false alarms; kindles the animosity of one part against another; foments, occasionally, riot and insurrection. It opens the door to foreign influence and corruption, which find a facilitated access to the government itself through the channels of party passions. Thus the policy and the will of one country are subjected to the policy and will of another.

There is an opinion, that parties in free countries are useful checks upon the administration of the Government, and serve to keep alive the spirit of Liberty. This, within certain limits, is probably true; and in Governments of a Monarchical cast, Patriotism may look with indulgence, if not with favor, upon the spirit of party. But in those of the popular character, in Governments purely elective, it is a spirit not to be encouraged. From their natural tendency, it is certain there will always be enough of that spirit for every salutary purpose. And, there being constant danger of excess, the effort ought to be, by force of public opinion, to mitigate and assuage it. A fire not to be quenched, it demands a uniform vigilance to prevent its bursting into a flame, lest, instead of warming, it should consume.

It is important, likewise, that the habits of thinking in a free country should inspire caution, in those intrusted with its administration, to confine themselves within their respective constitutional spheres, avoiding in the exercise of the powers of one department to encroach upon another. The spirit of encroachment tends to consolidate the powers of all the departments in one, and thus to create, whatever the form of government, a real despotism. A just estimate of that love of power, and proneness to abuse it, which predominates in the human heart, is sufficient to satisfy us of the truth of this position. The necessity of reciprocal checks in the exercise of political power, by dividing and distributing it into different depositories, and constituting each the Guardian of the Public Weal against invasions by the others, has been evinced by experiments ancient and modern; some of them in our country and under our own eyes. To preserve them must be as necessary as to institute them. If, in the opinion of the people, the distribution or modification of the constitutional powers be, in any particular, wrong, let it be corrected by an amendment, in the way which the Constitution designates. But let there be no change by usurpation; for, though this, in one instance, may be the instrument of good, it is the customary weapon by which free governments are destroyed. The precedent must always greatly overbalance, in permanent evil, any partial or transient benefit, which the use can at any time yield.

Of all the dispositions and habits, which lead to political prosperity, Religion and Morality are indispensible supports. In vain would that man claim the tribute of Patriotism, who should labor to subvert these great pillars of human happiness, these firmest props of the duties of Men and Citizens. The mere Politician, equally with the pious man, ought to respect and to cherish them. A volume could not trace all their connexions with private and public felicity. Let it simply be asked, Where is the security for property, for reputation, for life, if the sense of religious obligation *desert* the oaths, which are the instruments of investigation in Courts of Justice? And let us with caution indulge the supposition, that morality can be maintained without religion. Whatever may be conceded to the influence of refined education on minds of peculiar structure, reason and experience both forbid us to expect, that national morality can prevail in exclusion of religious principle.

It is substantially true, that virtue or morality is a necessary spring of popular government. The rule, indeed, extends with more or less force to every species of free government. Who, that is a sincere friend to it, can look with indifference upon attempts to shake the foundation of the fabric?

Promote, then, as an object of primary importance, institutions for the general diffusion of knowledge. In proportion as the structure of a government gives force to public opinion, it is essential that public opinion should be enlightened.

As a very important source of strength and security, cherish public credit. One method of preserving it is, to use it as sparingly as possible; avoiding occasions of expense by cultivating peace, but remembering also that timely disbursements to pre-

pare for danger frequently prevent much greater disbursements to repel it; avoiding, likewise, the accumulation of debt,
not only by shunning occasions of expense, but by vigorous
exertions in time of peace to discharge the debts, which unavoidable wars may have occasioned, not ungenerously throw-
ing upon posterity the burden, which we ourselves ought to
bear. The execution of these maxims belongs to your representatives, but it is necessary that public opinion should cooper-
ate. To facilitate to them the performance of their duty, it is
essential that you should practically bear in mind, that towards
the payment of debts there must be Revenue; that to have Revenue there must be taxes; that no taxes can be devised, which
are not more or less inconvenient and unpleasant; that the intrinsic embarrassment, inseparable from the selection of the
proper objects, (which is always a choice of difficulties,) ought
to be a decisive motive for a candid construction of the conduct of the government in making it, and for a spirit of acquiescence in the measures for obtaining Revenue, which the
public exigencies may, at any time, dictate.

Observe good faith and justice towards all Nations; cultivate
peace and harmony with all. Religion and Morality enjoin this
conduct; and can it be, that good policy does not equally enjoin it? It will be worthy of a free, enlightened, and, at no distant period, a great Nation, to give to mankind the
magnanimous and too novel example of a people always
guided by an exalted justice and benevolence. Who can doubt,
that, in the course of time and things, the fruits of such a plan
would richly repay any temporary advantages, which might be
lost by a steady adherence to it? Can it be, that Providence has
not connected the permanent felicity of a Nation with its Virtue? The experiment, at least, is recommended by every sentiment which ennobles human nature. Alas! is it rendered
impossible by its vices?

In the execution of such a plan, nothing is more essential,
than that permanent, inveterate antipathies against particular
Nations, and passionate attachments for others, should be excluded; and that, in place of them, just and amicable feelings
towards all should be cultivated. The Nation, which indulges

towards another an habitual hatred, or an habitual fondness, is in some degree a slave. It is a slave to its animosity or to its affection, either of which is sufficient to lead it astray from its duty and its interest. Antipathy in one nation against another disposes each more readily to offer insult and injury, to lay hold of slight causes of umbrage, and to be haughty and intractable, when accidental or trifling occasions of dispute occur. Hence frequent collisions, obstinate, envenomed, and bloody contests. The Nation, prompted by ill-will and resentment, sometimes impels to war the Government, contrary to the best calculations of policy. The Government sometimes participates in the national propensity, and adopts through passion what reason would reject; at other times, it makes the animosity of the Nation subservient to projects of hostility instigated by pride, ambition, and other sinister and pernicious motives. The peace often, sometimes perhaps the liberty, of Nations has been the victim.

So, likewise, a passionate attachment of one Nation for another produces a variety of evils. Sympathy for the favorite Nation, facilitating the illusion of an imaginary common interest, in cases where no real common interest exists and infusing into one the enmities of the other, betrays the former into a participation in the quarrels and wars of the latter, without adequate inducement or justification. It leads also, to concessions to the favorite Nation of privileges denied to others, which is apt doubly to injure the Nation making the concessions; by unnecessarily parting with what ought to have been retained, and by exciting jealousy, ill will, and a disposition to retaliate, in the parties from whom equal privileges are withheld; and it gives to ambitious, corrupted, or deluded citizens, (who devote themselves to the favorite nation,) facility to betray or sacrifice the interest of their own country, without odium, sometimes even with popularity; gilding with the appearances of a virtuous sense of obligation, a commendable deference for public opinion, or a laudable zeal for public good, the base or foolish compliances of ambition, corruption, or infatuation.

As avenues to foreign influence, in innumerable ways, such

373

attachments are particularly alarming, to the truly enlightened and independent Patriot. How many opportunities do they afford, to tamper with domestic factions, to practise the arts of seduction, to mislead public opinion, to influence or awe the Public Councils! Such an attachment of a small or weak, towards a great and powerful, nation, dooms the former to be the satellite of the latter.

Against the insidious wiles of foreign influence, (I conjure you to believe me, fellow-citizens,) the jealousy of a free people ought to be *constantly* awake; since history and experience prove, that foreign influence is one of the most baneful foes of Republican Government. But that jealousy, to be useful, must be impartial; else it becomes the instrument of the very influence to be avoided, instead of a defence against it. Excessive partiality for one foreign nation, and excessive dislike of another, cause those whom they actuate to see danger only on one side, and serve to veil and even second the arts of influence on the other. Real patriots, who may resist the intrigues of the favorite, are liable to become suspected and odious; while its tools and dupes usurp the applause and confidence of the people, to surrender their interests.

The great rule of conduct for us, in regard to foreign nations, is, in extending our commercial relations, to have with them as little *political* connection as possible. So far as we have already formed engagements, let them be fulfilled with perfect good faith. Here let us stop.

Europe has a set of primary interests, which to us have none, or a very remote relation. Hence she must be engaged in frequent controversies, the causes of which are essentially foreign to our concerns. Hence, therefore, it must be unwise in us to implicate ourselves by artificial ties, in the ordinary vicissitudes of her politics, or the ordinary combinations and collisions of her friendships or enmities.

Our detached and distant situation invites and enables us to pursue a different course. If we remain one people, under an efficient government, the period is not far off, when we may defy material injury from external annoyance; when we may take such an attitude as will cause the neutrality, we may at any time resolve upon, to be scrupulously respected; when belligerent nations, under the impossibility of making acquisitions upon us, will not lightly hazard them giving us provocation; when we may choose peace or war, as our interest, guided by justice, shall counsel.

Why forego the advantages of so peculiar a situation? Why quit our own, to stand upon foreign ground? Why, by interweaving our destiny with that of any part of Europe, entangle our peace and prosperity in the toils of European ambition, rivalship, interest, humor, or caprice?

It is our true policy to steer clear of permanent alliances with any portion of the foreign world, so far, I mean, as we are now at liberty to do it; for let me not be understood as capable of patronizing infidelity to existing engagements. I hold the maxim no less applicable to public than to private affairs, that honesty is always the best policy. I repeat it, therefore, let those engagements be observed in their genuine sense. But, in my opinion, it is unnecessary and would be unwise to extend them.

Taking care always to keep ourselves, by suitable establishments, on a respectable defensive posture, we may safely trust to temporary alliances, for extraordinary emergencies.

Harmony, and a liberal intercourse with all nations, are recommended by policy, humanity, and interest. But even our commercial policy should hold an equal and impartial hand; neither seeking nor granting exclusive favors or preferences; consulting the natural course of things; diffusing and diversifying, by gentle means, the streams of commerce, but forcing nothing; establishing, with powers so disposed, in order to give trade a stable course, to define the rights of our merchants, and to enable the government to support them, conventional rules of intercourse, the best that present circumstances and mutual opinion will permit, but temporary, and liable to be from time to time abandoned or varied, as experience and circumstances shall dictate; constantly keeping in view, that it is folly in one nation to look for disinterested favors from another; that it must pay with a portion of its independence for whatever it may accept under that character; that, by such acceptance, it may place itself in the condition of having given equivalents for nominal favors, and yet of being reproached with ingratitude for not giving more. There can be no greater error than to expect or calculate upon real favors from nation to nation. It is an illusion, which experience must cure, which a just pride ought to discard.

In offering to you, my countrymen, these counsels of an old and affectionate friend, I dare not hope they will make the strong and lasting impression I could wish; that they will control the usual current of the passions, or prevent our nation from running the course, which has hitherto marked the destiny of nations. But, if I may even flatter myself, that they may be productive of some partial benefit, some occasional good; that they may now and then recur to moderate the fury of party spirit, to warn against the mischiefs of foreign intrigue, to guard against the impostures of pretended patriotism; this hope will be a full recompense for the solicitude for your welfare, by which they have been dictated.

How far, in the discharge of my official duties, I have been guided by the principles which have been delineated, the public records and other evidences of my conduct must witness to you and to the world. To myself, the assurance of my own conscience is, that I have at least believed myself to be guided by them.

In relation to the still subsisting war in Europe, my Proclamation of the 22d of April, 1793, is the index to my Plan. Sanctioned by your approving voice, and by that of your Representatives in both Houses of Congress, the spirit of that measure has continually governed me, uninfluenced by any attempts to deter or divert me from it.

After deliberate examination, with the aid of the best lights I could obtain, I was well satisfied that our country, under all the circumstances of the case, had a right to take, and was bound in duty and interest to take, a neutral position. Having taken it, I determined, as far as should depend upon me, to maintain it, with moderation, perseverance, and firmness.

The considerations, which respect the right to hold this conduct, it is not necessary on this occasion to detail. I will only observe, that, according to my understanding of the matter, that right, so far from being denied by any of the Belligerent Powers, has been virtually admitted by all.

The duty of holding a neutral conduct may be inferred, without any thing more, from the obligation which justice and humanity impose on every nation, in cases in which it is free to act, to maintain inviolate the relations of peace and amity towards other nations.

The inducements of interest for observing that conduct will best be referred to your own reflections and experience. With me, a predominant motive has been to endeavor to gain time to our country to settle and mature its yet recent institutions, and to progress without interruption to that degree of strength and consistency, which is necessary to give it, humanly speaking, the command of its own fortunes.

Though, in reviewing the incidents of my administration, I am unconscious of intentional error, I am nevertheless too sensible of my defects, not to think it probable that I may have committed many errors. Whatever they may be, I fervently beseech the Almighty to avert or mitigate the evils to which they may tend. I shall also carry with me the hope, that my Country will never cease to view them with indulgence; and that, after forty-five years of my life dedicated to its service with an upright zeal, the faults of incompetent abilities will be consigned to oblivion, as myself must soon be to the mansions of rest.

Relying on its kindness in this as in other things, and actuated by that fervent love towards it, which is so natural to a man, who views in it the native soil of himself and his progenitors for several generations; I anticipate with pleasing expectation that retreat, in which I promise myself to realize, without alloy, the sweet enjoyment of partaking in the midst of my fellow-citizens, the benign influence of good laws under a free government, the ever favorite object of my heart, and the happy reward, as I trust, of our mutual cares, labors, and dangers.

GEORGE WASHINGTON.

United States, September 17th, 1796.

DEFINITIVE TREATY OF PEACE

BETWEEN THE UNITED STATES OF AMERICA, AND HIS BRITANNIC MAJESTY.

IN THE NAME OF THE MOST HOLY AND UNDIVIDED TRINITY.

IT having pleased the Divine Providence to dispose the hearts of the most serene and most potent prince, George the Third, by the grace of God King of Great Britain, France, and Ireland, Defender of the Faith, Duke of Brunswick and Luneburg, Arch Treasurer and Prince Elector of the holy Roman empire, &c. and of the United States of America, to forget all past misunderstandings and differences that have unhappily interrupted the good correspondence and friendship which they mutually wish to restore, and to establish such a beneficial and satisfactory intercourse between the two countries, upon the ground of reciprocal advantages and mutual convenience, as may promote and secure to both perpetual peace and harmony: And having, for this desirable end, already laid the foundation of peace and reconciliation, by the Provisional Articles, signed at Paris, on the thirtieth of November, one thousand seven hundred and eighty-two, by the Commissioners empowered on each part, which articles were agreed to be inserted in, and to constitute the Treaty of Peace proposed to be concluded between the Crown of Great Britain and the said United States, but which Treaty was not to be concluded until terms of peace should be agreed upon between Great Britain and France, and his Britannic Majesty should be ready to conclude such Treaty accordingly; and the Treaty between Great Britain and France having since been concluded, his Britannic

Majesty and the United States of America, in order to carry into full effect the Provisional Articles above mentioned, according to the tenor thereof, have constituted and appointed, that is to say: his Britannic Majesty on his part, David Hartley, esquire, member of the Parliament of Great Britain; and the said United States on their part, John Adams, esquire, late a Commissioner of the United States of America at the Court of Versailles, late Delegate in Congress from the State of Massachusetts, and Chief Justice of the said State, and Minister Plenipotentiary of the said United States to their High Mightinesses the States General of the United Netherlands; Benjamin Franklin, esquire, late Delegate in Congress from the State of Pennsylvania, President of the Convention of the said State, and Minister Plenipotentiary from the United States of America at the Court of Versailles; John Jay, esquire, late President of Congress, and Chief Justice of the State of New York, and Minister Plenipotentiary from the said United States at the Court of Madrid, to be the Plenipotentiaries for the concluding and signing the present definitive Treaty; who, after having reciprocally communicated their respective full powers, have agreed upon and confirmed the following articles:

ART. I. His Britannic Majesty acknowledges the said United States, namely, New Hampshire, Massachusetts Bay, Rhode Island and Providence Plantations, Connecticut, New York, New Jersey, Pennsylvania, Delaware, Maryland, Virginia, North Carolina, South Carolina, and Georgia, to be free, sovereign, and independent States; that he treats with them as such; and for himself, his heirs and successors, relinquishes all claims to the government, propriety, and territorial rights of the same, and every part thereof.

ART. 2. And that all disputes which might arise in future, on the subject of the boundaries of the said United States may be prevented, it is hereby agreed and declared, that the following are and shall be their boundaries, namely, from the northwest angle of Nova Scotia, namely, that angle which is formed by a line drawn due north from the source of St. Croix river to the Highlands; along the said Highlands which divide those rivers that empty themselves into the river St. Lawrence from those which fall into the Atlantic ocean, to the northwesternmost head of Connecticut river, thence down along the middle of that river, to the forty-fifth degree of north latitude; from thence, by a line due west on said latitude, until it strikes the river Iroquois or Cataraquy, thence along the middle of said river into lake Ontario, through the middle of said lake until it strikes the communication by water between that lake and lake Erie; thence along the middle of said communication into lake Erie, through the middle of said lake until it arrives at the water communication between that lake and lake Huron; thence along the middle of said water communication into the lake Huron; thence through the middle of said lake to the water communication between that lake and lake Superior; thence through lake Superior northward of the isles Royal and Philipeaux, to the Long Lake; thence through the middle of the said Long Lake, and the water communication between it and the lake of the Woods, to the said lake of the Woods; thence through the said lake to the most northwestern point thereof, and from thence on a due west course to the river Mississippi; thence by a line to be drawn along the middle of said river Mississippi until it shall intersect the northernmost part of the thirty-first degree of north latitude. South, by a line to be drawn due east from the determination of the line last mentioned, in the latitude of thirty-one degrees north of the equator, to the middle of the river Appalachicola or Catahouche; thence along the middle thereof to its junction with the Flint river; thence straight to the head of St. Mary's river; and thence down along the middle of St. Mary's river to the Atlantic ocean. East, by a line to be drawn along the middle of the river St. Croix, from its mouth, in the Bay of Fundy, to its source, and from its source, directly north, to the aforesaid Highlands, which divide the rivers that fall into the Atlantic ocean from those which fall into the river St. Lawrence: comprehending all islands within twenty leagues of any part of the shores of the United States, and lying between lines to be drawn due east from the points where the aforesaid boundaries between Nova Scotia on the one part, and East Florida on the other, shall respectively touch the bay of Fundy, and the Atlantic ocean; excepting such islands as now are, or heretofore have been, within the limits of the said Province of Nova Scotia.

ART. 3. It is agreed that the people of the United States shall continue to enjoy unmolested the right to take fish of every kind on the Grand Bank, and on all the other banks of Newfoundland; also, in the Gulf of St. Lawrence, and at all other places in the sea, where the inhabitants of both countries used at any time heretofore to fish; and also, that the inhabitants of the United States shall have liberty to take fish of every kind on such part of the coast of Newfoundland as British fishermen shall use; (but not to dry or cure the same on that island;) and also on the coasts, bays, and creeks, of all other of his Britannic Majesty's dominions in America; and that the American fishermen shall have liberty to dry and cure fish in any of the unsettled bays, harbors, and creeks of Nova Scotia, Magdalen Islands, and Labrador, so long as the same shall remain unsettled; but so soon as the same or either of them shall be settled, it shall not be lawful for the said fishermen to dry or cure fish at such settlement, without a previous agreement for that purpose with the inhabitants, proprietors, or possessors of the ground.

ART. 4. It is agreed that creditors on either side shall meet with no lawful impediment to the recovery of the full value in sterling money, of all bona fide debts heretofore contracted.

ART. 5. It is agreed that the Congress shall earnestly recommend it to the Legislatures of the respective States, to provide for the restitution of all estates, rights, and properties, which have been confiscated, belonging to real British subjects, and also of the estates, rights, and properties of persons resident in districts in the possession of his Majesty's arms and who have not borne arms against the said United States. And that persons of any other description shall have free liberty to go to any part or parts of any of the thirteen United States, and therein to remain twelve months, unmolested in their endeavors to obtain the restitution of such of their estates, rights, and properties, as may have been confiscated; and that Congress shall also earnestly recommend to the several States, a reconsideration and revision of all acts or laws regarding the premises, so as render the said laws or acts perfectly consistent, not only with justice and equity, but with that spirit of conciliation, which, on the return of the blessings of peace, should universally prevail. And that Congress shall also earnestly recommend to the several States, that the estates, rights, and properties of such last-mentioned persons, shall be restored to them, they refunding to any persons who may be now in possession, the bona fide price (where any has been given) which such persons may have paid on purchasing any of the said lands, rights, or properties, since the confiscation. And it is agreed, that all persons who have any interest in confiscated lands, either by debts, marriage settlements, or otherwise, shall meet with no lawful impediment in the prosecution of their just rights.

ART. 6. That there shall be no future confiscations made, nor any prosecutions commenced against any person or persons for, or by reason of, the part which he or they may have taken in the present war; and that no person shall, on that account, suffer any future loss or damage, either in his person, liberty, or property; and that those who may be in confinement on such charges, at the time of the ratification of the Treaty in America, shall be immediately set at liberty, and the prosecutions so commenced be discontinued.

ART. 7. There shall be a firm and perpetual peace between his Britannic Majesty and the said States, and between the subjects of the one and the citizens of the other, wherefore all hostilities, both by sea and land, shall from henceforth cease: all prisoners on both sides shall be set at liberty; and his Britannic Majesty shall, with all convenient speed, and without causing any destruction, or carrying away any negroes or other property of the American inhabitants, withdraw all his armies, garrisons, and fleets, from the said United States, and from every post, place, and harbor within the same; leaving in all fortifications the American artillery that may be therein; and shall also order and cause all archives, records, deeds, and papers, belonging to any of the said States, or their citizens, which, in the course of the war, may have fallen into the hands of his officers, to be forthwith restored and delivered to the proper States and persons to whom they belong.

ART. 8. The navigation of the river Mississippi, from its source to the ocean, shall forever remain free and open to the subjects of Great Britain, and the citizens of the United States.

ART. 9. In case it should so happen that any place or territory belonging to Great Britain or to the United States, should have been conquered by the arms of either from the other, before the arrival of the said Provisional Articles in America, it is agreed, that the same shall be restored without difficulty, and without requiring any compensation.

ART. 10. The solemn ratifications of the present Treaty, expedited in good and due form, shall be exchanged between the contracting parties, in the space of six months, or sooner if possible, to be computed from the day of the signature of the present Treaty. In witness whereof, we, the undersigned, their Ministers Plenipotentiary, have, in their name and in virtue of our full powers, signed with our hands the present definitive Treaty, and caused the seals of our arms to be affixed thereto. Done at Paris, this third day of September, in the year of our Lord one thousand seven hundred and eighty-three.

[L. S.]   D. HARTLEY,
[L. S.]   JOHN ADAMS,
[L. S.]   B. FRANKLIN,
[L. S.]   JOHN JAY.

AN ORDINANCE

FOR THE GOVERNMENT OF THE TERRITORY OF THE UNITED STATES NORTHWEST OF THE RIVER OHIO.

BE it ordained by the United States in Congress assembled, That the said Territory, for the purposes of temporary government, be one District; subject, however, to be divided into two Districts, as future circumstances may, in the opinion of Congress, make it expedient.

Be it ordained by the authority aforesaid, That the estates both of resident and non-resident proprietors in the said Territory, dying intestate, shall descend to, and be distributed among their children, and the descendants of a deceased child, in equal parts; the descendants of a deceased child or grandchild to take the share of their deceased parent in equal parts among them: and where there shall be no children or descendants, then in equal parts to the next of kin, in equal degree; and among collaterals, the children of a deceased brother or sister of the intestate shall have, in equal parts among them, their deceased parents' share; and there shall, in no case, be a distinction between kindred of the whole and half blood; saving in all cases to the widow of the intestate, her third part of the real estate for life, and one third part of the personal estate; and this law relative to descents and dower, shall remain in full force, until altered by the Legislature of the District. And until the Governor and Judges shall adopt laws as herein after mentioned, estates in the said Territory may be devised or bequeathed by wills in writing, signed and sealed by him or her, in whom the estate may be, (being of full age,) and attested by three witnesses; and real estates may be conveyed by lease and release, or bargain and sale, signed, sealed, and delivered, by the person, being of full age, in whom the estate may be, and attested by two witnesses, provided such wills be duly proved, and such conveyances be acknowledged, or the execution thereof duly proved, and be recorded within one year after proper magistrates, courts, and registers, shall be appointed for that purpose; and personal property may be transferred by delivery; saving, however, to the French and Canadian inhabitants, and other settlers of the Kaskaskies, Saint Vincents, and the neighboring villages, who have heretofore professed themselves citizens of Virginia, their laws and customs now in force among them, relative to the descent and conveyance of property.

Be it ordained by the authority aforesaid, That there shall be appointed, from time to time, by Congress, a Governor, whose commission shall continue in force for the term of three years, unless sooner revoked by Congress: he shall reside in the District, and have a freehold estate therein, in one thousand acres of land, while in the exercise of his office.

There shall be appointed, from time to time, by Congress, a Secretary, whose commission shall continue in force for four years, unless sooner revoked; he shall reside in the District, and have a freehold estate therein, in five hundred acres of land, while in the exercise of his office; it shall be his duty to keep and preserve the acts and laws passed by the Legislature, and the public records of the District, and the proceedings of the Governor in his executive department; and transmit authentic copies of such acts and proceedings, every six months, to the Secretary of Congress: There shall also be appointed a court, to consist of three Judges, any two of whom to form a court, who shall have a common law jurisdiction, and reside in the District, and have each therein a freehold estate, in five hundred acres of land, while in the exercise of their offices; and their commissions shall continue in force during good behavior.

The Governor and Judges, or a majority of them, shall adopt and publish in the District, such laws of the original States, criminal and civil, as may be necessary, and best suited to the circumstances of the District, and report them to Congress, from time to time; which laws shall be in force in the District until the organization of the General Assembly therein, unless disapproved of by Congress; but afterwards the Legislature shall have authority to alter them as they shall think fit.

The Governor for the time being, shall be commander-in-chief of the militia, appoint and commission all officers in the same, below the rank of general officers; all general officers shall be appointed and commissioned by Congress.

Previous to the organization of the General Assembly, the Governor shall appoint such magistrates and other civil officers, in each county or township, as he shall find necessary for the preservation of the peace and good order in the same. After the General Assembly shall be organized, the powers and duties of magistrates and other civil officers shall be regulated and defined by the said assembly; but all magistrates and other civil officers, not herein otherwise directed, shall, during the continuance of this temporary government, be appointed by the Governor.

For the prevention of crimes and injuries, the laws to be adopted or made shall have force in all parts of the District, and for the execution of process, criminal and civil, the Governor shall make proper divisions thereof; and he shall proceed from time to time, as circumstances may require, to lay out the parts of the District in which the Indian titles shall have been extinguished, into counties and townships, subject, however, to such alterations as may thereafter be made by the Legislature.

So soon as there shall be five thousand free male inhabitants, of full age, in the District, upon giving proof thereof to the Governor, they shall receive authority, with time and place, to elect Representatives from their counties or townships, to represent them in the General Assembly; provided that, for every five hundred free male inhabitants, there shall be one Representative, and so on, progressively, with the number of free male inhabitants, shall the right of representation increase, until the number of Representatives shall amount to twenty-five; after which the number and proportion of Representatives shall be regulated by the Legislature; provided, that no person be eligible or qualified to act as a Representative, unless he shall have been a citizen of one of the United States three years, and be a resident in the District, or unless he shall have resided in the District three years; and in either case, shall likewise hold in his own right, in fee simple, two hundred acres of land within the same; provided also, that a freehold in fifty acres of land in the District, having been a citizen of one of the States, and being resident in the District, or the like freehold and two years residence in the District, shall be necessary to qualify a man as an elector of a Representative.

The Representatives, thus elected, shall serve for the term of two years; and in case of the death of a Representative, or removal from office, the Governor shall issue a writ to the county or township, for which he was a member, to elect another in his stead, to serve for the residue of the term.

The General Assembly, or Legislature, shall consist of the Governor, Legislative Council, and a House of Representatives. The Legislative Council shall consist of five members, to continue in office five years, unless sooner removed by Congress; any three of whom to be a quorum: and the members of the Council shall be nominated and appointed in the following manner, to wit: As soon as Representatives shall be elected, the Governor shall appoint a time and place for them to meet together, and when met, they shall nominate ten persons, residents in the District, and each possessed of a freehold in five hundred acres of land, and return their names to Congress; five of whom Congress shall appoint and commission to serve as aforesaid: and whenever a vacancy shall happen in the Council, by death or removal from office, the House of Representatives shall nominate two persons, qualified as aforesaid, for each vacancy, and return their names to Congress; one of whom Congress shall appoint and commission for the residue of the term: And every five years, four months at least before the expiration of the time of service of the members of Council, the said House shall nominate ten persons, qualified as aforesaid, and return their names to Congress; five of whom Congress shall appoint and commission to serve as members of the Council five years, unless sooner removed. And the Governor, Legislative Council, and House of Representatives, shall have authority to make laws, in all cases, for the good government of the District, not repugnant to the principles and articles of this Ordinance established and declared. And all bills, having passed by a majority in the House, and by a majority in the Council, shall be referred to the Governor for his assent; but no bill or legislative act whatever, shall be of any force without his assent. The Governor shall have power to convene, prorogue, and dissolve, the General Assembly, when in his opinion it shall be expedient.

The Governor, Judges, Legislative Council, Secretary, and

such other officers as Congress shall appoint in the District, shall take an oath or affirmation of fidelity, and of office; the Governor before the President of Congress, and all other officers before the Governor. As soon as a Legislature shall be formed in the District, the Council and House assembled, in one room, shall have authority, by joint ballot, to elect a Delegate to Congress, who shall have a seat in Congress, with a right of debating, but not of voting during this temporary government.

And for extending the fundamental principles of civil and religious liberty, which form the basis whereon these republics, their laws, and constitutions, are erected; to fix and establish those principles as the basis of all laws, constitutions, and governments, which forever hereafter shall be formed in the said Territory; to provide, also, for the establishment of States, and permanent government therein, and for their admission to a share in the Federal councils on an equal footing with the original States, at as early periods as may be consistent with the general interest:

It is hereby ordained and declared, by the authority aforesaid, That the following Articles shall be considered as articles of compact, between the original States and the People and States in the said Territory, and forever remain unalterable, unless by common consent, to wit:

ART. 1. No person, demeaning himself in a peaceable and orderly manner, shall ever be molested on account of his mode of worship or religious sentiments, in the said Territory.

ART. 2. The inhabitants of the said Territory shall always be entitled to the benefits of the writ of habeas corpus, and of the trial by jury; of a proportionate representation of the people in the Legislature, and of judicial proceedings according to the course of the common law. All persons shall be bailable, unless for capital offences, where the proof shall be evident, or the presumption great. All fines shall be moderate; and no cruel or unusual punishment shall be inflicted. No man shall be deprived of his liberty or property, but by the judgement of his peers, or the law of the land, and should the public exigencies make it necessary, for the common preservation, to take any person's property, or to demand his particular services, full compensation shall be made for the same. And, in the just preservation of rights and property, it is understood and declared, that no law ought ever to be made, or have force in the said Territory, that shall, in any manner whatever, interfere with, or affect, private contracts or engagements, bona fide, and without fraud, previously formed.

ART. 3. Religion, morality, and knowledge, being necessary to good government and the happiness of mankind, schools and the means of education shall forever be encouraged. The utmost good faith shall always be observed towards the Indians; their lands and property shall never be taken from them without their consent; and in their property, rights, and liberty, they never shall be invaded or disturbed, unless in just and lawful wars authorized by Congress; but laws founded in justice and humanity shall, from time to time, be made, for preventing wrongs being done to them, and for preserving peace and friendship with them.

ART. 4. The said Territory, and the States which may be formed therein, shall forever remain a part of this Confederacy of the United States of America, subject to the articles of Confederation, and to such alterations therein as shall be constitutionally made; and to all the acts and ordinances of the United States in Congress assembled, conformable thereto. The inhabitants and settlers in the said Territory shall be subject to pay a part of the Federal debts, contracted or to be contracted, and a proportional part of the expenses of government, to be apportioned on them by Congress, according to the same common rule and measure by which apportionments thereof shall be made on the other States; and the taxes for paying their proportion, shall be laid and levied by the authority and direction of the Legislatures of the District or Districts, or new States, as in the original States, within the time agreed upon by the United States in Congress assembled. The Legislatures of those Districts, or new States, shall never interfere with the primary disposal of the soil by the United States in Congress assembled, nor with any regulations Congress may find necessary, for securing the title in such soil, to the bona fide purchasers. No tax shall be imposed on lands the property of the United States; and in no case shall non-resident proprietors be taxed higher than residents. The navigable waters leading into the Mississippi and St. Lawrence, and the carrying places between the same, shall be common highways, and forever free, as well to the inhabitants of the said Territory, as to the citizens of the United States, and those of any other States that may be admitted into the Confederacy, without any tax, impost, or duty therefore.

ART. 5. There shall be formed in the said Territory, not less than three, nor more than five States; and the boundaries of the States, as soon as Virginia shall alter her act of cession, and consent to the same, shall become fixed and established as follows, to wit: the western State in the said Territory, shall be bounded by the Mississippi, the Ohio, and Wabash rivers; a direct line drawn from the Wabash and Post Vincents, due north, to the Territorial line between the United States and Canada; and by the said Territorial line to the lake of the Woods and Mississippi. The middle States shall be bounded by the said direct line, the Wabash, from Post Vincents to the Ohio, by the Ohio, by a direct line drawn due north from the mouth of the Great Miami to the said Territorial line, and by the said Territorial line. The eastern State shall be bounded by the last mentioned direct line, the Ohio, Pennsylvania, and the said Territorial line: provided however, and it is further understood and declared, that the boundaries of these three States shall be subject so far to be altered, that, if Congress shall hereafter find it expedient, they shall have authority to form one or two States in that part of the said Territory which lies north of an east and west line drawn through the southerly bend or extreme of lake Michigan. And whenever any of the said States shall have sixty thousand free inhabitants therein, such State shall be admitted, by its delegates, into the Congress of the United States, on an equal footing with the original States, in all respects whatever; and shall be at liberty to form a permanent Constitution and State government; provided the Constitution and government, so to be formed, shall be republican, and in conformity to the principles contained in these Articles; and, so far as it can be consistent with the general interest of the Confederacy, such admission shall be allowed at an earlier period, and when there may be a less number of free inhabitants in the State than sixty thousand.

ART. 6. There shall be neither slavery nor involuntary servitude in the said Territory, otherwise than in the punishment of crimes, whereof the party shall have been duly convicted: provided always, that any person escaping into the same, from whom labor or service is lawfully claimed in any one of the original States, such fugitive may be lawfully reclaimed, and conveyed to the person claiming his or her labor or service as aforesaid.

Be it ordained by the authority aforesaid, That the resolutions of the 23d of April, 1784, relative to the subject of this Ordinance, be, and the same are hereby repealed and declared null and void. Done, &c.

XIII.

A GLOSSARY

OF THE LEGAL AND OTHER NOT-EASILY-UNDERSTOOD WORDS AND PHRASES.

A fortiori, literally, for the stronger ground, or reason.

Allegiance, the tie, or duty, which binds the subject or citizen of a State to aid and assist the State, or Sovereignty, in return for the protection afforded by the latter. It imports, therefore, the obligation of a subject, or citizen, to be faithful to the State.

Ambassador, a public minister, of the highest grade, sent abroad by a sovereign state, or prince, to transact public business with a foreign government, in behalf of his own. There are three grades of foreign ministers. (1.) *Ambassadors,* who have the highest rank and privileges, and who represent, personally, their sovereign. (2.) *Ministers Plenipotentiary,* who have full powers to act for their sovereign or country. (3.) *Ministers Resident,* who generally possess, or may possess, the same powers, but hold a subordinate rank to Ministers Plenipotentiary. The explanation of the peculiar rights and duties of each class belongs, properly, to a treatise on the law of nations.

Arrest, the seizure and detention of the person of a party, by a public officer, under a writ or process from some court or magistrate. Thus, when a sheriff takes a man in custody, under a writ, we say, the sheriff arrests him, or he is under arrest.

Arrest of judgement, an order of a court, directing that no judgement be rendered in a case, from an error of law in the proceedings.

Articles of Confederation, the form of a general government, adopted by the States, during the Revolution, for their union. It was framed by the Continental Congress, in 1778; and was finally adopted, by all the States, in 1781, and remained in force until the present Constitution of the United States was adopted, in 1788. The articles will be found, at large, in the Appendix to this Volume, pp. 279—289.

Autre Droit, in the right of another, and not in one's own personal right. Thus, an administrator or executor, who collects a debt due to the estate of the deceased party, receives it not on his personal account, but in the right, or as representative, of another.

Bail, a person, who becomes surety for another's appearance in a court of justice, to answer to some civil suit, or criminal accusation; and usually, also, that he shall abide the judgement of the court thereon.

Bailable, literally, where bail may be taken. Thus, a suit or criminal accusation is said to be bailable, where the party is entitled, after arrest, to be discharged on giving bail.

Bill. This word has various senses, according to the things, to which it is applied. It may be generally defined, to be a formal, written Instrument. When we speak of a Bill before a Legislature, we mean, a written Instrument, containing a proposed Law, drawn up in the proper form. When the Bill is said to be passed by the Legislature, we mean, that it has received the final assent of the Legislature. When the Bill is passed, and is approved by the Executive, or otherwise becomes a Law, we call it an Act, or Statute.

Bill of Credit, a written Instrument, which contains a promise or agreement of the State to pay or allow a certain sum of money to the bearer or holder thereof. It is issued on the credit of the State, and is designed to circulate as currency.

Bill of Rights, a written Instrument, containing a public declaration of certain general rights of the people, which are held fundamental to their security and protection.

Bills for raising Revenue. These are written Instruments, containing laws proposed to be passed by the Legislature, to create a revenue, or income, to the Government; such as a Bill to lay and collect a tax, or duty, on houses, or lands, or goods.

Bona fide, a phrase borrowed from the Latin language, and literally meaning, "in good faith." We commonly apply it to a person, who acts honestly and conscientiously in doing any thing, without suspecting or knowing it to be wrong.

Bottomry Bond, literally, a Bond given by a master or owner of a ship, or other vessel, pledging the bottom of the vessel, that is, the vessel itself, for the repayment of money borrowed upon the credit of the vessel, and payable upon the contingency, that the vessel performs the voyage specified in the bond.

Cabinet, an abbreviated expression for Cabinet Council, meaning the Ministers of the State, or Heads of the Departments of the Government, who are convened by the Executive Magistrate, to assist and advise him in the Government. Thus, in the United States, we say, the Heads of the Departments of State, of War, of the Treasury, of the Navy, of the Post Office, and of the Law, (the Attorney General,) constitute the Cabinet, that is, they are the private confidential advisers and council of the President.

Cessio Bonorum, literally, a Cession or Transfer of the Goods or Property of a party. It is a phrase derived from the Roman or civil law, and means, that a debtor has made a cession, or assignment, of his property, for the benefit of his creditors.

Charter. In a general sense, this word means any written Instrument conferring rights or creating obligations, from the Latin word *charta,* paper or parchment, on which something is written. But, in legal language, a Charter usually means a written Instrument, or grant, under the public seal of the Government, conferring certain rights, privileges, and authorities, of a public nature, upon certain citizens or subjects. Such were the original Charters of Government, granted by the Crown to the American Colonies.

Commission, a written Document, signed by the Executive, or other proper officer of the Government, conferring an authority, or appointment to office, on some person. Commissions to public officers, appointed by the President of the United States, are signed by the President, and have the great seal of the United States annexed thereto. To commission, is to give or grant such commission to the proper party.

Confederation, Articles of, see *Articles of Confederation.*

Consul, a commercial Agent of the Government, appointed and resident in a foreign country, to attend to the commercial rights and privileges of his own country, and its citizens, in such foreign country.

Continental Congress, the general appellation of the general Congress or Legislature, in which all the States of the Union were represented, by their Delegates, during the American Revolution. It was called 'Continental,' as being for the whole of the Continent of America, embraced within the limits of the United States, in contradistinction to a Provincial Congress, which was the Legislative Body of a single State, Colony, or Province, of the Union.

Conveyance, a transfer, in writing, by one person to another, of his right and title to land or other property. It is usually by an Instrument under the seal of the person making the transfer.

Copyright, the right of an Author to the exclusive publication and sale of his works, for the period, which is prescribed by law for its continuance, upon his complying with the requisites of law, in order to secure the same.

Crown. This word is used as equivalent to King, Sovereign, or reigning Monarch. Thus, we say, indifferently, such grant was made by, or such a power exists in, the Crown, the King, or the Sovereign.

Declaration of Independence, the Act by which the United States severed their connexion with the British Crown. It may be found, at length, in the Appendix to this Volume, pp. 275—279.

Declaration of Rights, of the Continental Congress, a declaration, published October 14, 1774, and which may be found, at length, in the Appendix to this Volume, pp. 271—274.

Defendant, the person against whom any suit is brought; but, in a more limited sense, it means the person, against whom any suit is brought, who appears in court to defend, or contest, the suit.

Duty on Tonnage, a tax laid on ships and vessels, in proportion to their tonnage; as, for example, a tax of six cents a ton on the tonnage of every American ship, or a tax of fifty cents a ton on that of every foreign ship, arriving in the ports of the United States.

Embargo, a restraint, or detainment, of ships and vessels, from sailing out of port, imposed by the authority of the Government. It is usually imposed for temporary purposes, in contemplation of war, or on account of some immediate and impending public danger.

Equity, This word is commonly used as equivalent to natural justice, in contradistinction to strict Law. In the Law, it is used, to express the jurisdiction, which belongs to Courts of Equity, to enforce rights and remedy wrongs, in favor of parties; which rights and wrongs Courts of common Law have no authority to enforce or redress.

Estate, the right and interest, which a man has in property. *Real Estate* is the right and interest, which a man has in land, or other things of a kindred and permanent nature; such, for example, as an interest in a mill, in a waterfall, or in a private way. *Personal Estate* is the right or interest, which a man has in goods, merchandises, and other movable property, or debts and credits.

Estoppel is, in Law, the stopping, or precluding, or preventing, a man from setting up any fact, or previous act, to contradict or invalidate, what he has since done or admitted. Thus, if a man makes a conveyance, by deed, of land, stating therein that he has a good title thereto, he shall be estopped to deny that he had any title.

Excise. This word ordinarily means a tax, or duty, laid upon some commodity or thing used, or manufactured, or sold, in a country. Thus, a tax laid upon all coaches used, or upon all spirits manufactured, or upon all goods sold at auction, in a country, is called an excise. It is commonly used in contradistinction to "imposts," the latter word being applied to taxes levied on goods upon their importation from a foreign country, whereas excises are taxes on things already in the country, or to be sold or manufactured there, and are therefore commonly called "internal taxes."

Ex post facto, literally, after the act is done. The phrase is usually applied to laws passed to punish an act as a crime, when it was not so at the time, when the act was done. Hence such laws are called *Ex post facto* laws.

Felony. This word was originally applied to crimes, which the common law punished by a forfeiture of the lands and goods of the offender, it being supposed to be derived from the feudal law, in which *"fee"* signified the fief, feud, or estate of the tenant, and *"lon,"* which signified price or value. It is now commonly applied to designate such crimes as are punished capitally, that is, by death.

Franchise, a right or privilege, granted by the King or Government to one or more persons, which does not belong to subjects or citizens generally; and which cannot properly be exercised by them, without such grant. Thus, to be and act as a corporation, is a franchise.

General Issue, a law phrase, signifying a general denial, by the Defendant in a suit, of all the charges made by the Plaintiff, in his written statements, or allegations, (commonly called a declaration,) against the Defendant, for which the suit is brought. Thus, if an action is brought by A against B, for an assault and battery of A, and B pleads, that he is not guilty, this is called the general issue; that is, the Defendant denies the whole matter charged against him. The Reply of the Plaintiff, putting the matter of fact on trial, by the Jury, is called joining the issue. So, where a party, charged with a crime, pleads not guilty, that is the general issue.

Grantee, the person to whom a grant is made. The person, who makes the grant, is called the *Grantor.*

Habeas Corpus, literally, Have you the Body. The phrase designates the most emphatic words of a writ, issued by a Judge or Court, commanding a person, who has another in custody, or in imprisonment, to have his body (Habeas Corpus) before the Judge or Court, at a particular time and place, and to state the cause of his imprisonment. The person, whether a sheriff, gaoler, or other person, is bound to produce the body of the prisoner at the time and place appointed; and, if the prisoner is illegally or improperly in custody, the Judge or Court will discharge him. Hence it is deemed the great security of the personal liberty of the citizen against oppression and illegal confinement.

Impeachment, in a juridical sense, is a written, formal accusation of a person, as being guilty of some public offence or misdemeanor. When the charges against him are specially described and set forth in writing, they are called Articles of Impeachment. When, for example, the House of Representatives of the United States prefers or offers to the Senate written charges, against any public officer, as being guilty of high crimes and misdemeanors, on which it requires him to be put upon trial, it is called an Impeachment.

In Capite, literally, in chief, or of the head. Tenants *in capite,* are those tenants of land, who hold them directly, or immediately, from and under the King, by his gift or grant, in contradistinction to persons who hold by the grant of, or under, other persons.

Indictment is a formal written accusation, by a Grand Jury, charging a person to be guilty of a particular crime or misdemeanor, which is particularly described and set forth in the indictment.

Infamous crime. This phrase means, in common language, a crime, which is attended with infamy. In Law, it is usually applied to such gross, or atrocious crimes, as involve deep moral turpitude and disgrace.

Injunction, the name of a writ or process, which enjoins or commands a man to do or not to do a particular act or thing; and is a common process issued by Courts of Equity, in proper cases. An injunction of a judgement is an order to the party, who has obtained a judgement in a suit, not to enforce that judgement by an execution, or otherwise.

Insolvency, an inability of a debtor to pay all his debts. *Insolvent laws* are such as are made for the relief of debtors unable to pay all their debts.

Ipso facto, literally, by this very act. It means, that a certain result immediately follows from that act. Thus, we say, if a man conveys his estate to another, he ceases, *ipso facto,* (by this very act,) to be the owner thereof.

Jure Belli, literally, by the law or right of war.

Jurisprudence is, properly speaking, the Science of the Law, in which sense, it includes all the principles and doctrines of the Law. The word is sometimes used in a more limited sense, and means only the expositions and interpretations of the Law, by Judicial Tribunals.

Jury, a body composed of twelve men, selected to try questions of fact in civil and criminal suits, and who are under oath or solemn affirmation, to decide the facts truly and faithfully, according to the evidence laid before them. The points, which they are to try, are generally founded upon the written allegations of the parties, (called the pleadings,) and the points, on which the parties require their decision, are called the *issues,* and the decisions on those points made by the jury, after hearing the case, are called their verdict, or finding of the truth of the facts. The jury for the trial of causes is sometimes called the *petit,* (or small,) or *traverse jury,* (that is, a jury to try questions of fact, which are traversed or denied between the parties.)

Jury, Grand, a body composed of not less than twelve, nor more than twenty-three men, who, under oath, hear the proof of any particular crime, or offence, with which any person is charged, and if they believe him guilty on the evidence, they present an indictment against him.

Law, Civil. The phrase, "civil law," sometimes means the law, which respects the private rights and property of persons, in contradistinction to criminal law, which respects public offences. Sometimes, it means the Roman Law, which is commonly called the civil law. Sometimes, civil law is used in contradistinction to military law, the latter being applicable only to persons in the military or naval service.

Law, Common. The phrase, "common law," is used, in England, to express all the doctrines and principles of Law, which are recognized and enforced in its jurisprudence, and are not founded upon any positive existing act or statute of Parliament. It consists of all the general customs and usages, which regulate the rights of property, and all those general principles of justice and interpretation, which are acted upon in Courts of Justice, and all those remedies, which are applied for the redress of wrongs, which cannot be traced up to any positive act or statute. The phrase, "common law," is sometimes used to distinguish the English law from the Roman, which is commonly called the "civil law;" and sometimes merely to express, that it is the law applicable, in common to the whole kingdom. The common Law of each of the American States is that portion of the English common Law, which has been adopted by the particular State, in connexion with its own peculiar and settled usages and customs, and which is not prescribed by any act or statute of the State Legislature.

Law, Constitutional. Constitutional Law is that branch of the Law, which relates to the exposition and interpretation of the Constitution of the State or Nation.

Law, Merchant. That branch of the Laws of a State or Nation, which treats of rights, duties, contracts, &c., respecting trade, and commerce, and navigation, and shipping, and sales, and insurance, and bills of exchange, and promissory notes, &c. &c.

Law, Municipal. Municipal Law means the law of a particular community, State, or Nation, in contradistinction to the law of foreign communities, States, or Nations.

Law of Nations. The Law of Nations is properly that, which regulates the rights and duties of Nations, in respect to each other, and the respective subjects and citizens thereof. That branch, which respects the rights and intercourse of the Nations, in their sovereign capacities, is often called public international law; that, which respects the private rights and intercourse of the respective subjects and citizens thereof, is called private international law.

Laws, Insolvent. Laws made respecting debtors, who are unable to pay their debts, and distributing their property among their creditors.

Laws, Inspection. Inspection laws are such laws as are made by a particular State, to ascertain and fix the quality, character, and relative value, of its own products or manufactures. In order to ascertain these facts, the products or manufactures are examined, or inspected, by skilful persons, who are often called inspectors; as, for example, inspectors of provisions, inspectors of flour, inspectors of ashes, &c.

Letters of Marque and Reprisal. These are letters under seal, or commissions, granted by a government to one or more of its citizens, to make seizure or reprisal of the property of an enemy, or of persons, who belong to another government, which government has refused to do justice to the citizens of the country granting the letters of marque and reprisal.

Magna Charta, or *Magna Carta,* literally, the Great Charter. This name is given to a formal written charter, granted by King John, and confirmed by King Henry III., of England, which solemnly recognised and secured certain enumerated rights, privileges, and liberties, as belonging to the people of England, which have ever since constituted a fundamental part of the constitution of government of England. Among other important rights, it secured the right of a trial by jury in civil and criminal cases, and the right of the subject to the free enjoyment of his life, his liberty, and his property, unless declared forfeited by the judgement of his peers, (a jury,) or by the Law of the land. Several of its provisions constitute a part of the Bill of Rights set forth in our present State and National Constitutions.

Malversations in Office. This phrase is applied to official misdemeanors, corruptions, extortions, and other wrongful conduct, by public officers.

Mandamus, literally, "we command." This is a writ issued by a Court of Justice to some Corporation, public officer, or other person, commanding them to do some particular thing, therein specified, which appertains to their office or duty. It is called a Mandamus, from this word being in the original writ, which was formerly in Latin.

Material Men. Those persons are called, in Admiralty Courts, material men, who supply ships with provisions, or equipments, or other outfits, or furnish materials for repairs, and make the repairs on ships.

Mesne Process, literally, intermediate process, as contradistinguished from final process, in any suit. In strictness, the writ first issued, to bring a party before a court, in a suit, is called original process; the writ of execution, which issues to enforce the judgement in the suit, is called the final process; and all other process or writs, issued in that suit, are mesne process. But, in America, mesne process is ordinarily used to describe all process issued in a suit, which is not final process.

Ministers Plenipotentiary,
Ministers Resident.   See *Ambassadors.*

Ordinance of 1787, for the settlement and government of the North Western Territory of the United States, may be found, at length, in the Appendix to this Volume, pp. 329—337.

Parliament. This is the appellation, by which the Legislature of Great Britain is ordinarily designated. It is composed of the House of Lords, and House of Commons.

Patent, an abbreviated expression, signifying letters-patent, or open letters, or grants of the government, under the great seal thereof, granting some right, privilege, or property, to a person, who is thence called the Patentee. Thus, the government grants the public lands, by a patent, to the purchaser. So, a copy-right in a book, or an exclusive right to an invention, is granted by a patent. When the word patent is used in conversation, it ordinarily is limited to a patent-right for an invention.

Patentee The party, who is the grantee of a patent from the government.

Peers. Peers, ordinarily, means the nobility of Great Britain, who have a seat in the House of Lords. They are called peers, from the Latin word, *pares,* equals. But the word is also used to signify, the pares, or jurymen, who are entitled to try questions of fact in civil and criminal cases. The trial by jury is therefore often called a trial by his (the defendant's) peers.

Personal Estate. See *Estate.*

Plaintiff, the party, who brings a suit against another, for redress of some private wrong or breach of contract. He is so called, because he makes a plaint or complaint against the wrongdoer.

Plea, the written defence of the Defendant in any suit, in denial or avoidance of the matter charged by the Plaintiff in that suit against him.

Plea, Special. It is a special justification or excuse, set forth in writing by the Defendant in a suit, which bars or destroys the Plaintiff's right in that suit. It is used in contradistinction, generally, to the general issue. A justification admits the act charged by the Plaintiff to be done or omitted, and justifies the Defendant in such act or omission. Whereas the general issue usually denies, that the act has ever been done or omitted.

Plurality of Votes. A person is said to have a plurality of votes, who has more votes than any other single candidate for the same office. A person is said to have a majority of votes, who has a larger number than all the other candidates have, adding all their votes together.

Primà facie means, literally, upon the first view or appearance. It commonly applies to cases of evidence or presumption, where the meaning is, that the evidence or presumption is to be taken to be sufficient to prove certain facts, until other evidence or presumptions are introduced to control it.

Prison Liberties, or *Gaol Limits.* To every public gaol or prison, there are certain limited spaces, or local limits, outside of the walls of the gaol or prison, within which persons imprisoned for debts are entitled to reside, or be, upon complying with the conditions and securities required to be given, that they will commit no escape. These limits, or liberties, are commonly called the gaol or prison limits or liberties.

Privies, in a legal sense, are those, who claim any right or property from or under another person. Thus, the heir, or devisee, of an ancestor, is a privy under the latter. An executor is a privy under his intestate. A purchaser is a privy in estate from the seller.

Process of Law. Process means the writs and other compulsive written orders, issued in any civil or criminal case, to compel the appearance of a party or witness, or to enforce obedience to the judgement, or other order of a court of justice.

Property in Contingency, is property, to which there is no absolute right or title in a party, but its vesting in him is dependent upon a future uncertain event. Thus, a legacy to a man, who is under age, if he arrives at twenty-one years, is property in contingency.

Proprietary. This phrase is equivalent to owner or proprietor. But it is usually limited to persons, who possess a right to territory, with the powers of government therein. Thus, Penn was called the Proprietary of Pennsylvania, and Lord Baltimore, of Maryland; because, by grants from the King of England, not only the territory of those Colonies, but the right of governing them, was vested in them.

Pro tempore, literally, for a time. It means, that a person is not the regular officer holding an office, but one holding it for a short and uncertain period. Thus, the Vice President of the United States is the regular President of the Senate; but, in his absence, the Senate may appoint a President, *pro tempore,* to perform his duties.

Provincial Congress, see *Continental Congress.*

Real Estate, see *Estate.*

Records of a Court. These are the written memorials of the transactions of a court of justice, drawn up in form by its regular officers, and styled records, because the acts and doings of the Court are therein recorded fully and truly, so as to be received as absolutely correct.

Replication is the written reply of the Plaintiff in a suit, to the plea put in by the Defendant in the same suit. Its true object is, to deny or destroy the validity of the plea, as a bar to the suit.

Reprieve. When a criminal has been condemned, by the sentence of a court of justice, to suffer a particular punishment at a particular time, and the execution of that sentence is postponed, suspended, or withdrawn, for an interval of time, by the proper authority, it is called a reprieve; from *reprendre,* to take back.

Return-Day of Process. Whenever a writ or process is issued by a court of justice, to an officer, or other person, to be by him executed, according to the command therein stated, it usually contains a fixed time, when the officer is to make a return of that writ or process, with a written statement of his acts or proceedings done under it. That time is the return-day; and that written statement is technically called his Return.

Right, Possessory. A man, who is in possession of property, having a right to possess it, is said to have a possessory right. Thus, a man, who hires a horse and chaise for a journey, has a possessory right to the horse and chaise for that journey, although the person, who lets them, is the general owner. So a man in possession of land, as a tenant, has a possessory right in the land, although it is owned by his landlord.

Sergeant-at-Arms. The name of the officer of a legislative body, who serves processes, and executes the order of that body upon solemn occasions.

Socage, a word of feudal origin, and, in that system, the tenure, by which a man holds lands, is to render therefor some certain and determinate service, in contradistinction to tenure of lands by uncertain and precarious services, where the tenant was obliged to render such service as the grantor might, from time to time, require of him. *Free Socage* is a tenure by certain and honorable service.

Stamp Act. An act or statute, which requires certain papers and enumerated documents to be stamped with a stamp by the government, before they have any validity; and imposes a certain tax or duty for the stamping such papers or documents. Thus, if the government should declare, that every deed or promissory note should be written on paper stamped by the government, and require the party to pay a fixed sum or tax for such stamped paper, the Act or Law, making such provisions, would be called a Stamp Act.

Stand seised. A man is said to stand seised of land, who is in possession of it under a claim or title to it, either in fee, or, at least, for life.

State Trials are trials for crimes or offences in Courts of justice. They are called State trials, because the State or Government prosecutes the suit or indictment.

Statute. An act or law, passed by a Legislature. It is called a Statute, from *Statutum,* a thing ordered or appointed by the Legislature.

Statute of Limitations. A statute or law, which limited the time within which a suit or action may be brought in a court of justice. Such statutes exist in every State in the Union.

Suit at Law is the remedy, which a person, aggrieved by any wrong done to him, seeks, in a court of law, for redress of the wrong.

Tonnage Duty is a tax or duty laid by the Legislature, or other competent authority, upon ships or vessels, in proportion to their tonnage.

Tort is a wrong or injury done by one man to another, or to his property or rights. It includes all trespasses; but is a word of larger signification.

Treaty of Peace, of 1783, is the treaty made between Great Britain and the American States, by which Great Britain acknowledged our Independence, and surrendered her claims to our Territory. It closed the War for our Independence; and will be found in the Appendix to the present Volume, pp. 324—329.

Trespass is a wrong or injury done by one man to another, or to his property or rights. When the word is used, alone, it means some wrong done by violence, or force, or some illegal act. Thus, if a man unlawfully strikes another, or unlawfully takes possession of the land or goods of another, he is said to be guilty of a trespass.

V. is often put for *versus,* or against. Thus, a suit is said to be by A *versus* B.

Vivà Voce, literally, by the living voice, or orally. Thus, when a witness gives his testimony in open court, in the presence of the audience, and answers, by word of mouth, we say, his testimony is *vivà voce.* If his testimony is written down, and read, it is called his Deposition.

Warrant is a written, sealed order, command, or writ, requiring and authorizing an officer or other person to do a particular act. It is usually applied to the process, by which criminals are arrested for trial or examination.

Writ of Error is a writ, which authorizes a Court of justice to bring a record before it, either of the same court, or of another court, in order to examine and decide, whether there is any error of law in the judgement, or other proceedings in that record; and, if there be, to correct the error.

Writ of Habeas Corpus, see *Habeas Corpus.*